# POCKET
*Book of*
# KNOWLEDGE

# Contents

# GRUESOME
# HISTORIES

Written by Susan Mayes

Illustrated by Celia Witchard

# A Word of Warning

Is your knowledge of the past everything it could be?  Do you hunger for the details behind all those dull dates and events?

This book contains a grim feast of delightfully unpleasant facts that didn't quite make it into your school textbooks, but maybe should have done!

A word of warning...avoid eating and drinking whilst devouring gruesome historical information; it could damage your health, not to mention the new carpet!

Just to give you an idea of what to expect, here's a little taster of things to come...

The Romans may have been pioneering and powerful people, but some of their habits seem a mite nasty by today's standards.  Find out about life in the public loo and after-dinner puking.

Discover the delights that awaited girls in Ancient Greece – providing they were not abandoned at birth, that is!

Preserved bodies, otherwise known as *mummies*, will keep you riveted to the spot.  Read about *natural mummies* and about the not-so-natural.  Ooh-er!

Enter the grisly world of old-fashioned medicine, but only if you are feeling strong and reckless. Definitely not one for the squeamish!

What was life like at sea? Is there any truth behind the tales of pillaging pirates, maggot-infested biscuits and rat-ridden ships? (Ahoy Jim lad!)

Find out about day-to-day life behind the castle walls in peacetime and in wartime. It wasn't all a bed of roses then, especially where punishments were concerned.

Has this got you interested? Are you hungry for more? Then turn the pages and read on...

# EARLY NASTIES

$A$n *archaeologist* is someone who studies ancient things...and we're talking a teeny bit more ancient than your grandma or your old, toothless moggy! Well, quite a lot more ancient actually.

Here are a few of the not-so-nice things that archaeologists have found out about people who lived long before us.

## WHAT A WAY TO GO!

Many thousands of years ago, in ancient societies, dying was an important business. Some civilisations built a *funeral pyre* – that's a big bonfire – and put the dead body on top. Then the whole thing was burned, accompanied by the odd sacrificial victim or two. Nice, eh? Afterwards, the bones might have been laid to rest in a burial chamber, along with a few essentials for the dead person to use in the next life. (Well, you never know what you might need!)

*Funeral pyre*

## A TIGHT SQUEEZE

Human remains have been found buried inside huge clay jars, of all things. Not the most comfortable resting place you could imagine!

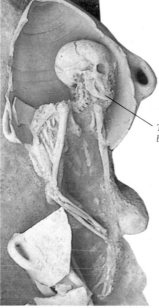

*This skeleton was found buried in a jar, in Jordan.*

## WHAT A PONG!

In the past, on the islands of the South Pacific, a substance called *ambergris* was used as a basis for perfumes. It was made from the intestines of the sperm whale and had a strong pong!

## SWEET BREATH

If you had bad breath, *frankincense* (the resin from a type of spruce tree) was the thing to take. Who needs a refreshing packet of strong mints!

*Frankincense*

# Horrid Roman Habits

The Ancient Romans were around from 753 BC, for about 1,163 years. They were powerful, intelligent people who did lots of good things, but they had a few horrid habits that you really MUST know about.

## At Your Convenience

Plumbing was one of the Romans' strong points. They built public toilets where multi-seater loos were placed over a water channel, with running water to wash the waste to the public sewer.

In those days, they didn't have loo rolls. They used a stick with a piece of sponge on the end. Nice, eh?

## A Day Out

For a fun day in Roman times you could take a trip to Rome and go to the Colosseum – a big building used for entertainment and sport. One of the highlights in this 50,000-seater stadium was when trained fighters called *gladiators* fought each other to the death, for public amusement.

*Gladiator's helmet*

## MEAL TIME

The Romans loved their nosh. The rich ones in particular took hours over their main meal. It was polite to belch during a good feed, and they HAD to eat with their hands, because they didn't have forks. Sounds ideal!

## SICKY-ICKY

There was often so much food around at Roman meals, that the only way to get through it all was to make yourself sick, to make space for another helping. Some houses had a special room called a *vomitorium*, where you could go to puke in peace. The other option was to vomit on the floor. Uuugh!

## ROMAN REVENGE

If you had an enemy in Roman times, you could seek revenge by visiting your nearest temple and placing a curse on them.

*This curse is written on a lead plaque.*

# ERUPTION AND DESTRUCTION

One of the most famous gruesome tales is about the destruction of the Italian cities of Pompeii and Herculaneum. They were buried when the nearby volcano, Mount Vesuvius, erupted in 79 AD.

On 24th August, 79 AD, people in Pompeii and the nearby city of Herculaneum were going about their daily business...eating, shopping, having a snooze.

Without warning, Vesuvius erupted and buried Pompeii under several metres of volcanic ash. Herculaneum was swamped by volcanic mud which was 20 m (65 ft) deep in places. That's five times more than covered Pompeii.

*Volcanic ash rained down on Pompeii for several hours.*

## GRUESOME FINDS

The buried cities of Pompeii and Herculaneum were more or less forgotten until excavations started in the 18th century. Little by little, the remains were revealed. Many gruesome finds tell the tale of what happened during those terrifying hours all those years ago.

One poor guard dog was chained to his post when disaster struck.

One person was found sitting huddled, covering his face in his last moments of life.

*This mother was trying to shield her child when they died.*

*Body cavity is discovered*

*Cavity is filled with wet plaster of Paris*

## PLASTER CASTS

Human and animal remains were not found complete. Over the years, the bodies had decayed, leaving shapes where they used to be inside the hardened volcanic rock.

When archaeologists discovered the cavities, they filled them with plaster to make solid shapes of what used to be inside.

# A Grisly Greek Beginning

Growing up in Ancient Greece wasn't a bundle of laughs. The life of a child was a bit of an ordeal, especially when there was a good chance that you wouldn't be allowed to live. Yikes!

## New Babies

A baby's future rested in the hands of its father. If it was a girl or if it was puny, or if the family was poor, it might be abandoned and left in the open air to die!

A few abandoned babies were lucky and were saved by other families and brought up as slaves. If a baby was accepted by its own family and named on the tenth day of its life, it was treated kindly. Phew!

## Believe It or Not...

Children were considered to be young adults at about the age of 12 or 13. They had to dedicate their toys to the god Apollo or the goddess Artemis. This was the sign that they had reached the end of childhood.

*Clay toys*

## A BOY'S LIFE

Boys went to school at about 7 years of age. Each had a personal slave called a pedagogue who carried their books!

At school they learned reading, writing and arithmetic, plus music. So far, so good, but... they had to learn lots of poetry by heart and learn to discuss subjects in an interesting and intelligent way. This was called debating. Uh oh!

## A GIRL'S LIFE

Greek girls were not as important as the boys. They didn't go to school; they stayed at home where mum taught them to spin, weave and look after the house. (Big deal!) A few richer girls might have been taught to read and write by a personal tutor.

Girls married at 13 or 14. A girl's father chose her husband and she would only gain a little in importance if she had a baby boy. Huh!

# BEASTLY BODIES

The preserved bodies of people or animals are called *mummies*. If people die or are buried in the right conditions, they may be mummified by accident. Mummies still have skin on them, so skeletons don't count.

*Mummy of Eskimo baby*

For the brave and strong-stomached only! Do NOT read this while eating your tea!

## DEEP FREEZE

When someone dies, invisible little nasties called *bacteria* make the body decay or, to put it another way, rot. But if bodies are buried in very cold, icy places, they become frozen, so decay never starts.

The six-month-old Eskimo boy on the left died around 1475. His body lay protected from the sun and snow and was freeze-dried by the Arctic air. Seven other well-preserved bodies were discovered with him, on a cliff in Greenland.

## BOG PEOPLE

*Peatbogs* are wet, earthy places which are perfect for preserving bodies. This is because there isn't any of the oxygen which bacteria need to make things decay.

Tollund Man was the name given to a natural mummy found in a Danish peatbog. The body is over 2,200 years old, but it is perfectly preserved.

## SAND MUMMY

The earliest known Egyptian mummies are around 5,000 years old. Wow...that's some old person!

The dead body was buried in a shallow hole in the desert and covered with sand. This mummified the body really well. The sand mummy in this picture still has her hair. She is known as Gingerella!

## GOOD LUCK MUMMIES

In 16th- and 17th-century England, builders used to board up a dead animal in the house they were finishing, along with a few lucky bits and pieces. The cold draughts often freeze-dried the dead offering and mummified it.

# Making a Mummy

The Egyptians believed in life after death, or the *afterlife*. They wanted to preserve a dead person's body in a lifelike way, to prepare him or her for a better future life. Here's how they did it.

## Embalming

First, remove all the vital organs, except the heart which may be needed in the next world. Wash the body in wine and spices, then cover with a special salt. Leave for 70 days. Then pour over liquid resin and rub in oil, wax and other stuff, to prevent cracking. Lastly, pack with linen, sand or sawdust to achieve a good body shape.

## Wrapping Up

Next, wrap the mummy in hundreds of metres of linen cloth. Do layers of bandage alternated with large sheets of material, called *shrouds.* Do up to 20 layers in this way. But DON'T forget to wrap the fingers and toes individually!

## THE MUMMY'S MASK

Make a decorative mask to protect the mummy's head, or to replace it if you have accidentally lost or damaged the real thing! Painted papier mâché will do for poorer mummies, but go for gold if they are rich ones! Also add charms called *amulets*, to protect the body from evil and to bring good luck.

## MUMMY CASES

Place your completed work of art in a decorated coffin, called a *mummy case*, to protect it from wild animals and tomb thieves. Place in a second case, just to be on the safe side.

## STONE COFFIN

Lastly, if your mummy is a VIP, place in a stone coffin, called a *sarcophagus*. There... that didn't take long, did it?

# DEAD IMPORTANT

A *pharaoh* was an Egyptian king. The Egyptians believed that their pharaoh was a living god, so when he died they took the best possible care of him. As well as receiving all the routine after-death perks described on pages 18 and 19, there were other delights in store.

## PYRAMIDS

During a pharaoh's lifetime, he had an enormous pyramid built as a tomb and final resting place for his body. It was meant to help him achieve eternal life.

## THE FUNERAL

A pharaoh's funeral was a grand affair. His mummified body was taken to the pyramid in a procession led by priests. He was accompanied by professional mourners who did loads of wailing and throwing around of sand... a bit of a palaver!

## TAKING IT WITH YOU

Mummies were buried with their own kit of useful things for the afterlife. If you were a VIP, this kit might include statues, furniture, jewellery and model workers called *shabtis* to do all the hard graft.

*Pendant buried with the famous pharaoh, Tutankhamun*

## THE 'OPENING OF THE MOUTH' CEREMONY

This ceremony was performed to restore the mummy's senses so it could eat, drink and generally live it up in the afterlife. The ceremony was performed by priests who touched the mummy's mouth with ritual instruments.

## SPOOKY SPELLS

The ultimate Egyptian handbook was called *The Book of the Dead*. This handy little volume contained a collection of spells. Each one was a prayer or a plea from the dead person and was meant to help them on the tricky trip to the next world.

# MUMMY MANIA

The Egyptians set a bit of a trend in mummification. Not only did they preserve their human loved ones, but they preserved other things besides. The fashion has been continued over the centuries, with some pretty weird results.

## MUMMIFIED MOGGIES AND DOGGIES

The Egyptians kept cats as pets. They were sacred animals and anyone who killed a cat could be punished with death. (Yikes!) Some families took pussy to be embalmed when it passed on. Even dead wild dogs got special treatment.

*Mummy of a wild dog*

### BELIEVE IT OR NOT...

When a cat died, the owners may have shaved their eyebrows. Why?

As a mark of respect, of course!

## ANIMALS OF IMPORTANCE

The Egyptians believed that different animals were the representatives of different gods. If you thought that mummified cats and dogs were weird, take a look at this collection.

Coffin for the smallest creature to be embalmed – a scarab beetle

Gold case for a bird called an ibis

Bronze case for the mummy of a shrew mouse

## MEET THE FAMILY

In Sicily, there are about 6,000 mummies in an underground cemetery, called a *catacomb*. The oldest ones are nearly 400 years old.

In the past, families took their children to visit their long-dead great-grandparents. They had a comfortable chat with the dead and even took a picnic to eat outside. You can still visit the mummies today.

## FISHY FRAUD

Imaginary creatures called *mermaids* and *mermen* were popular in 17th-century Europe. The mummified merman on the left was given to an English prince by someone who claimed that it had been caught by a Japanese fisherman. Hmmm! It was REALLY made from a monkey's head and a fish's tail.

# CREEPY CURES

Back in ancient times, when people didn't know a lot about the causes of illness, there were some pretty odd cures around. It's a wonder people survived at all when you look at some of the remedies they came up with.

## HEAD HOLES

In Stone Age times, they developed a nifty little medical routine for releasing the evil spirits and demons that caused mental problems and other illnesses. It was called *trepanning* and involved drilling a hole in the head to let the demons out. Ouch! A lie down in a dark room gets my vote every time!

*Trepanned skull with three holes*

## MEDICINE MEN

The North American Indians had doctors called *shamans*. They were men or women who

had the power to heal the sick. If you were feeling a bit rough, then the shaman would conduct a dramatic ceremony to make your mind reject sickness. Just what the doctor ordered!

## MAGIC AND MEDICINE

In Egyptian times, doctors and magicians worked together to cure some problems. A mixture of medicines and spells was used if the patient had a snake or scorpion bite. Magic alone could be used to help prevent possible injury from a hungry crocodile.

## LITTLE REMINDERS

The Romans used to ask the gods for a cure to their illnesses. They left models of the body part they were having problems with, to remind the gods of the cures they had asked for. The mind boggles!

## PREVENTATIVE MEDICINE

Roman soldiers were fed a daily ration of garlic to keep them healthy. Imagine the smell as the army approached. It's no wonder that the Romans conquered so many countries!

*Garlic*

*Mustard had healing properties*

*Fenugreek (used for treating pneumonia)*

# "Now This Won't Hurt..."

Does the sight of a needle make your tummy wobble? Well this little assortment of historical medical procedures will have it heaving in no time! Rest assured – they were the 'in thing' at the time they were used.

*Bronze cupping vessel*

## Cupping

In Roman times, they did a thing called *cupping* to draw poison from the body. Like squeezing a spot? No...nothing as comfortable as that!

A cup with a piece of burning cloth was pressed on the skin. The burning used up all the oxygen in the cup and sucked it on to the body, drawing out all the nasties. Jolly painful!

## Urine-testing

The life of medieval doctors was not all a bundle of laughs. An important way of finding out what was wrong with a patient was to test their urine. There were up to 30 things to note, including the colour, the smell and, wait for it...the taste! Uuugh!

## BLOOD-LETTING

The ancient practice of *blood-letting* was very popular in the Middle Ages. If you were feeling ill in any way, draining a bit of blood from the body was supposed to make you feel a whole lot better. Not so sure myself! Blood-sucking relatives of earthworms called *leeches* were used as a slow way of blood-letting. Just pop one on the skin, let it drink five times its own weight in blood (no problem for a leech), then peel off.

*Leeches*

## BLOOD TRANSFUSIONS

Once it had been discovered that blood flowed around the body in a particular way, more experiments began. (Uh oh!) They tried replacing the blood of sick people with the blood of animals. Needless to say, it didn't work.

# TOOLS OF THE TRADE

Here's a gruesome little history quiz to entertain you and your friends on wet afternoons. Look at this awesome collection of historical medical tools and decide what each one was used for.

1 (a) Early African probes for digging decayed bits from teeth
  (b) Early Chinese acupuncture needles, used to relieve health problems
  (c) Sharp thorns used by Australian Aborigines to sew up wounds

2 (a) Machine used in the 1800s for making tablets
  (b) Late 19th-century antiseptic machine
  (c) A 19th-century machine used to test urine samples

3 (a) A late Roman device for holding a wound open during surgery
  (b) An Egyptian charm pinned to clothing to ward off illness
  (c) A Roman holder for false teeth

4 (a) A 19th-century oxygen mask
  (b) A false nose
  (c) A Roman heel support

5 (a) Tool for removing tonsils
  (b) Tool for holding operating instruments in antiseptic
  (c) Tool for removing appendix

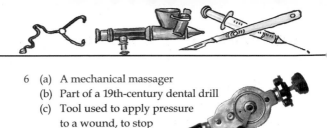

6 (a) A mechanical massager
  (b) Part of a 19th-century dental drill
  (c) Tool used to apply pressure
      to a wound, to stop
      blood flow

7 (a) Tool used for ear examinations
  (b) A 19th-century
      ear syringe
  (c) Microscope for
      examining
      blood samples

8 (a) Prototype
      syringe for
      taking blood samples
  (b) Late 18th-century syringe for
      injecting cordials into the stomach
  (c) Early 19th-century stethoscope

9 (a) A 17th-century model for teaching
      bone-setting
  (b) A 17th-century frame to
      hold patients still during
      an operation
  (c) Early Chinese support to teach
      children good body posture

10 (a) A 17th-century scalpel
   (b) A 17th-century tongue depressor
       for inspecting the back of the throat
   (c) A 16th-century spatula for mixing
       and applying ointments

Answers

1 (c) 2 (b) 3 (c) 4 (b) 5 (a) 6 (a) 7 (a) 8 (c) 9 (a) 10 (b)

# ODIOUS OPERATIONS

Before the mid-19th century, having an operation was a hideous and agonizing event – one to miss if humanly possible. But things DID get better, thank goodness! Here's a quick rundown on a few operation procedures.

## OPERATING WITH ANTS

In the ancient world, surgery in India was quite a sophisticated affair. They had some unlikely little helpers in the form of black ants. These made a strong *antiseptic* acid and were used as clips instead of stitches.

## HAIRCUT OR OPERATION?

Until the 16th century, doctors were not well-thought-of. Many surgeons combined surgery with being a barber and had an even worse reputation. (Surprise, surprise!) However, once they set up special training colleges, things began to look up for them.

## LET'S HEAR IT FOR JOSEPH LISTER

Joseph Lister (1827-1912) introduced the use of antiseptics. This helped to prevent people from dying from infection after operations. Hoorah!

*Machine for spraying carbolic steam*

## FREE FROM PAIN

There were no anaesthetics
before the 19th century, so
people having operations
had to either drink loads of
alcohol, be knocked out or
faint in agony. NOT nice!

In the mid-19th century,
*anaesthesia* was developed,
so patients slept during
operations. Hoorah,
HOORAH!

### BELIEVE IT OR NOT...

Today, a surgeon's basic tools would still be recognized
by a surgeon from Ancient Greece or Rome.

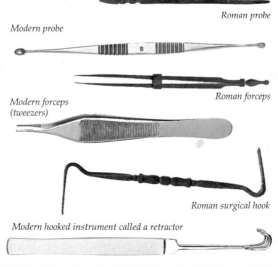

*Roman probe*

*Modern probe*

*Modern forceps
(tweezers)*

*Roman forceps*

*Roman surgical hook*

*Modern hooked instrument called a retractor*

# SETTING SAIL

From around the 15th century, sailing became a popular way of exploring. Later, trading ships carried goodies to different countries around the world. Life at sea wasn't all plain sailing though. Conditions were cramped and filthy, and the sailors had to be tough.

*Merchant ship*

## SHIPS' LOOS

A ship's loos were called the *heads*, or *seats of ease*. They were very basic – a hole cut in the deck with a seat on top. If a sailor couldn't get to the official loos, he used a bucket instead. Care had to be taken when emptying it overboard!

## MAGGOTY BISCUITS

Biscuits featured heavily in a sailor's diet, and we're not talking nice chocolaty ones either. They were rock hard and infested with maggots and weevils, which the sailors usually ended up eating. Yuck!

## SICK SAILORS

Being ill on a ship was to be avoided at all costs. Medical treatment was horribly primitive and if you got injured in battle you stood a good chance of dying from the treatment intended to save you.

## Scurvy

*Scurvy* was a disease which caused problems including weakness, tender gums, loss of teeth and bleeding under the skin. Mmm... nice! In 1747, it was discovered that feeding the crew with fresh fruit and vegetables packed with vitamin C helped prevent this nasty illness.

## Fresh Meat

Live animals were kept on ships to provide sailors with fresh meat. Good idea...but imagine the stink!

## Slave Ships

In the 17th century, seven million people were taken from Africa to work as slaves in the West Indies and America. The conditions on the slave ships which transported them were horrific and many of the slaves died on the journey.

## Getting Ratty

A ship's *hold*, where the cargo was stored, was usually crawling with rats infested with germ-carrying fleas. The rats ate the sailors' food and even gnawed through the wood of the boat! Little blighters!

*Most ships had a population of rats.*

# PILLAGING PIRATES

*Fierce-looking carved Viking head*

Pirates lived at sea and robbed other ships. There have been pirates around ever since there were ships for them to plunder. Here are some of the things that those raucous rogues got up to.

## VIKING PIRATES

From the 8th to the 11th centuries, Viking ships struck terror into the hearts of Northern Europeans. Viking pirates were legendary for their attacks on ships and raids on villages.

## FEARSOME FIENDS

Pirates encouraged the reputation they had of being fierce and cruel. They knew that their victims would give in more easily if they were threatened with torture and death. Well, who wouldn't?

*Every pirate had his own Jolly Roger design.*

## JOLLY ROGER

This is the famous name of the pirate flag. The skull and crossbones on a black background was a warning to the victims to surrender without a fight. A plain red flag was feared most of all as it meant that the pirates would give no mercy.

## A CAREER MOVE

Many ordinary sailors became pirates. They saw piracy as a life of freedom with a chance of becoming wealthy. Hah, hah, hah, haaaah!

*Gold doubloon*

*Silver coins – called pieces of eight*

## WOMEN PIRATES

Piracy was for men, so if a woman fancied a stab at it she had to disguise herself as a bloke. She had to dress in men's clothes, and take up drinking and swearing.

## RULES AND REGULATIONS

Here are a few typical rules that some pirates agreed to obey:

☠ Everyone is entitled to vote and to a share of the booze.

☠ Don't play cards or games for money.

☠ Candles out by eight o'clock.

☠ No boys or women on board.

☠ Keep weapons clean.

☠ Desertion in a battle is punished with death or marooning.

# KNIGHT LIFE

The life of a knight involved lots of riding around on horseback in heavy armour and being generally bold and loyal.

## EARLY KNIGHTS

In the 11th century, a group of brave blokes became socially recognized and very important. They were called *knights*. These champion chaps were warriors who fought on horseback, serving the local lord, count or duke.

## STARTING YOUNG

A boy of noble birth, destined to become a knight, was sent to a nobleman's house at 7 years old, to become his *page*.

At about 14, he became a knight's *squire*. Basically, this meant that he looked after the armour and horses, and learned to shoot with a bow.

A good squire became a knight at the age of 21, after only 14 years of training!

## KNIGHT ATTIRE

Knights wore heavy armour to protect them when fighting. Their gear changed over the centuries, but it still looks pretty uncomfortable to the modern eye.

A suit of armour weighed about 20-25 kg (44-55 lb), but the knight was still able to run, lie down and mount his horse. There was one drawback though; armour was hot...VERY hot! Phewee!

## HORSE ARMOUR

A knight's horse got to wear armour too. After all, the nag was a vital and expensive piece of the knight's equipment.

## TOURNAMENTS

In a tournament, two teams of knights fought a mock battle. At first, proper battle armour and weapons were used, but by the 13th century blunted weapons were introduced. What a relief!

## JOUSTING

A popular pursuit with knights, this one. In a *joust*, two knights on horseback fought one-to-one. They used long weapons called *lances* to push each other off their horses. Ouch!

*Horse's headgear*

# BATTLE STATIONS

There have been battles all over the world throughout time. To save you from the horror of lots of boring dates, here are some entertaining snippets of info about life in battle.

## GREAT BATTLES

The great battles of history were often short. This was because it took so much effort and strength to swing the heavy swords and wield the spears that were used at the time, that the fighters soon became exhausted.

## BELIEVE IT OR NOT...

The longest continuous war was between a number of European countries and it lasted from 1618 to 1648. It became known as the Thirty Years' War. Imaginative, eh?

## A SCARY SIGHT

The part of an army on horseback is called the *cavalry*. In the past, this was split into light cavalry and heavy cavalry. The light cavalry found out what the enemy was up to and chased after beaten soldiers. The heavy cavalry charged the enemy in solid lines on the battlefield. This scary sight sent many enemies running in the opposite direction.

## WHOOPS!

Doing *drill* is when soldiers train to use weapons really efficiently, to make a strong fighting unit. Unfortunately, French soldiers in the Napoleonic era (the late 1700s) were not too hot on drill. Many of them were shot by men behind them. Careless!

*Rifle drill*

## BATTLE WOUNDS

In the past, disease was a big wartime killer. Thousands of men died in battle, but thousands more died because their wounds were not properly cleaned and the operating instruments were dirty! Yuck!

## IMPORTANT COLOURS

A regiment's colours is the name given to its flag, with its own special design. In battle, soldiers risked their lives to protect their colours, to stop the enemy from seizing them. The colours would often be passed from person to person as each bearer was shot down. Steer clear of the flag, I say!

# CASTLE CAPERS

Castle-building started in the 9th and 10th centuries. Early ones were made of earth and timber; later ones were made of stone. The people who lived there included the nobleman and his family, a page, a knight, a priest and a fool (for entertainment).

## SMELLY WALLS

When a castle was built, its walls were waterproofed with a smelly mixture of clay, animal dung and horsehair. Perfect all-weather protection!

## CASTLE CUISINE

Food served in a castle included meat, fish, poultry, game, eggs, vegetables and fruit. As they didn't have refrigerators then, some meat was salted to preserve it. Rich sauces came in handy for disguising the taste of over-ripe meat. Delicious!

## FOOD TASTERS

Before royalty or a noble family ate, a food taster had to sample each dish to check for poison. On the whole this was probably a pleasant occupation, unless you worked for an unpopular boss and ended up dead!

## LOO LIFE

Castle loos were called *garderobes*. They either stuck out from castle walls, emptying into the *moat* (the watery bit around the castle) or drained into a *cesspit* (place for collecting sewage).

## HEADS OVERHEAD!

In wartime, castles were attacked by hostile armies. One of the grisly things attackers did was to catapult severed heads over the castle walls. Dead animals were popular ammunition too, as the attackers hoped to spread disease in the castle.

The people in the castle often had their own smelly form of ammunition – human excrement!

## MURDER HOLES

Holes in the roof near the main entrance of Bodiam Castle were called *murder holes*. They were used for dumping scalding water, hot sand, stones or boiling oil on the attackers. Nice!

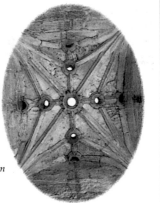

*Murder holes in Bodiam Castle*

# GHASTLY PUNISHMENTS

Prisoners were often kept in castles. Important prisoners were treated quite well, but others were not so lucky. Here are some of the punishments which befell the more unfortunate.

## DUCKING

This is nothing to do with those sweet little quacking creatures...well, not directly anyway. Ducking was a punishment where the offender was tied into a *ducking stool* and ducked (surprise, surprise!) in the moat or the village pond. VERY humiliating and VERY wet!

## BRANDING

An immediate punishment for a wrongdoer was to have a burn mark branded on the body with a hot *branding iron*. The face was one of the worst places to be branded because everyone could see that you had been up to no good!

## CHAINED UP

A prisoner could be chained to the wall with a *manacle* – a heavy metal chain with a locking iron ring. This was REALLY heavy and VERY uncomfortable.

*Manacle*

## SMALL CELLS

Prisoners were often barred into small cells inside the castle. These had a stone bench seat, a small wooden door for passing food through, and not much else.

## BURNING AT THE STAKE

This was a hideous yet popular method of execution during the 16th century. People who refused to follow the state religion sometimes met this fiery end.

A Frenchwoman called Joan of Arc was accused of witchcraft and burned at the stake in 1431.

## HANGING, DRAWING AND QUARTERING

Really very unpleasant this – NOT one to dwell on. The penalty for plotting against the king was to be hung, then have your innards removed, and finally...to be chopped up into four bits. Uuugh!

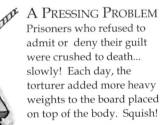

## A PRESSING PROBLEM

Prisoners who refused to admit or deny their guilt were crushed to death... slowly! Each day, the torturer added more heavy weights to the board placed on top of the body. Squish!

# PLAGUE

In the 14th century, a killer plague known as the Black Death spread worldwide and wiped out just about everyone who caught it. Here are some plague facts...for the more gruesome reader!

## DEATH TOLL
It is thought that the Black Death killed a shocking 25 million people in Europe alone. Symptoms included the skin turning black and a high fever.

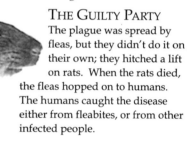

## THE GUILTY PARTY
The plague was spread by fleas, but they didn't do it on their own; they hitched a lift on rats. When the rats died, the fleas hopped on to humans. The humans caught the disease either from fleabites, or from other infected people.

## A LACK OF PRIESTS
Around the time of the plague, people believed that it was important to make a final confession of their sins to a priest. However, so many priests died that most people had to be buried without prayers or a proper ceremony.

## AN UNLIKELY CURE

The gold and silver *pomander* below was filled with nice-smelling petals and herbs. The smell was supposed to freshen the air and keep the plague away. Some chance!

*Each section had a different herb in it.*

## AFTER THE PLAGUE

Life wasn't a lot of fun for the people who survived the plague, although it was probably better than being dead! So many people had been killed that the survivors had to work much harder, and they didn't get any extra money either!

# Historical Food Facts

Here are a few tantalising historical food facts. Maybe you could memorise them and recall them next time you sit down to a family meal!

## Mixed Blessings

Festival time in the castle was a gastronomic delight, but the castle cooks did some weird things with the menu. Mixing sweet and savoury things was common, so you could end up munching on roast heron, a sweet pie, fish and dates – all in the same course. Mmm-mmmm!

## Overcooked

The remains of food were found at Pompeii in Italy, which was buried in ash after Mount Vesuvius erupted in 79 AD. The not-so-tasty morsels included a loaf of bread, figs and a bowl of preserved eggs.

## Leather Lunch

A band of 17th-century pirates became so hungry that they had to eat their leather satchels. A recipe left by one

of them told of slicing the leather up, tenderising it with stones, removing the hair and then roasting or grilling it. An extra tip recommended serving with plenty of water!

## ROMAN DELICACIES

Do you fancy a change from your usual supper time snack? Why not try out a dish described by one ancient writer – dormice cooked in honey and poppy seeds.

## DEAD TASTY

Egyptian mummies had food buried with them (among other things), for the afterlife. Let's hope that they didn't have to eat too much of the tough bread that they ate in real life. It was so hard that their teeth got badly worn.

## WHO ATE WHAT?

One of the ways archaeologists find out what people (and animals) ate long ago is by studying *coprolites* (preserved excrement). When cut up, they reveal fragments of plant and bone, and also eggs of infesting parasites. Oh sorry...were you eating?

# FASHION VICTIMS

Clothes have been worn for many
thousands of years, and a jolly good job
too! There have been many weird and
wonderful fashion items, but many of the
makers and wearers became victims of
their finery.

## BELIEVE IT OR NOT...

Some of the earliest cloth was made
from tree bark. It was soaked in
water and pounded to soften it.
Then it was oiled and painted,
ready to wear. Comfy...NOT!

## TAILOR-MADE

In medieval times, wealthy people employed a tailor to
make their clothes. He spent so much time bent over
sewing in his workshop, that a bad stomach and a curved
spine were hard to avoid.

## ARCTIC ATTIRE

Surviving in the freezing Arctic is a
chilly business. It's probably just
as well that it's cold when you
consider what some of the
traditional clothes were
made of.

*Jackets made from strips
of seal or walrus intestine
were popular!*

## BIG BELLIES
A peculiar fashion started in 16th-century Spain. Men had the fronts of their jackets padded with an artificial belly made from horsehair, rags or wool. Very attractive!

## PLENTIFUL PETTICOATS
Talk about fashion victims! In the early 1800s, a lady had to wear up to six petticoats under her skirt to achieve the right fullness and look. One of these was stiffened with horsehair.

## WALKING TALL
So you thought that platform shoes were a fairly recent invention, did you? Around the 15th century, Italian footwear included chunky *chopines*, which were worn over shoes in wet weather. Things got ridiculous when some reached a height of 76 cm (30 in). Fancy tottering around in those!

## SQUASHED FEET
Around 1,000 years ago, it became fashionable for young Chinese girls to have their feet bound up tightly. This made their feet painfully deformed, but small feet were considered beautiful.

# SICKENING SNIPPETS

If you've managed to get through all the fascinating facts in this book and still have space left for more, here are some final snippets to complete the gruesome experience.

## UNFORTUNATE INSIGHT

Giordano Bruno was burned at the stake at the end of the 16th century for saying that the universe was made up of millions of planets and Earth was one of them. Not far from the truth there Giordano! Bad luck!

## A BAD MOVE

Colonel Pierrepont designed the first traffic island in Piccadilly, London. When it was installed, he stepped back to admire it and was killed by a passing hansom cab.

## DEADLY TREASURE

Countess Arco of Austria found a chest full of gold coins in her garden and took it everywhere with her, strapped to the luggage rack of her coach. One day, on a particularly bumpy journey, the chest was jolted off the rack and fell on the countess' head, killing her outright.

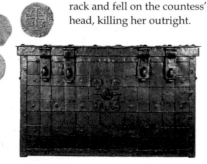

## DEAD PROFESSIONAL

Anne Boleyn, the second
wife of Henry VIII,
rehearsed her execution
the night before.
There's nothing like
being prepared for
the big event, is there?

## KILLER BATHS

In 1903, two tramps were arrested in St Louis, Missouri,
and were given their first baths. A nice experience you
might think. Not really...both tramps died soon after this
cleansing ordeal!

## SPOOKY PREDICTION

In 1869, a lady in the court of the
French emperor, Napoleon III,
told him that she dreamed she
had seen his state coach being
blown up by a bomb...so the
emperor never rode in his coach.
It was probably just as well, as it
was sold to Tsar Alexander II of
Russia who was assassinated
while driving in it, in 1881.

**Acknowledgements:** (KEY: b=bottom, c=centre, l=left, r=right, t=top)
95th Rifles and Re-enactment Living History Unit; British Museum; Chateau
de Loches; Museo Archeologico di Napoli; Museum of London; National
Maritime Museum, Greenwich, London; Natural History Museum; Pitt Rivers
Museum; Science Museum, London; Viking Ship Museum, Oslo, Norway;
Warwick Castle.

**Picture Credits:** The Greenland Museum: 16; Scarab Pectoral, from the tomb
of Tutankhamun, c. 1361-52 BC, Egyptian National Museum,
Cairo/Giraudon/Bridgeman Art Library, London: 21t; Whydah International:
46b; Trustees of the British Museum:23bl.

**Additional Photography:** Geoff Brightling, Jane Burton, Tina Chambers,
Geoff Dann, David Exton, Christi Graham and Nick Nichols of the
British Museum, Peter Hayman, Dave King, John Lepine, Liz McAulay,
James Stevenson, Jane Stockman, J Tubb, Adrian Whicher.

Every effort has been made to trace the copyright holders. Funfax Ltd
apologises for any unintentional omissions and would be pleased, in such
cases, to add an acknowledgement in further editions.

# INSIDE
# OUT

Written by Susan Mayes

Illustrated by Andrew Peters
and Simon Tegg

# YOUR BRILLIANT BODY

Congratulations! You are the proud owner of a brilliant, sophisticated machine. What do you mean, "No I'm not!"? YES YOU ARE! Your body is a clever and complicated thing, made of lots of different parts which do their own special jobs. To give you a taste of the wonders to come, here are a few of the marvellous things that your body can do.

Your brain is the high-tech control centre of your whole system.

Your muscles help you to run, jump, swim and much, much more.

Your skin holds all your bits in and helps to keep you at the right temperature.

Your skeleton is a rigid framework that helps to keep your body shape. Without it, you would be a floppy mound of flesh. Yuck!

Somewhere between your mouth and your bottom, there is a lengthy network of tubing called your *digestive system*. This takes all the goodness out of your food, to keep you going and keep you growing.

Seeing, hearing, smelling, tasting, feeling – your body does all this.

Your lungs expand to help you breathe fresh air, then they cunningly get rid of the old air. Clever, eh?

Your blood has numerous jobs to do and your heart works night and day to pump it around your body.

So you see...you really ARE something special (as if you needed convincing!). For the gory and the not-so-gory details, read on.

Lungs

# EARLY WEIRD IDEAS

Today, scientists know an amazing amount about the human body, but things were different hundreds of years ago. Some of the ideas they came up with were quite accurate, but some were way out. Uh oh!

## DISCOVERIES AND MISTAKES

Claudius Galen was a know-it-all doctor from Ancient Greece. He made lots of discoveries, but he made lots of mistakes, too. He had so much authority and such a high opinion of himself, that no one really questioned his findings for around fourteen centuries.

## MINI MACHINES

Italian, Giorgio Baglivi (1668-1707), had over-simplified beliefs about the body, which he saw as a set of small machines. He thought of blood vessels as a system of water pipes and the lungs as bellows. Good try, Giorgio, but not quite there!

## BLOODY THOUGHTS

Blood is blood! That's what people believed around the 17th century. They tried *transfusing* (transferring) it from one person to another and even between animals and people. But blood is NOT the same in everyone and everything, so people tended to die from the experiments.

## THE FOUR HUMOURS

In ancient times, doctors believed that four body fluids determined a person's character. An imbalance in the amounts of *blood, mucus* (phlegm), *black bile* and *yellow bile* could make a person cheerful or miserable, for instance. Laxatives, bleeding or a change of diet were prescribed to alter the balance. Hmmmm!

# All Shapes and Sizes

$W$e all start off small, but each of us grows to a slightly different shape and size. There are lots of variations on the body theme.

## A Basic Framework

The shape you are is mostly controlled by the size and shape of the bones in your skeleton. For instance, some people have broad shoulders and others have narrow ones. Even if you are as tall as your friend, your proportions may be different.

## Believe It or Not...

Robert Wadlow of Alton in Illinois, USA, grew to an incredible height of 2.7 m (just under 9 ft). Now THAT'S tall!

## Healthy Living

Eating and exercise make a difference to the way you look. If you eat more than you need, your body stores the extra food as fat. If you do lots of exercise, you get bulging muscles.

## BODY MEASUREMENTS

Way back in history, before there were rulers or tape measures, people used body parts for measuring. Although the size of the parts varied from person to person, the measurements seemed accurate enough as a guide for building.

| Egyptian Measuring System | |
|---|---|
| Body Part | Name |
| Width of finger | Zebo |
| Width of palm | Shep |
| Width of outspread fingers | Span |
| Fingertip to elbow point | Royal cubit |

## LET'S FACE FACTS

Would you say that both sides of your face are the same? It's a weird fact, but faces are not *symmetrical* (exactly the same on each side).

*Face looks the same on each side*

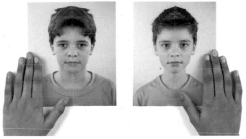

*Here, each picture has one side of face as its mirror image, showing that the face isn't really symmetrical*

# Your Basic Ingredients

Every bit of the human body is made up of tiny living parts called *cells* – millions and millions of them, actually! Jam-packed, or what? They are so small that they can only be seen with a powerful microscope.

## WHAT'S IN A CELL?

The important part of a cell is in the middle. This is called the *nucleus,* and it controls the way the cell works.

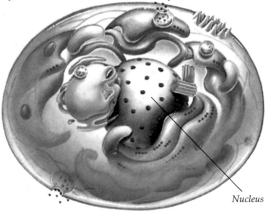

*Nucleus*

## WET, OR WHAT?

Your body is about two-thirds water. Most of this is in your cells and the liquid parts, such as your blood. Even your tough bones are one-third water. Incredible, isn't it?

Red blood cells
carry oxygen around
the body

## DIFFERENT JOBS

You have lots of different
cells and each type has a
different job.

Muscle cells
get shorter to
move the body

Nerve cells
send messages from
one part of the body
to another

## LONG AND SHORT LIVES

Different types of cells have different life spans. The cells
that line your intestines only live for a few hours because
they get rubbed away by digested food squeezing past.
Bone cells last for many years.

## REPAIRS

Just in case you are worrying about your body wearing
away altogether, here's some good news. It is making
new cells all the time, to replace the dead ones. Hoorah!

## GROWING

While you are growing into an adult,
your body makes more and more
cells. That's how you get
bigger. Each cell
grows and then
divides into
two cells.

Cell growing and
dividing into two

# BONES

Thank goodness for bones! They form the rigid frame (your skeleton) inside your body which protects your soft organs and stops you from collapsing in a heap. You have 206 bones altogether, but only the main ones are named here.

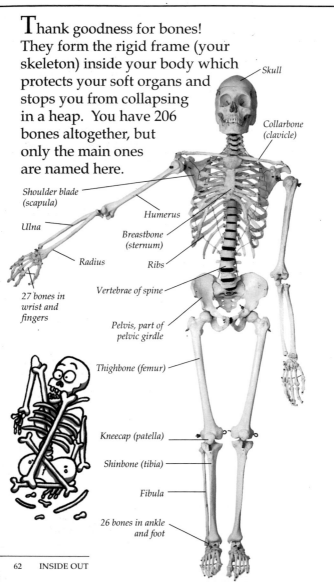

Skull

Collarbone (clavicle)

Shoulder blade (scapula)

Humerus

Ulna

Breastbone (sternum)

Radius

Ribs

27 bones in wrist and fingers

Vertebrae of spine

Pelvis, part of pelvic girdle

Thighbone (femur)

Kneecap (patella)

Shinbone (tibia)

Fibula

26 bones in ankle and foot

## INSIDE BONES

Bones are not solid. A long bone, like the thighbone, has a space for the *marrow* that makes new cells for your blood. The hard outer bone is built from thousands of closely arranged rods, which make it light and strong.

*Marrow*

*Thousands of tiny rods in outer bone*

## JOINTS

Having a strong, sturdy framework would be useless if it didn't move easily. Luckily, a system of joints allows you to do more or less as you like. Where two bones meet, *ligaments* (straps) hold the bones together, so that they can move but not come apart. Phew!

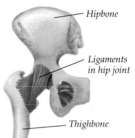

*Hipbone*

*Ligaments in hip joint*

*Thighbone*

## THE SMALLEST BONE

The *stirrup bone*, one of the three bones in the middle of your ear, is the smallest bone in your body. It's REALLY tiny.

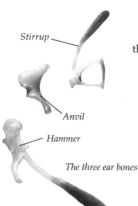

*Stirrup*

*Anvil*

*Hammer*

*The three ear bones*

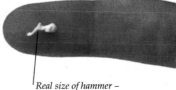

*Real size of hammer – stirrup is half this size!*

# How You Move

There are over 600 strong, stretchy muscles in your body. Most of them are joined to your bones and are used to move them into position.

## Big and Small

Your biggest muscles are in your buttocks and thighs. The smallest ones are inside your ear and are as thin as cotton thread.

## Working in Pairs

Most muscles work in pairs. This is because they can only pull, not push. So if one muscle pulls to move a bone, the other muscle has to pull the bone the other way, to return it to its natural position.

*Biceps muscle pulls upper arm to bend elbow*

*Triceps muscle pulls lower arm to straighten elbow*

## SMILING'S EASY

You have around 30-40
muscles in your face. It
only takes about 10 of
them to smile, but it takes
about 12 to frown. So
stick with the smiles!

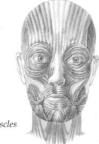

*Face muscles*

*Frowning*                    *Smiling*

## CRAMP

Sometimes, muscles become hard and tight, causing a
few painful moments of agony called *cramp*. Aaaagh!
This happens because the muscles have not been well-
used for a while.

## FULL-TIME MUSCLES

Your heart, stomach and intestines are all partly made of
muscle which never tires. Your heart muscle is called the
*cardiac muscle* and beats all your life. That's a relief!

## EXERCISE

Your muscles can adjust themselves depending on how
much they are used. If you use them a lot, they will
become bigger and stronger. The amount of time they can
work without getting tired increases, too.

# Super Skin

Not only is your skin a handy, tight-fitting bag that keeps your innards where they should be, but it does a lot more, too. At a maximum of 5 mm (1/4 in) thick, it is one of the body's vital organs.

## Skin Colour

Your skin has a dye called *melanin* in it, which gives it its colour. A person with dark skin has more melanin in their skin than a person with fair skin. In a light-skinned person, more melanin is made when they are in the sun, to protect them from the sun's rays.

## Hot and Cold

If your body gets too hot, sweat starts to ooze out of *sweat glands*, on to your body surface through *pores*. It *evaporates* (dries up), taking the body heat with it, so you feel cooler. Yippee!

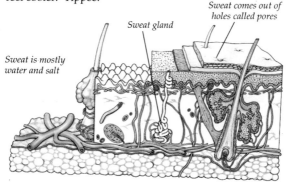

*Sweat comes out of holes called pores*

*Sweat gland*

*Sweat is mostly water and salt*

---

### Believe It or Not...

About 4 kg (9 lb) of your skin wears away and flakes off each year. Yikes! It gets rubbed against clothes, sheets and other things, and drops away. Yuck!

---

## GOOSEPIMPLES

You have lots of small, fine hairs on your skin – about three to five million actually. When you get cold, muscles under your skin tighten and make the hairs stand up on end. That's what makes goosepimples.

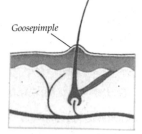

*Goosepimple*

*Hairs stand up on end to trap air and retain heat*

## TOUCH

You feel things with millions of tiny sensors in your skin, called *nerve endings*. When you touch something, your skin sends a message to your brain, telling it if things are hot, cold, rough, smooth, and so on.

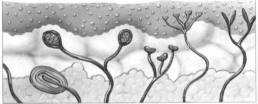

*Different types of nerve endings*

## NAILS

Like your skin and hair, your nails are made of hard, tough stuff called *keratin*. Your toenails grow three or four times more slowly than your fingernails. Fascinating, eh?

*Some people let their nails grow so long that they begin to curl. Gruesome!*

# EYES AND SEEING

Sight is one of the five senses which let you experience the world around you. An incredible two-thirds of your mind's attention is taken up by what you see.

## WHAT'S WHAT
Each bit of your eye has a different job to do.

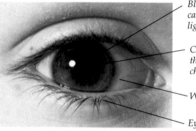

*Black dot is really a hole called the pupil – lets light into your eye*

*Coloured part is called the iris – muscles in it change size of pupil*

*White of eye*

*Eyelashes keep out dust and dirt*

## HOW YOU SEE
Light rays shine in through your pupil. A clear disc behind, called the *lens*, bends the rays to make an upside-down image of the thing you are looking at appear on the *retina*, at the back. The retina turns the picture into nerve signals which go to your brain. The brain turns the picture the right way up. Got that?

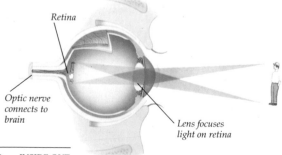

*Retina*

*Optic nerve connects to brain*

*Lens focuses light on retina*

## WEARING GLASSES

If the lenses in your eyes don't work very well, they need a bit of extra help. The lenses in glasses help the lenses in your eyes to get the picture on to the retina properly.

## PUPIL PUZZLE

When it is dark, your pupils open wide to let as much light in as possible, to help you see. In a bright light, your pupils shrink to protect your eye. Amazing!

## CRYING YOUR EYES OUT

Tears are made by a *tear gland* behind each upper eyelid. They flow out along tiny tubes called *ducts* and smear over your eye when you blink. Used tears drain into your nose through *tear ducts*. That's why having a good cry makes your nose run. Sniff, sniff!

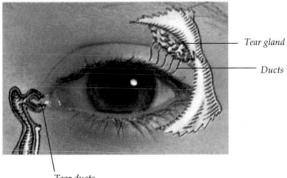

Tear gland

Ducts

Tear ducts

# EARS AND HEARING

You can only see a part of your ear – the flappy bit on the outside. The rest is inside your head.

## WHAT'S INSIDE?

Sound travels down the *ear canal* and hits the *eardrum*, making it vibrate. This makes three tiny bones vibrate too, passing the vibrations even further inside. They travel through liquid in a curly tube called the *cochlea*, pulling on tiny hairs inside. The hairs make nerve signals which go to the brain. Complicated, isn't it?

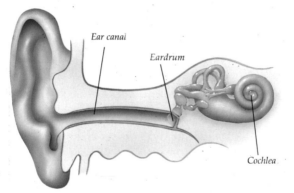

Ear canal

Eardrum

Cochlea

## HEARING YOURSELF

When you munch food or talk, your ear receives sound waves through the bones in your head, as well as through the air. So the way you sound to YOU is different from the way you sound to other people. (That's why you sound strange when you hear a recording of your voice.)

## BALANCE

Your ears help you balance...honestly! Fluid in parts called the *semicircular canals* is swirled by head movements, sending messages to your brain about your body's position. Then you adjust the rest of your body, to balance.

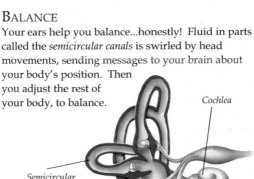

Cochlea

Semicircular canals

## BELIEVE IT OR NOT...

Dancers and skaters can spin without falling over by keeping their head level and focusing on one point. This stops the fluid in their semicircular canals from slopping around too much and making them dizzy.

## LOUD AND QUIET

Your little lugs are incredibly sensitive. They can hear loud sounds, of course, but they can also pick up the tiniest sounds, too.

As people get older, their ears become less sensitive, which is why you have to talk loudly and clearly to make some old people hear.

# SMELL AND TASTE

Imagine not being able to smell or taste things. Eating in particular would be a pretty dull experience.

## A SMELLY BUSINESS

As well as helping you breathe, your nose helps you smell. Smells are made of microscopic particles called *molecules*. Tiny hairy sensors in your nostrils detect the molecules and tell your brain. Simple!

## EARLY WARNING SYSTEM

Your nose can be a very handy early warning system. It can sniff the smoke from a fire, it can smell food when it's going off, or it can even get a whiff of your socks when they need a wash! Poo-eeeee!

## TANTALISING TASTES

Your tongue is covered with thousands of microscopic sensors called *taste buds*. Most of them are along the tip, the sides and the back. Each part detects a different sort of taste.

*Back tastes bitter things (coffee, for instance)*

*Middle sides taste sour foods*

*Sides detect salt*

*Tip tastes sweetness*

## YUCK!

When you were younger, did you think that some kinds of food tasted REALLY revolting, but you like them now? If so, this could partly be because some of your taste buds die as you grow older, so things don't taste as strong. A baby has over 10,000 taste buds whereas an older person has about 5,000.

## BLOCKED NOSE

If you have a blocked nose, you can't smell your food, and you probably can't taste it either. This is because the two senses work very closely together, so they are both affected by the problem.

*Putting a clip on the nose makes tasting very tricky.*

# LOOKING AT TEETH

Your teeth are vital for making your food small enough to swallow easily. They are really tough, to withstand a lifetime of cutting and grinding.

*Crown is the part you see*

## INSIDE A TOOTH

There are two main parts to a tooth. The *crown* is the part above the gum and the *root* holds the tooth firmly in place in the jawbone.

*Enamel outer casing – enamel is the hardest substance in the body*

*Blood vessels*

*Dentine absorbs jolts*

*Cement*

*Jawbone*

## GROWING TEETH

A newborn baby's teeth are usually hidden in its gums. As it grows, its teeth grow too. They begin to show at about six months. The first teeth to grow are called *milk teeth* – there are 20 of them. By six years old, these start to fall out and are replaced by the adult set which takes their place. Adults have 32 teeth.

## DIFFERENT JOBS

You have four different types of teeth for doing different cutting jobs. The chisel-shaped *incisors* cut and slice; the pointed *canines* grip and tear; the broad, flat *premolars* and *molars* crush and chew. Munch, crunch, slurp!

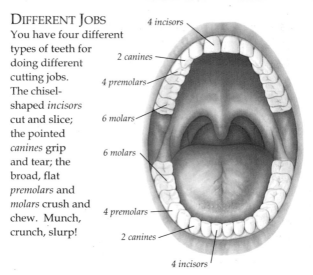

4 incisors

2 canines

4 premolars

6 molars

6 molars

4 premolars

2 canines

4 incisors

### BELIEVE IT OR NOT...

You make about 1.5 litres (2.6 pt) of *saliva* (spit) a day. Gulp! It helps soften your food, making chewing and swallowing easier.

## HEALTHY GNASHERS

If you take care of your teeth, they should last a lifetime. Cleaning them regularly gets rid of tiny bits of food which stick to them and lurk in crevices. The fragments make acids which rot your teeth; sugary things are the worst offenders!

# Food's Journey

When you munch your way through your favourite meal, your food is starting a journey which lasts about a day. It travels down a long, winding tube called the *alimentary canal* which begins at your mouth and ends at your bottom. Follow the journey over the next four pages.

## Chewing and Swallowing

Some kinds of food need chewing more than others, to get them ready to swallow. Your tongue pushes the food to the back of your throat, then muscles push it downwards.

## Choking

Have you ever tucked into some tasty morsel and choked on it? Usually, your windpipe closes when you swallow, to stop food from going down it. Sometimes it doesn't close in time, so a bit 'goes down the wrong way', making you choke. This usually sends the food back up again.

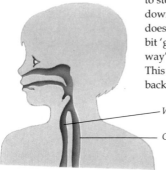

— *Windpipe*

— *Gullet*

## AND THEN...

After you have swallowed, the food travels in soft lumps down your *gullet* and into your *stomach*. This stretches as it fills and can hold 2 litres (3.5 pt) or more. Blimey! The stomach mashes the food up into a soupy mixture.

### BELIEVE IT OR NOT...
Your stomach has a slimy lining. This stops the strong chemicals that digest food from digesting your stomach as well. Eeek!

### BURPING
A potentially embarrassing quirk of your digestive system, this one! Eating fast, or talking while you eat, makes you swallow air with your food. Your body may send the air back up as a BURP! Oooh...pardon me!

Gullet

Stomach

# The Journey Continues

Right...so you've toured the mouth, the gullet and the stomach. Here's what happens next...

## Into the Intestines

After about three hours, the 'soup' in your stomach moves to your *small intestine*. This is a long, curled-up tube where the *nutrients* (good things) in the 'soup' are taken into the blood.

*Thousands of tiny folds on the walls of the small intestine called villi – blood flows around the villi to carry away nutrients*

## Large Intestine

The large intestine is fatter than the small intestine, but nowhere near as long. Water and salts are absorbed into the first part, called the *colon*. *Faeces* (solid waste) collects in the last part, called the *rectum*, and gets pushed out through your *anus* (bottom) when you go to the toilet.

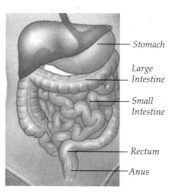

Stomach

Large Intestine

Small Intestine

Rectum

Anus

## WASTE WATER

In case you were wondering about waste water, which no doubt you were, this is turned into *urine* (wee) in your kidneys. It is stored in your bladder until you go to the toilet.

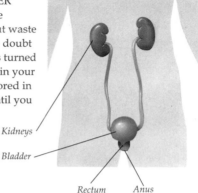

*Kidneys*

*Bladder*

*Rectum*  *Anus*

## RUMBLING TUM

Don't be embarrassed about your rumbling tum. It's only your digestive system squeezing and churning gas and digestive juices...so forget the blushes!

## UPSET STOMACH

If you eat food that's gone off, your body tries to get rid of it. Your stomach muscles push it back up your gullet and you are sick, or it may speed through you and emerge at the other end as diarrhoea. Sorry...were you eating?

# BREATHING

$W$hat do you have in common with snails and rabbits? Well, among other things, you need oxygen to keep you alive. Here is how YOU get it...

## BREATHING IN AND OUT

When you breathe, your lungs become bigger to make space for the air. This goes in through your nose or your mouth, down your windpipe and into your lungs. When you breathe out, your lungs return to their smaller size and the air is pushed out.

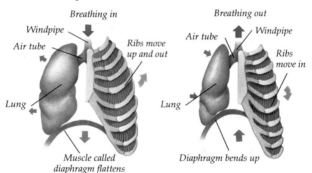

Breathing in

Windpipe

Air tube

Ribs move up and out

Lung

Muscle called diaphragm flattens

Breathing out

Air tube

Windpipe

Ribs move in

Lung

Diaphragm bends up

## THE INSIDE STORY

In your lungs, the air travels to the ends of the air tubes and into bunches of *air sacs*. The oxygen seeps through the sac walls, into your blood. This carries oxygen to your cells, to keep you alive. Your blood carries a waste gas called *carbon dioxide* back to your lungs and you breathe it out. Clever, eh?

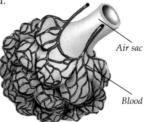

Air sac

Blood

## SEEING YOUR BREATH

On chilly days, you can see smoky clouds when you breathe out. This is because your breath contains water vapour and when it meets the cold air, it condenses into tiny droplets which look like puffs of smoke.

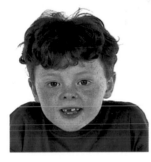

## HICCUPS

The big muscle (your diaphragm) below your lungs sometimes gets out of control. This makes your breath come in gasps which sound like "hic"!

## YAWNING

If you breathe slowly, your lungs don't get rid of all the carbon dioxide. Your brain tells your lungs to take an extra-deep breath to blow out the old air. This is a yawn.

## YOUR VOICE BOX

When you breathe out, air flows past two flaps called *vocal cords*, at the top of your windpipe. This makes them vibrate, creating a sound. Your mouth shapes the sounds into words, and hey presto...you speak!

# BLOOD BASICS

A word of warning – these pages are not for the squeamish who have a thing about blood. For the more strong-hearted amongst you, read on to discover some fascinating blood facts.

## BLOOD FLOW

Your heart pumps blood out into your blood vessels. There are three different types of vessels for getting the blood around your body.

*Heart*

*Arteries carry blood away from heart – usually contain bright red blood high in oxygen. Remember: arteries = away.*

*Veins carry blood which is low in oxygen back to heart*

*Capillaries – network of microscopic vessels at the end of arteries – let oxygen and nutrients into body tissue, then join veins*

## HEARTBEATS

Your heart is a hollow muscle about the size of your clenched fist. The left side pumps blood with oxygen out into your blood vessels. The right side pumps the blood from your body back to your lungs to collect more oxygen. Got that?

An adult's heart beats (or pulses) between 60-80 times a minute when they are resting. A child's beats 90-100 times. Feel your inner wrist with two fingertips and you will feel your pulse.

## What Blood Is

Your blood is a combination of things. About half is a pale yellow fluid called *plasma.* The other half is made up of *red cells, white cells* and *platelets.*

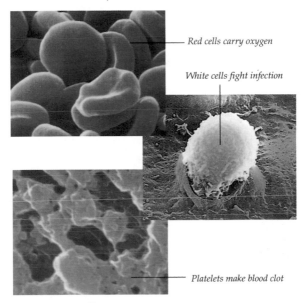

Red cells carry oxygen

White cells fight infection

Platelets make blood clot

## Clots and Scabs

A nice one to discuss with friends at meal time! If you cut yourself, the blood of the wound forms a clot which seals the leak. This dries and hardens, making a tough scab which protects the skin underneath while it heals. Don't pick!

## Hot and Cold

Blood is handy stuff when it comes to heating you up or cooling you down. It takes warmth from busy organs and muscles to cooler parts, to even out your body temperature.

# Brain Power

Your brain looks like a big, grey walnut and it fits cosily into the top part of your skull. It controls everything your body does, including your thoughts, feelings, memories and movements.

## Three-part Wonder

The human brain has three main parts. Each part does a different job.

*The cerebrum is the thinking part – it deals with hearing, touch, sight and body movements.*

*The cerebellum controls balance and skilled movements.*

*The brainstem controls automatic actions, like breathing.*

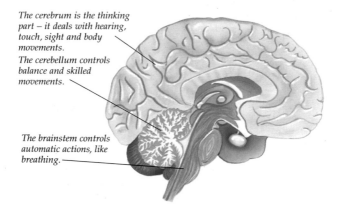

## Believe It or Not...

If your wrinkly cerebrum was unfolded and flattened out, you could cover the kitchen table with it. Handy if the tablecloth is in the wash!

## MEMORY

Your brain controls different types of memory, so you remember some things for longer than others.

Your sensory memory helps you make sense of where you are, so you can move around without bumping into things.

Your short-term memory deals with information you have just received, but it only remembers things for a short while. A new telephone number may slip your mind within a minute or two.

## LEARNING

How good you are at learning mostly depends on the power of your memory.

One type of learning involves physical skills, where you learn by remembering what works and what doesn't.

A second kind of learning is to do with thinking ideas through and ways of working things out.

A third kind of learning is to do with storing facts and figures, so you can use them later.

# A Bundle of Nerves

Your nervous system is like a network of telephone wires which run all over your body. It passes messages between your brain, spinal cord and body at lightning speed. The messages travel as tiny electrical signals.

## Two Main Parts

Your brain is your body's control centre and your spinal cord has many millions of nerves in it. Together they are known as the *central nervous system*. The rest of your nerves spread out through your body and are called the *peripheral nervous system*.

Brain

Spinal cord

## Pins and Needles

If you lean on a part of your body for too long, nerves get squashed and can't work properly. You feel a tingle which is your nerves sending you the signal to move.

## How it Works

Here is an example showing you how your nervous system operates:

1. Eyes see a delicious cake and nose smells it.

2. Nerve endings in eyes and nose send a message to the brain to let it know.

3. Brain notices: "CAKE!"

4. Message from brain tells hand: "Pick it up and place it in mouth."

5. Hand does as it's told.

## Early Warning

Pain is not nice, but it is very useful. If you have a rotten tooth, the nerve endings send messages to your brain and you feel pain which warns you to do something about the damage...like go to the dentist, for instance.

## Danger!

If you touch something that's very hot, you soon pull away. To make this happen as quickly as possible, the message doesn't go to your brain; it goes via your spinal cord to your muscles, to make you move. Your reaction is called a *reflex* and it happens without you thinking about it.

# Sleeping and Dreaming

While you sleep, your body and brain don't shut down – they just slow down a bit. Your body carries on growing and repairing itself and your brain keeps all your vital functions going. It may also do some of that weird stuff called dreaming.

## Believe It or Not...
You sleep for about a third of your life. Zzzzzzzzz!

## Baby Sleep
A baby growing in its mother's tummy wakes and sleeps just like you. Some unborn babies even suck their thumbs! After being born, some young babies sleep for as long as 18 hours a day, but they wake up every few hours to feed. They don't know about day and night at first.

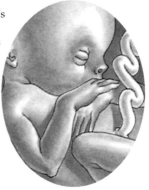

## Brain Recovery
Your brain needs you to sleep, to give it a chance to recover from the mental exercises of the day. At night, it goes through cycles of deep sleep and shallow sleep. During deep sleep, parts of the nervous system are active, and this is when REM occurs.

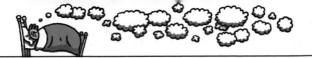

## REM Sleep

*REM sleep* is a stage of the sleeping cycle when your eyes move beneath your eyelids. (REM stands for rapid eye movement.) This is the time when most dreams happen. People woken during REM sleep can usually remember vivid dreams.

## What's In a Dream?

Dreams can be scary, sad, funny, or completely peculiar! Nobody is really sure why they happen or what they mean, but they could be a way of making sense of what has happened to you.

Many people believe that every dream has a meaning. For instance, if you dream about giving someone flowers, it may mean you love them. Ooh-er!

# Male and Female

When boys and girls are very small, there are very few obvious differences between them. As they grow up, the differences become much clearer. Here is what it's all about...

## Growing Up

Your body changes and grows from the moment you are born, but some major changes happen between the ages of about nine and fifteen. The changes are called *puberty*, and they make it possible for a male and female to make a baby.

## Male Bits

A male's body makes millions of microscopic tadpole-shaped sex cells called *sperm*. They are made in his two *testicles*, which hang behind his *penis*.

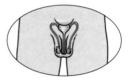

*Male's reproductive organs*

Sperm can travel from the testicles along the *sperm ducts* and *urethra*, and out of the penis.

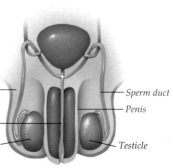

*Scrotum – protective covering for testicles*

*Urethra (urine never comes out of here at the same time as sperm)*

*Testicle*

*Sperm duct*

*Penis*

*Testicle*

## Believe It or Not...

In each testicle, there are 500 m (547 yd) of tiny, tightly-coiled tubes. Blimey, boys!

## FEMALE BITS

A female's body makes sex cells. (One of these can only become a baby when it joins with a male's sex cell.) Here is the journey that a female's sex cell makes:

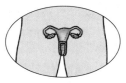

*Female's reproductive organs*

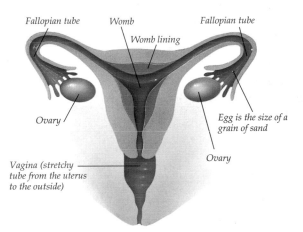

Fallopian tube     Womb     Fallopian tube

Womb lining

Ovary

Egg is the size of a grain of sand

Ovary

Vagina (stretchy tube from the uterus to the outside)

A female's sex cell is called an *egg cell* or *ovum*. Lots are stored in her *ovaries*.

Once a month, an egg cell from one of the ovaries travels down one of the *fallopian tubes*, towards the *womb* (also called the *uterus*).

Each month, the lining of the womb gets thick and soft, ready for a baby to start growing.

If the egg cell doesn't meet a male's sex cell, the womb's lining breaks up and passes out through the *vagina*, with the egg. This is called having a *period*.

# MAKING A BABY

A baby can only start to grow when an egg and a sperm meet and join. It takes nine months for the baby to grow to its full size; then it is ready to be born.

## GETTING TOGETHER

Before a baby can begin to grow, a man and woman get together and cuddle very closely. Soon, the man's penis becomes stiffer and slips easily inside the woman's vagina. This is called *making love* or *having sex*.

## THE EGGS JOIN

Millions of tiny sperm cells come out of the man's penis

and swim through the woman's vagina and womb, then up the fallopian tubes. If there is an egg cell in one of the tubes, just one of the sperm may wriggle inside (left). The other sperm die.

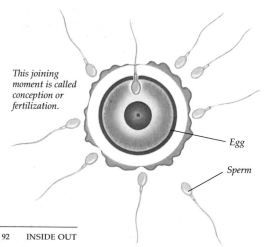

*This joining moment is called conception or fertilization.*

Egg

Sperm

## A Brand New Start

The fertilized egg contains the code for a new person to start growing. It floats down the fallopian tube to the womb, where it settles comfortably in the soft lining. It starts to divide from one cell into the millions which make up a new baby.

## The Baby Grows

The baby grows in the womb for nine months, attached by its *umbilical cord*. It gets food and oxygen from its mother's blood through this.

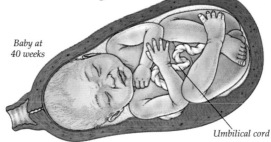

*Baby at 40 weeks*

*Umbilical cord*

## Being Born

After nine months, the womb squeezes and squeezes to push the baby headfirst (sometimes it's the other way up) down the mother's vagina. Immediately after the birth, the umbilical cord is cut off (it doesn't hurt). The little bit that's left dries up and drops off after a few days, leaving a *belly button*.

# THE WAY YOU ARE

You have your very own special set of instructions called your *genetic code*. This is what makes you YOU.

## CHROMOSOMES
The instructions that make you the way you are, are called *genes* (NOT jeans!). They are carried in your cells, in threads called *chromosomes*.

*Part of a chromosome; each bead-like bit is a gene*

## YOUR PERSONAL RECIPE
Many things about you depend on your genes – for example the colour of your hair, whether it's straight or curly, the size of your features and how tall you are. Because you get your genes from both parents, you are probably like both of them in some ways.

## IDENTICAL TWINS
Sometimes, a single egg splits into two halves after conception. The two halves grow into separate babies called *identical twins*. They share the same genetic code, so they look exactly the same.

*Identical twins are always the same sex.*

## FRATERNAL TWINS

Sometimes, two sperm join with two different eggs at the same time, and two babies grow in the womb. They are called *fraternal twins* (or *non-identical twins*) but they are not always the same sex and often look very different.

*Fraternal twins can look very different.*

## BOY OR GIRL?

Whether you are a boy or a girl depends on the sex chromosome in the egg and the sex chromosome in the sperm that joined to make you. There are two kinds of sex chromosome – X and Y. All eggs carry an X chromosome and all sperm carry either an X or a Y chromosome.

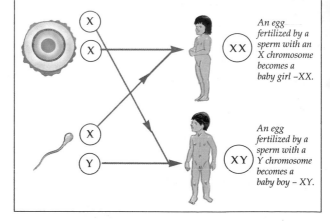

*An egg fertilized by a sperm with an X chromosome becomes a baby girl –XX.*

*An egg fertilized by a sperm with a Y chromosome becomes a baby boy – XY.*

# GERM INVASION

When you're ill, you often feel dreadful – tired, achy, a sore throat...uuugh! Swot up on germs and you'll understand the reasons why.

## WHAT GERMS ARE

Germs are tiny living things that are all around you. They are on your skin, in the air, in your food... everywhere. There are three main kinds called *bacteria, viruses* and *fungi*. Bacteria cause illnesses such as ear infections. Viruses cause things such as chickenpox. Fungi are germs which grow on your body – athlete's foot, for instance.

## WHEN YOU GET ILL

Bacteria and viruses have their own ways of attacking your system. Bacteria can attack your cells with poison, or spread infection around via your blood. Viruses get into cells and make new viruses, which then go on the rampage.

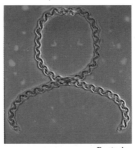

*Bacteria*

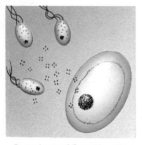

*Bacteria attacking with poison*

*Virus entering a cell to reproduce*

## BLOOD

As your blood circulates, it can carry and spread germs, but it fights them too. The white cells in your blood stick to germs, surround them and digest them. Delicious!

*White cell surrounding germs*

## CLEANING UP

Liquid called *lymph* runs around your body in a network of tubes, carrying dead germs and cells to *lymph nodes*. Then white blood cells clean the nodes out. Nifty, eh?

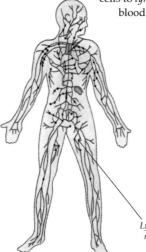

*Lymph node*

## YOUR IMMUNE SYSTEM

When you are ill, your body makes *antibodies* which help do away with the germs. They stay in your body and attack the same kind of germ if it appears again – so you only get most infections once. This is called *being immune*.

## UNABLE TO FIGHT

Some people get a virus called *HIV*, which causes an illness called *AIDS*. This stops their bodies from being able to protect against infections or fight them.

# ALLERGIES

Some people's bodies have a peculiar habit of fighting ordinary things as if they were germs. This is called *having an allergy*.

### DIFFERENT TYPES
Some people are *allergic* (or sensitive) to things they breathe in. Dust, fur, pollen and even feathers can make their eyes itch and water, and they sneeze uncontrollably. Other people are allergic to certain foods and they get tummy ache or even a rash.

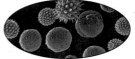

*Magnified pollen grains*

### BUT WHY?
The thing which causes an allergy is called an *allergen*. When it gets into the body of an allergic person, they make antibodies to fight it. A chemical called *histamine* is made and this causes all the annoying symptoms, such as the sneezing.

### ASTHMA
People with asthma have difficulty in breathing. This can be because an allergy to something makes their air tubes get really narrow, so less air gets through. They wheeze and cough as they try to take in more air.

*Normal open airway*

*Airway during an asthma attack*

## ACCIDENTS

"Oh DO be careful!" can sound annoying when you've just had an accident. After all...you didn't WANT to hurt yourself. Bruises or breaks can be painful, but they mend eventually, thank goodness!

## BRUISES

When you walk into a table or trip over the dog, you may get a bruise – not very pretty, but fairly harmless. This happens because your blood vessels get damaged and blood leaks out under your skin.

## BROKEN BONES

A broken bone can be repaired, so don't despair if you get a break! The bone must be set in the right position and kept still. It takes up to two to three months for new cells to grow over the break and join the bits together.

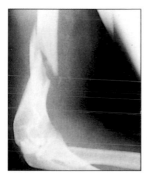

*X-ray shows broken arm on day of break*

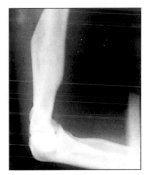

*X-ray of arm a few months later*

**Acknowledgements:** (KEY: a=above, b=bottom/below, c=centre, l=left, r=right, t=top) Gordon Models (back cover cr); Dr A V Mitchell; Museum of Natural History of the University of Florence, Zoology Section "La Specola".

**Picture Credits:** Mary Evans Picture Library: 67b; Images Colour Library: 57bl; Science Photo Library/CNRI: 83cla; 83clb; 96cr; /Gopal Murti: 61br; /NIBSC: 83cr; /D Phillips: 92cl; /David Scharf: 98cr.

**Additional Photography:** Andy Crawford, Geoff Dann, Steve Gorton, Dave King, Liberto Perugi, Susanna Price, Tim Ridley, Dave Rudkin.

**Additional Illustrations:** Karen Coehran, Giulanio Fornari, Mick Gillah, Tony Graham, Selwyn Hutchinson, John Temperton, Spike Walker (Microworld Services), John Woodcock.

**Models:** Dean Atta, Marvin Campbell, Puishan Chan, Ebu Djemal, Shonagh & Callie Munday, Aaron O'Connor, Kieron Parris, Jay Tan, Jessica Whiteman, Snezana Zivojinovic.

# PREDATOR

Written by Susan Mayes

Illustrated by Gary Boller

# MEET THE PREDATORS

Predators hunt, kill and EAT other animals. Think of sharp teeth, needle-like claws and powerful jaws and you've got your average predator. Yikes!

*T. rex*

There are really obvious examples like the long-dead dinosaur, Tyrannosaurus rex, or a lion. But what about that sweet, cuddly little creature at home that you call Tiddles? Yes...your beloved moggy is a predator too! (Sorry to break it to you like that!)

Predators come in all shapes and sizes, and with slight variations. Swimmers such as sharks and leopard seals use their lethal teeth to do away with their victims.

Fliers such as owls and bats come out at night to track down their evening meal.

*Barn owl*

Snakes slither in search of prey and kill using their poisonous bite, or by giving a suffocating hug (depending on the type of snake). You should see the size of some of the things they gulp down...ENORMOUS!

*Boa constrictor*

Then there are plants...yes, plants! Have you ever considered that they kill for food? Well...not all of them, but certain types live on a tasty diet of flies and other unsuspecting creatures that come their way.

Don't forget the mini killers either. Ants and spiders are among the small predators you'll come across. Maybe not that frightening if you're an average human, but pretty scary if you're their next snack!

*Venus flytrap*

*Tarantula*

Now don't let any of this put you off. The sight of a mouse's tail hanging out of Tiddles' mouth may not be all that appealing, but that's life...that's nature! Prepare to be fascinated, gripped and maybe even slightly appalled...but be warned...you may have trouble tearing yourself away!

# PREHISTORIC KILLERS

Many millions of years ago, before your granny was born, dinosaurs roamed the Earth. Some were peaceful plant-eaters called *herbivores*, and others were hunting meat-eaters called *carnivores*. These meat-eating beasties chased and ate other dinosaurs, or fed on dead bodies that they found. Mmm-mmmm!

*How thecodontians changed*

## BEFORE THE DINOSAURS

Before dinosaurs came on the scene, their crocodile-like ancestors, the thecodontians (pronounced *theck-oh-don-tee-ons*) were the VIPs. Over millions of years, these cumbersome creatures changed the way they moved their legs and became smaller and faster moving.

## STAURIKOSAURUS

Staurikosaurus (*store-rick-oh-saw-rus*) was one of the first meat-eating dinosaurs. It sped along nimbly on its long back legs, in an upright position, and snapped up prey with its tooth-lined jaws.

*Staurikosaurus was about 2 m (6 ft 6 in) long.*

## COMPSOGNATHUS

Compsognathus *(comp-sog-nay-thus)* was one of the smallest
known meat-eating dinosaurs. Although the little fella
was 1 m (3 ft) long, a lot of this was tail.
Its body was about the size
of a chicken's.

*Compsognathus probably
ate little creatures such
as lizards or dragonflies.*

## DEINONYCHUS

Deinonychus *(die-non-i-kus)*
was a gruesome beast!
It was 2.4-3.4 m (8-11 ft) long (not huge by dinosaur
standards) and boy, was it FIERCE! These dinosaurs
hunted in packs, leaping on an unsuspecting
plant-eater and slashing at it with their claws.

*Long arms
with three-
fingered
claws*

*Sickle-like claw on
second toe of foot*

## TERRIBLE CLAW

The name Deinonychus means 'terrible claw'. The claw
behind the name is on
each back foot. These
vicious weapons were
held up out of the way
when the dinosaur ran.
They flicked forwards
for slashing and
attacking. Ouch!

*Position when
not in use*

*Position for attack*

# INTRODUCING T. REX

Tyrannosaurus rex (or *T. rex* for short) was mighty big, mighty strong, mighty heavy and mighty FEROCIOUS! It was the largest land-living meat-eater that we know about. Here are some fearsome facts about this big brute.

## LAST ONE OUT

T. rex lived a mere 65 million years ago. In fact, it was one of the last dinosaurs to become extinct (to die out). Scientists know when this happened but they are not sure why. Something violent probably happened to change the world's climate.

## THE BIGGEST BEAST

T. rex was the largest of the meat-eating dinosaurs. It was about 14 m (46 ft) long and 6 m (18 ft) tall. Imagine meeting THAT on your way home from school! Aaaagh!

## WHAT LEGS!

T. rex's leg bones were thick to support its incredible weight. Powerful, rippling muscles helped this giant thunder along in pursuit of a meal.

## WEEDY ARMS

For a muscly monster, T. rex had really weedy arms. They were short, with two claws on each one. It probably used them to push itself up after taking a well-earned break from hunting and killing.

## GRUESOME GNASHERS

The gaping mouth of T. rex was full of serrated teeth for tearing its victims apart. These knife-like weapons were as long as 18 cm (7 in), which is a little bigger than the height of this book. Ooh-er!

## EATING OUT

Most dinosaurs would have looked like a tasty snack to T. rex. However, some dinosaurs were harder to attack than others. T. rex would have had a tricky time fighting the armoured plant-eater shown here.

*Edmontonia
(Ed-mon-tone-ee-ah)*

# LIONS AND TIGERS

Lions and tigers are probably the best-known of the big cat family. These magnificent, powerful beasts are fantastic hunting machines.

*Lion*

## DESIGNED FOR HUNTING

Big cats are perfectly (or should that be *purrfectly?*) designed for hunting and the lion is no exception. It is intelligent, strong and fast.

## GROUP HUNTING

Lions live in Africa and in a small forest in India. They are the only cats that hunt in groups. Most of the hunting is done by the females. They have massive paws for swiping prey and sharp teeth for snapping bones.

## TIGER TERRITORY

Tigers live in lots of different parts of the world including the rain forests of Southeast Asia and in freezing cold Siberia. The tiger is the biggest and most powerful of all the big cats.

## NOT SO FAST!

Tigers cannot run fast for very long, but they make up for this with their great strength, attacking large prey without much problem. They are also good swimmers...handy for relaxing and keeping cool!

*Tiger*

*Massive paws for swiping prey*

## HIDE AND SNEAK

A tiger's black and orange stripes match the patches of sun on the grass and trees, so the beasty doesn't stand out. This helps it hide and sneak up on its prey without being seen. Surprise, surprise!

## BELIEVE IT OR NOT...

Siberian tigers are the biggest tigers, weighing up to 384 kg (845 lb). They can jump 12 m (40 ft) – over four times their body length!

# MORE WILD PUSSYCATS

$S$mall wild cats are different from big ones because of their size...obviously! But another main difference is that they cannot roar. (Grrr-aah!) For more fascinating feline facts, read on...

## EARLY MOGGIES

The earliest fossil ancestors of the cat family come from about 50 million years ago. Another type of early moggy was the sabre-toothed cat. It had dagger-like teeth in its upper jaw.

*Smilodon (smil-oh-don) – a sabre-toothed cat that became extinct about 11,000 years ago*

## CHEETAHS

The cheetah is different from all other cats because it is better at running than leaping. When it is running at full speed, it can reach 96 km/h (60 mph).

## LEOPARDS

Leopards are secretive creatures, living alone and hunting mostly at night. They are agile climbers and can easily scale a vertical tree. Carrying dead prey up into the branches is no problem.

*Lazing around is just the thing after a big meal.*

### JAGUARS

Jaguars hunt alone, killing creatures such as sloths, tapirs and turtles. Although they can climb, they are much happier hunting at ground level and in water. River turtles and even crocodiles make particularly tasty snacks!

### BELIEVE IT OR NOT...

A black panther is just a leopard with different colouring. It has spots, but you have to look really closely to see them amongst all the dark fur. (Careful though!)

### PUMAS

Pumas (also known as cougars) search huge distances for their next meal. Once they have caught it, they may drag it 400 m (1,300 ft) to hide it from scavengers. Good idea!

# THE GREAT WHITE SHARK

The mere mention of a great white shark can transform even the butchest male into a quaking wreck. But does this awesome, swimming predator deserve its reputation as a bloodthirsty killer? Read on and make up your own mind.

## VITAL STATISTICS
At their largest, great white sharks can grow to over 6 m (20 ft) long. They can weigh more than 2 tonnes.

## BELIEVE IT OR NOT....
One of the largest sets of great white shark jaws in the world is 57.5 cm (22.5 in) wide. You would have no trouble slipping in there quite comfortably!

*Great white shark jaws*

## FILM STAR STATUS
A great white shark was the star of a scary 1970s film called *Jaws*. In the film, it was responsible for killing unsuspecting swimmers, but in reality attacks on people are rare. Phew!

## CRAFTY COLOURING
This lethal creature's pale colouring helps it blend into the watery scenery and sneak up on its prey. From underneath, its white belly looks like a bright patch of sunlight on the water.

## On the Menu

A great white shark's diet changes as it grows up. Young, small sharks like a tasty bit of fish. The older ones prefer a more varied menu which includes seals, porpoises, sea lions, some sea birds and even other sharks. Yikes!

## Eye Eye

When a great white shark goes in for the kill, its eyes roll back in their sockets, so that the whites of the eyes show. This helps protect the vital eye parts from being scratched by the flailing victim.

*Sharp, serrated tooth of a great white shark (actual size)*

*Model of a male great white shark*

# SHARKS AND A KILLER WHALE

There are up to 400 species of shark lurking in the oceans of the world. Here are just a few fishy snippets to whet your appetite, with a killer whale thrown in for good measure.

## SIXTH SENSE

Sharks have the same five senses as us humans – they can hear, see, taste, smell and touch. But they also have special pores (NOT paws!) on their heads which can sense electrical signals generated by swimming supper. Smart, eh?

## BENDY BODY

The leopard shark spends a lot of time lurking near the sea bed. Its flexible body gives it a handy advantage when hunting, as it can turn around easily in small spaces. Nifty, eh?

*Leopard shark*

## HAMMERHEAD

The hammerhead shark got its name because it looks as if it has swallowed a hammer! Its eyes are on the end of the sticking out bits and its nostrils are widely spaced at the front. This wide head is good at sensing nearby nosh.

*Open mouth of a basking shark*

## BIG BASKER

The basking shark doesn't go in for big meals; it prefers snacking. It swims along with its big mouth wide open and filters all the tiny creatures out of the water. Every minute or so, it swallows its catch.

## COOKIECUTTERS

The cookiecutter shark is a small creature with a nasty eating habit. It uses its lips to suck on to its chosen victim

(whales, seals and dolphins are popular). Then it bites and swivels around, tearing off the flesh. Ouch!

## KILLER WHALE

An adult male killer whale (or *orca*) can grow to 9 m (30 ft) long. It's a fearsome hunter and consumes anything from little fish to whales ten times its size. Gutsy or what?

# Other Hunters Of The Deep

There's nothing quite like a swim in the sea...bobbing around on the crest of a wave. Next time you go for a dip, give a moment's thought to some of the hunters that roam the oceans of the world.

## Ugly Mug

The deep-sea angler fish is no beauty, so it's just as well that it lurks in the dark depths of the ocean. Some species of angler fish lure their prey with a luminous spine. Then they clamp their victim in sharp-toothed jaws and swallow them whole! Greedy!

## Eight-armed Hunter

At night, the common octopus sneaks up on its victim and pounces. It wraps its supper in its eight arms, injects its stomach juices into the creature, then sucks out the squidgy flesh. Slurp!

*Big, stretchy belly has space for huge prey*

*Arms hold prey*

*Suckers grip rocks*

## FEELING BLUE

The blue-ringed octopus (shown here) could fit in a person's hand, but DON'T try it, as this little monster has a lethal bite. Look out for its warning system – blue-ringed spots appear on its skin if it is irritated, or when it is feeding. "Leave me ALONE!"

## SQUID ATTACK!

Squid can grow big...one tonne big. That really is some GIANT! Sperm whales often have scars where squid suckers have zapped on to get a grip.

## NEW GNASHERS

*Wolffish*

The wolffish crunches through the hard shells of sea urchins, mussels and crabs with its fang-like teeth. When the front set of teeth are worn down, they are replaced by a new set of gnashers which grow in behind the first set.

# ARCTIC ATTACKERS

In the freezing cold Arctic, a meal is not always easy to come by. Many animals that live there have to be ruthless killers to make sure that they get the food they need to survive.

## POWERFUL HUNTER

The polar bear is the most powerful hunter in the Arctic. It lies patiently by a hole in the ice, waiting for a seal to come up for air. When the unsuspecting victim pops up, the bear swipes it with its huge paw and bites it at the back of the skull. End of story!

*Hollow hairs trap warm air near body*

## HUNTING PRACTICE

Polar bear cubs at play are a delightful sight. It's easy to forget that their games help them learn and practise the skills they need to become hunters, like their parents.

## A MIXED MENU

A grizzly bear's diet changes at different times of the year, depending on what is available. Small mammals, fish and insects are all popular, and plants are a healthy extra.

## STEALTHY STOAT

The stoat (or *ermine*) looks sweet and furry, but it is really a merciless killer. It chases little rodents called *lemmings* through their underground tunnels. Vroom!

## WICKED WOLVERINE

This fearsome creature is a relative of the stoat. It is heavily built and VERY strong. It has no problem killing its main prey – reindeer. Just look at those vicious teeth and claws!

*Wolverine*

# WOLVES

Wolves live in groups called packs, with up to 20 family members. They manage to survive in the freezing Arctic because of their thick fur and group-hunting habits.

## CAMOUFLAGED COAT

Wolves living in the Arctic parts of North America and Eurasia often have a white coat. This cunning disguise helps them to hunt against a snowy background without being seen by their prey. Boo!!

### BELIEVE IT OR NOT...

A wolf can jump as far as 4.5 m (15 ft). It can also leap upwards, sideways and backwards. What a nimble athlete!

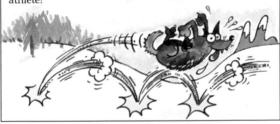

## HOWLING TOGETHER

Before a hunt, all the wolves in the pack have a good howling session, to show that they are ready for 'the off'. One of them starts, then the others gradually join in. A-ooooh!

## CANINE CUISINE

Wolves mostly hunt large hoofed animals such as moose, caribou and musk oxen. They run down their prey together in a team effort.

### SPECIAL FEATURES

A wolf is a superbly designed hunter. Here are a few points which make it so good at the job:

*Ears hear sounds up to 3 km (2 miles) away. (Eyesight is poor!)*

*A keen nose smells when a live meal is in the area.*

*Powerful jaws are home to 42 teeth for gripping and tearing flesh.*

*A strong body and long legs are excellent for chasing prey.*

# DEADLY DOGS

There are about 37 species in the dog family. All members of the family are carnivores (meat-eaters), so bad luck prey of all sizes! Here are a few morsels of information about wild dogs, for you to get your teeth into.

## AFRICAN HUNTING DOGS

These odd-looking creatures live on African grasslands, in big family packs. When they are hunting, their strong scent helps them keep in contact and their white-tipped tails make it easier to spot each other.

After a kill, the hunters regurgitate (vomit) bits of food for the puppies and the other dogs who stayed behind. Tasty!

## LONE HUNTER

The red fox is one of the most common carnivores in the world. (Sorry, foxy!) It has a taste for rodents and rabbits, so it helps keep down the numbers of these creatures in the wild.

*Red fox*

## HOT FOX

The fennec fox lives in the Sahara desert and the Arabian desert. Keen eyes, a sensitive nose and ENORMOUS ears help this little fox to hunt on even the darkest desert night (it's too hot to hunt in the day). Phew!

## COLD FOX

The Arctic fox's thick fur and furry feet help to keep out the cold. It feeds on birds which live on the ground, lemmings and other small rodents. It can stand temperatures as cold as –50°C (–58°F). Brrrrrr!

*Fennec fox*

## DINGOES

Dingoes are wild dogs that live in Australia. They gather into big packs to hunt large prey. Sheep and rabbits are popular supper specials.

*Dingo*

# CUDDLY KILLERS

Now for the moment all you cat-lovers have been waiting for. It's time to feature that furry little bundle of fun...the domestic moggy. A word of warning – don't be TOO shocked by what follows!

## WHY CATS HUNT

Domestic cats don't often hunt because they are hungry. It's because chasing live food is a fun game that they enjoy playing. Well...it makes a change from hanging around on the windowsill.

## WHAT'S ON THE MENU?

Basically, anything that moves is likely to be swiped by your darling pet. Creatures like birds and rodents are best for chasing though...so lock up your hamsters! If Tiddles proudly presents you with extra breakfast, try not to be cross. It's a prized gift showing that she thinks of you as an important part of her family. (Thanks, Tiddles!)

## GETTING THE HANG OF IT

Cats learn how to hunt by watching what other cats do and by trying it out for themselves. If a kitten has a non-hunting mother, then the chances are that it won't be destined for a life of mousing!

*PLAY-FIGHTING*
*This game helps them test their strength and learn new skills.*

## ESSENTIAL HUNTING SKILLS

Tiddles approaches her victim by slinking stealthily along the ground.

She pauses to watch it, then slinks on again.

When she is close enough, Tiddles prepares to jump. Her feet tread and her tail twitches.

She shoots forwards and leaps on her prey, pinning it down.

### PLAYING AROUND

Cats often play with their prey before killing it.

One bite with her sharp teeth and it's "goodbye Mr Mouse"!

The game is much more fun (for the cat!) if the poor creature struggles between attacks. Sorry, but it's a fact of cat life!

# Jungle Hunters

The jungles of the world are home to predators great and small. Tigers have already had their turn, and snakes and crocodiles are lurking a few pages on. It's time to feature a motley assortment of other jungle hunters who don't deserve to be left out.

## Water Dragons

Water dragons are lizards that live in the forests of Southeast Asia and Australia. They live mainly in trees growing near water, where they search for eggs and nestlings to eat. If they are disturbed, they drop into the water below. Wheeeeeee... splosh!

*Water dragon*

## The Giant Otter

A giant otter is happiest in the water. It makes its home in holes in the river bank or under tree roots. This big creature's favourite menu includes fish, eggs, water mammals and birds.

### THE MARBLED SCORPION
Although this fearsome little creature has a poisonous sting in its tail, this is mainly for defending itself. It overpowers the small creatures that it hunts using its jaws and front claws.

*Marbled scorpion*

### GONE FISHING
The fishing bat (or bulldog bat) preys on fish. It skims low over the water and lifts them out with its sharp, hooked claws. It either eats its prey while flying (an impressive trick!) or carries it to its roost to dine in comfort.

### SINISTER CENTIPEDE
The giant tiger centipede really ISN'T something you would like to meet on a ramble through the jungle. Its orange and black stripes warn that it is poisonous. It injects its victims with venom using the sharply-tipped claws on its first pair of legs. Steer clear!

# Hungry Plants

Insects make a tasty snack for many creatures, but they are also food for plants in some parts of the world. (Yes...plants!) If the soil is poor quality, the plants need the extra food to survive. They entice and trap creepy crawly victims for their next meal.

## Death Traps

Pitcher plants have jug-like traps at the ends of their leaves. Each one has a lid over the top to keep the rain out, and sweet nectar around the rim. Insects catching a niff of the nectar land on the slippery rim, fall inside and drown in the liquid at the bottom. Glug, glug...

*Pitcher plant*

*Dead insects are slowly digested in liquid*

## A Sticky End

The leaves of sundew plants are covered in tiny hairs which make droplets of sticky, gluey stuff. An insect landing to investigate sticks to the hairs which fold over and trap it. Farewell little fly!

## A WATERY GRAVE

Bladderworts are water plants which develop tiny bladders on their delicate leaves. If a tiny water creature passes by, a bladder snaps open and the creature gets sucked inside. Woosh!

## SNAPPY KILLER

A venus flytrap looks and smells attractive to an unwary insect. A safe landing place with a supply of nectar...what could be better? But within seconds of touchdown, the two halves of the leaf snap shut. If the plant senses that its victim contains protein, the trap closes fully and digestion starts. Yummy!

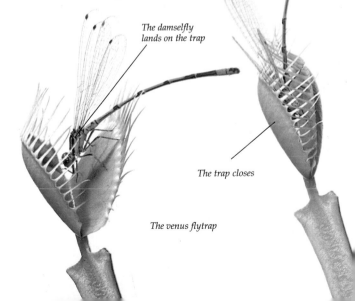

*The damselfly lands on the trap*

*The trap closes*

*The venus flytrap*

# MINI KILLERS

There are many small-scale meat-eaters around the world that kill to survive, including one third of insects. Take a look at these little beasties to see what they get up to.

## PERILOUS PRAYING MANTIS

The praying mantis is cunningly disguised in green, so it looks like a leaf. It grabs its prey with spiky front legs and slices through the doomed victim's body casing with its powerful, sharp jaws. Then it scoops out the innards. Mmm-mmm!

*Praying mantis*

## SOUP AGAIN!

A diving beetle *larva* (that's the beetle in the early stages of its life) has a gruesome way of killing. It spears its prey with its pointed fangs and squirts juices into it, dissolving the victim's body into a soupy mush which the larva then sucks up. Shloop, slurp!

## PARALYSED PREY

Most hunting wasps are plant-eaters and only hunt prey to feed their young. The world's largest wasp, the tarantula hawk wasp, paralyses a spider with her sting, then lays an egg on it. When it hatches, the grub feeds on the fresh, living meat. Yuck!

*Adult hunting wasp*

## FEARSOME ANT

All ants have strong jaws called *mandibles* for chopping up food. The bulldog ant is a particularly fierce customer as it eats other insects. It has extra big mandibles which it uses for catching its victim and chopping it up into easy-to-eat pieces.

## SPIDER SUPPERTIME

Who could forget spiders... those sinister scuttlers? Spiders the world over live on the creatures they catch. Many (but not all) of them trap their victims in a silky

*Bulldog ant*

web, inject them with paralysing poison, then suck up the body juices. Easy when you know how!

## BELIEVE IT OR NOT...

The pygmy shrew is no creepy crawly, but it deserves a mention as it is one of the tiniest mammals. It dines on earthworms and other small creatures. It has to eat almost its own weight in food each day. Imagine that!

# EAGLES

Eagles are the most powerful birds of prey. They have excellent eyesight, huge wings and strong legs and feet. These special features help them to hunt and capture their tasty victims.

*Golden eagle*

## HOT AIR

Natural currents of hot air rise into the sky. They are called *thermals*. Eagles use these thermals to lift them up higher into the air. Wheeee...

If you are a small, scurrying creature, it would be handy to know how to spot an eagle before it spots you! Keep an eye out for giveaway signs: wings with finger-like tips and a wide tail.

## MAGNIFICENT KILLERS

The golden eagle has huge talons (claws), a hooked beak and really fantastic eyesight. When hunting, it soars high in the sky, searching for prey. Suddenly, it swoops and grabs a victim, killing it with its crushing claws.

*Golden eagle*

## LAZY HUNTER

The bateleur eagle feeds mostly on carrion – that's dead and rotting flesh to you! It makes fierce attacks on other carrion-feeding birds and robs them of their nosh. However, it sometimes makes the effort and kills for itself.

*Bateleur eagle*

*When angry or excited, it raises its crest.*

## HUGE HARPY

The harpy eagle lives in the rain forests of South Mexico to North Argentina. It is the largest eagle in the world and has feet the size of an adult's hand, so don't mess with this one! It uses its enormous talons to snatch prey such as howler monkeys or sloths from the branches. Blimey!

*Harpy eagle*

# More Killer Birds

We all need to eat to survive, but look at the lengths that some birds go to, to catch their daily supply of food.

## Sick Supper

The Andean condor is the world's heaviest bird of prey. It flies over the Andes looking for dead, sick or wounded animals to eat. There is usually plenty of food around because living conditions there are difficult. That's handy!

## Dive, Dive, Dive!

The brown pelican is the only pelican that dives for food. When it spots its fishy prey, it dives down into the water from as high as 15 m (50 ft). It scoops up food in the stretchy pouch under its beak, coming up to the surface to dine.

## The Lanner Falcon

The lanner falcon hunts and lives in the desert. It's partial to birds called *sandgrouse* and hovers in the sky, looking out for them. When it spots one, it swoops down, catching the creature in midair, or on the ground.

*Hooked beak rips flesh*

*Lethal talons catch prey*

## LEFTOVERS

Predatory birds which feed
on other birds and small
mammals cannot chew their
food as they have no teeth.
To get rid of the undigested
bits of bone, fur and feathers,
they puke up pellets containing
the leftovers. Nice one!

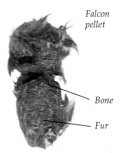

*Falcon pellet*

*Bone*

*Fur*

## BELIEVE IT OR NOT...

The gannet is a sea bird which puts on an impressive
display when it goes fishing.
It folds its wings and plunges from as high as 30 m
(100 ft) to dive-bomb shoals of fish in the water below.
That's some stunt!

## PIRATE BIRD

The skua is a ruthless hunter with a reputation
as 'pirate of the skies'. It chases other birds
and forces them to vomit up their food
for it to eat. It also steals
the eggs
and young
of other birds,
as well as killing
ducks and gulls.
Boooo! Hisssss!

*Skua*

# Night Hunters

Animals which come out at night are called *nocturnal* animals. Those which hunt live prey are specially developed for catching their evening snack in darkness...and that's without the aid of a torch!

## Owls

Most owls sleep in the day and hunt at night. Their brilliant eyesight and sharp hearing help them catch scurrying mice and small birds.

The barn owl has fringed feathers which muffle the sound of its moving wings, so small animals cannot hear it coming. Eeek!

*Barn owl*

## Enormous Eyes

The bushbaby has huge eyes and ears to help it hunt at night. Its enormous eyes can see flying insects in the dark and its sensitive ears can hear them. It clings to the branch with its back feet and stretches to snatch the flying midnight snack with its hands. Clever, eh?

*Bushbaby*

## NIGHT MONKEY
The douroucouli, or night monkey, is the only monkey in the world to come out at night. It likes to eat fruit and leaves, but it also leaps from branch to branch, hunting for insects and other small animals.

*Bat*

## HUNTING BY SOUND
Bats sleep during the day, hanging upside down by their feet. At night, they come out to hunt for insects. They make high-pitched sounds which bounce off flying insects, so they can home in on the echo and...crunch, slurp!

## FURRY FIEND
The red-kneed tarantula lives in the rain forest. It stays in its silk-lined burrow in the day and comes out at night. It hunts insects and small creatures which it paralyses by injecting with venom. Lovely!

# Sssssssnakes

Snakes are long, slithering, hissing, legless reptiles. They are ALL meat-eaters, but only about one tenth of them are dangerous to people. Snakes live all over the world, except in very cold places, so if you're feeling weak at the knees...start packing those winter woollies!

## Sensing Prey

Snakes have poor eyesight and hearing, but they make up for this in other ways. They have no external (outside) ears, but they can sense vibrations with an inner ear. Some snakes have little heat-sensitive holes in their lips for detecting warm-blooded prey. Ooh-er!

## Believe It or Not...

Giant snakes can swallow REALLY big animals. If a constrictor eats something like a whole leopard (yes, a WHOLE leopard), it probably won't eat anything else for a year. Surprise, surprise!

## BEASTLY BOA CONSTRICTOR

For those of you who like a gruesome tale, here are the details of how a boa constrictor consumes its prey.

The snake attacks its victim and clamps the wriggling creature in its jaws. Then it starts to coil around it, gripping tighter and tighter, suffocating it.

Once the victim's heart stops beating, the snake adjusts the animal's position so that it will slip down the throat nice and easily.

The snake moves its flexible jaws from side to side, easing the animal down. Small creatures disappear quickly but larger ones take an hour or more.

## POISONOUS FANGS

Vipers, cobras and sea snakes are among the most dangerous snakes of all. Their venomous fangs contain a poisonous cocktail which subdues victims, ready for killing. Byeee...I'm off!

*Red spitting cobra ejects venom from tiny holes in fangs*

# MAKE IT SNAPPY!

Crocodiles and their snappy relatives are an ancient group of animals related to the dinosaurs. They lurk around the tropical regions of the world.

## SNAPPING SKULLS

Take a peek at the terrifying teeth in the skull of this snappy hunter... if you dare!

*A crocodile's teeth are brilliant for gripping and piercing, but pretty useless for slicing and chewing. It has to tear chunks of flesh off prey such as buffalo.*

*Nile crocodile*

## A QUICK BURST

Nile crocodiles can grow frighteningly big, but even the small ones can overpower and kill large animals, including people! They lurk in the watery depths for a lot of the time, but they put on a quick burst of speed to catch prey. They drag it underwater to drown it.

## THE BIGGEST

The biggest crocodile in the world is the aggressive estuarine (or saltwater) crocodile. Some as long as 8 m (26 ft) have been recorded. If you want to avoid these beasties, steer clear of the area from southern India to northern Australia.

## A NON-CROCODILE SNAPPER

The alligator snapping turtle is a dangerous creature. It lies motionless on the river bed with its mouth wide open. It is almost invisible to passing fish, except for a strange worm-like bit on the end of its tongue. "Ah, food," the fish thinks as it gets up close, and...SNAP, gulp...gone!

*Strong jaws slice fish in half*

# LETHAL LIZARDS

There are over 3,000 species of lizard. Many of them are predators and feed on insects, mammals, birds and other reptiles.

*Basilisk lizards*

## RUNNING ON WATER

The basilisk (or Jesus Christ) lizard can run on water. Yes...run on water! It has large back feet with a flap of skin on its hind toes. This big surface area helps the lizard chase prey across water as well as across land. Wow!

## EYED LIZARDS

The eyed lizard is a fast mover whose favourite food is

crickets and grasshoppers. It gives chase and grabs its victim in its jaws. A violent shake is all that it takes to stun the creature. Then the lizard passes the meal to the back of its throat with short, snapping movements.

## FATTER WITH AGE

The tegu lizard starts life as a slim young thing, but it gets fatter as it gets older. This is because of all the birds, mammals and other lizards that it eats. Burp!

*Tegu lizard*

## THE BIGGEST LIZARD

The komodo dragon is the largest living lizard in the world. It attacks animals such as wild boar, deer and water buffalo, cutting off chunks of flesh with its serrated teeth. One captured giant was 3.10 m (10 ft 2 in) long and weighed 165.6 kg (365 lb). Yikes!

*Chameleon*

## CAMOUFLAGE

Chameleons have a useful trick which helps them hunt successfully. They can change colour to blend in with the background, so ambushing prey becomes much easier. This skill is also handy when avoiding being spotted by enemies. Pretty smart, eh?

# Frogs and Toads

Frogs and toads belong to a group of animals called *amphibians* that typically live on land but breed in water. Their long back legs give them extra power to chase and catch the insects and other creatures that they feast upon.

## Wide-mouthed Toad

The ornate horned toad has a huge mouth which is ideal for catching big insects, frogs and mice. It sits and waits for nosh to come its way. Its camouflaged skin helps it blend into the background and surprise the next victim to pass by.

## Creeping Toads

The common toad watches its prey closely. It even stalks it with movements like a cat's when it hunts live food. Once it is close enough, it leans over, darts its tongue out and snatches up the tasty morsel. It blinks as it swallows, as this helps to push the food down. Gulp!

*Common toad*

## HUNTER AND HUNTED

Poison-dart frogs live in Central and South America and are very brightly coloured. Although they are predators, they are also in danger of being hunted and eaten by other creatures. (Uh, oh!) The bright colours warn other predators that they are poisonous to eat, so "STAY AWAY"!

*This spotted poison-dart frog comes from Costa Rica, Panama and Columbia.*

## FROGS IN THE LOO

White's tree frog has round, sticky toe-pads and feeds on anything that is small enough for it to swallow. It lives in forests, but it is also known to Australians because it lives in their water barrels and, wait for it...in their loos! So if you're down under, check down under before you get comfortable!

# PREDATOR PUZZLE

Okay, clever clogs! So you've read all about those beastly predators. How many of the fascinating, fearsome facts have you managed to gobble up? Score two points for every correct answer, plus extra points where they are available.

**1 A BLACK PANTHER IS REALLY A TYPE OF WHAT?**

(a) Jaguar    (b) Leopard    (c) Puma

**2 WHICH ARCTIC KILLER ENJOYS A MAIN DIET OF REINDEER?**

(a) Wolverine
(b) Polar bear
(c) Grizzly bear

**3 WHERE ARE A SHARK'S SENSORY PORES?**

(a) Along its back
(b) On its head
(c) On its fins

**4 WHICH SHARK GULPS DOWN SMALL CREATURES EVERY FEW MINUTES?**

(a) Basking shark    (b) Leopard shark    (c) Cookiecutter shark

**5 WHICH MEMBER OF THE DOG FAMILY IS THE ODD ONE OUT? (SCORE AN EXTRA POINT IF YOU CAN SAY WHY.)**

(a) Wolf    (b) African hunting dog    (c) Red fox

6 WHICH OF THESE MEAT-EATING PLANTS IS THE ODD ONE OUT? (SCORE AN EXTRA POINT IF YOU CAN SAY WHY.)
(a) Pitcher plant  (b) Bladderwort  (c) Venus flytrap

7 WHICH DINOSAUR BECAME FAMOUS FOR ITS SLASHING CLAWS?
(a)   Deinonychus
(b)   Staurikosaurus
(c)   Tyrannosaurus rex

8 WHICH IS THE LARGEST LIZARD IN THE WORLD?
(a)   The water dragon
(b)   The basilisk lizard
(c)   The komodo dragon

9 WHICH BIRD HAS A REPUTATION AS 'PIRATE OF THE SKIES'?

(a) Golden eagle     (b) Andean Condor     (c)   Skua

10 WHICH OF THESE NIGHT HUNTERS IS THE ODD ONE OUT? (YET ANOTHER POINT AVAILABLE IF YOU KNOW WHY.)
(a)   Bat
(b)   Bushbaby
(c)   Owl

---

ANSWERS

1 b  2 a  3 b  4 a  5 c (It is a lone hunter. The others are pack hunters.)  6 a (It doesn't have moving parts like the other plants.)  7 a  8 c  9 c
10 a (It has poor eyesight. The others have excellent eyesight.)

SCORES

1-9 Could do better! Grrrr!
10-19 Pretty good, but you need to feast on a few more facts!
20-23 Excellent! Fact eater extraordinaire!

(KEY: a=above, b=bottom/below, c=centre, l=left, r=right, t=top)

**Picture credits:** Planet Earth Pictures/M&C Denis-Hout 110b; Wild Images
Ltd/Dutcher Film Productions 120b; Bruce Coleman Ltd/John Shaw 121;
Oxford Scientific Film/Kathie Atkinson 131a;

**Additional photography by:** Jane Burton, Peter Chadwick, Andy Crawford,
Geoff Dann,  Colin Keaton, Frank Greenaway, Dave King, Karl Shone,
Kim Taylor, Harry Taylor, Jerry Young.

Every effort has been made to trace the copyright holders.  Funfax Ltd
apologises for any unintentional omissions and would be pleased, in such
cases, to add an acknowledgement in further editions.

# JUNGLE TRAIL

Written by Fiona Waters

Illustrated by Gary Boller

# WHAT IS A RAIN FOREST?

About a third of the Earth's land is covered in forests. The largest forest of all is called the taiga and it runs across Canada, Scandinavia and the Russian Federation. It is always bitterly cold there and, for several months of the year, dark all the time. The tropical rain forests are very different.

Rain forests are always hot, about 27-28°C (80-82°F), and it rains every day. The warm, damp *environment* is very good for plants and animals, and the forests are home to about half the world's plant and animal *species*.

*Green area = rain forest*

## ANT-ASTIC

The largest rain forest is around the Amazon River in South America. It covers an area of 7 million sq km

(2.7 million sq miles). A single tree in the Amazon basin can be home to as many as 43 different species of ant!

*Amazon rain forest*

## GOING DOWN

A rain forest consists of several layers of *vegetation* (plant life). At the very top is the *emergent* layer formed by the tops of the very highest trees.

*Emergent layer*

Next down is the *canopy* layer. Most of the animals and birds live here as there is plenty of food, water and light.

*Canopy*

Below the canopy is the *understorey* where climbing plants twine themselves around the tree trunk.

*Understorey*

*Forest floor*

Finally, at the bottom there is the *forest floor*. Not much grows here apart from *fungi* and *parasites*, and plants wherever the light manages to get through.

# From the Top. . .

*Liverwort*

In some rain forests there is a layer even higher than the emergent layer called the *cloud forest*. This area is shrouded in heavy mist and is cool and very damp, so all the trees are covered in mosses and seaweed-like plants called liverworts.

## The Top Floor

In most rain forests, the emergent layer trees are far taller than any of the others, rising to as high as 60-70 m (200-230 ft) above the ground. The tallest broad-leaved rain forest tree recorded is a tualang at 87 m (285 ft) tall.

## Roof-top Inhabitants

The black and white colobus monkey lives up in the tree tops where it feeds on the leaves. It has to be very wary of one of its neighbours, the harpy eagle. One of the world's largest eagles, this bird is quite happy to have a sloth or a monkey for supper! Delicious!

*Colobus monkey*

## LEAFY CANOPY

At the canopy level, 25-45 m (82-148ft) above the forest floor, it is leafy all the year round. Some trees may shed their leaves, but only for a few days. Most of the leaves have a shiny surface so that the rainwater slides off quickly to prevent the growth of *algae*, a type of plant. Ingenious!

*Typical rain forest leaf*

## TARZAN'S ROPES

At canopy level, there are many plants that need light to survive, so they use the tall rain forest trees as supports to climb up. They are called *lianas*, and they can grow amazingly quickly, forming natural ropes. The fictional character Tarzan used lianas to swing from tree to tree across the jungle!

## HIDDEN LIFE

The canopy is teeming with life. Birds, butterflies, animals, insects, flowers and plants are in super abundance here. Many are never seen on the forest floor and it wasn't until biologists erected walkways high up in the trees that many species became known.

*White-lipped tree frog*

# . . . To the Bottom

The forest floor is very shady and the air is almost completely still. Only about two per cent of the light reaches it through the canopy. The ground is carpeted with roots and twigs, and only when a tree falls down, letting more light through, do other plants shoot up.

Extra light can make giant bamboos put on a huge spurt of growth – up to 23 cm (9 in) a day!

## Mushrooms on Toast?

Fungi grow very quickly in the *humidity* (dampness) of the forest floor. They take *nutrients* (mineral nourishment) from the dead leaves and are often very brightly coloured, and highly poisonous.

## Deep-rooted

Because rain forest trees have to grow to such huge heights to find light, they are in danger of toppling over. They avoid this by producing *buttress roots* which spread out to an enormous size. They sometimes spread up the tree to a height of 9 m (30 ft).

## WET UNDERFOOT

With all the rain that it gets, the rain forest is running with water which eventually drains into the rivers. When rain forest rivers flood, *swamp forests* are created where the *silt* (a muddy deposit) covers the surrounding land. Where the rivers go into the sea, *mangrove swamps* are formed. These swamplands are home to many thousands of fish, snakes and plants.

## DANGER!

There are dangers lurking in the rain forest. Piranha fish are found in rain forest waters. With their rows of sharp, triangular teeth they are to be avoided. When water levels are low in the dry season, they gather in shoals of 20 or more and are able to attack quite large prey.

*Piranha fish*

*Anaconda*

The anaconda snake keeps close to swamps and is an excellent swimmer. It sneaks up on small animals drinking at the water's edge and squeezes them to death. Yuck!

# CENTRAL AMERICAN JUNGLES

The narrow neck of land called an *isthmus,* that joins North and South America, was once the centre of two amazing civilizations – the Mayans and the Aztecs. They left behind many examples of pottery showing the rich variety of animals to be found there.

## DISAPPEARING RAIN FOREST
Almost all the Caribbean islands were covered with rain forests at one time, but they have gradually been cleared to make way for sugar *plantations.* Sugar cane is one of the major crops in Central America.

## NOISY TREE-DWELLERS
Macaws are vividly-coloured, noisy birds which live high up in the trees, with their nests often over 30 m (98 ft) above the ground. They are expert fliers with short, broad wings and can actually brake before landing on a tree or branch. They live on seeds which they crack open with their pincer-like beaks.

## GOLDEN BEETLE

The jewel-like golden beetle is about 3 cm (over 1 in) long and lives only in Costa Rica. The adults chomp their way through leaves, while the young, called *larvae*, feed on soft rotting plants.

*Golden beetle*

## SMALL IS BEAUTIFUL

Although the countries in Central America are small, they are amazingly rich in resources. They export many tropical crops such as avocado pears, pawpaws, vanilla and allspice.

## BELIEVE IT OR NOT...

The tiny Central American republic of Panama has more birds than the whole of North America.

# SOUTH AMERICAN JUNGLE

South America is a place of extremes. Here are some of its main features:

- The world's longest mountain chain, the Andes, dominates South America and is 7,200 km (4,500 miles) long.

- The Amazon River is over 6,000 km (3,700 miles) long.

- The Atacama Desert in Chile is the world's driest place.

- Over 11,700 mm (460 in) of rain falls in parts of Colombia. Don't forget your umbrella!

## BELIEVE IT OR NOT...

About 180,000 cu m (6.4 million cu ft) of water pours out of the Amazon River into the Atlantic Ocean every second. The river could fill St Paul's Cathedral in London in just over a second. Phew!

## BIG, BIGGER AND BEST

The Amazonian rain forest is home to about one fifth of the world's bird and flowering plant species, and about one tenth of the world's mammal species. The three-toed sloth (on the left) lives here, doing very little apart from hanging upside-down!

## GOLDEN MONKEY

The golden tamarin monkey can only be found in Atlantic coastal rain forests. Tamarins were recently close to *extinction* (dying out) as they were exported as pets, and too much of their natural habitat was being destroyed.

*Golden tamarin*

## LIP GLOSS

One of the ingredients in lipstick is often *carnauba wax* which comes from the Brazilian wax palm. Young leaves are picked and dried in the sun until the wax flakes off. About 1,300 leaves are needed to get only 1 kg (2.2 lb) of wax.

*Wax palm*

## SPECIAL BREW

The Amazon lily is believed to have mysterious powers. Tribes in Colombia and Ecuador boil the whole plant, including the bulb, to make a tea that the men drink before they go hunting.

# Exotic Specimens

Next time you consider going on a trek through the rain forest, make a note to look out for the exotic specimens shown on these pages.

## Leafy Canal

When the leaves of water lilies first emerge they are rolled up in tubes underwater. In the spring, the leaves come to the surface and open out to lie flat. The leaves of the Amazonian water lily can reach a diameter of more than 2 m (6 ft) and can support the weight of a young child.

## High-rise Roots

Usually, trees cannot grow in waterlogged soil as the ground is too unstable and is very low in *oxygen,* which tree roots need. Mangrove trees have adapted to their watery surroundings by having two kinds of roots. *Stilt roots* come from the tree trunk and put an anchor down in the mud. *Breathing roots*, called *pneumatophores* (on the right), come up out of the water so that they can take in oxygen. Smart, huh?

## Float Like a Butterfly

Gorgeously-coloured butterflies are to be found all over the world in tropical rain forests, but the biggest variety live in South America. With no winter and many different plants to feed on, butterflies flourish here. Some look quite spectacular with glowing colours, while others are so well *camouflaged* that they are almost totally hidden.

*South American camouflaged butterfly*

*Swallowtail*

## Bright Lights

Collecting jungle insects for research is always difficult. They are attracted by *ultraviolet light*, so scientists rig up large bags with a light above them and the insects usually fall for it! Every bag may contain thousands of different species.

# African Rain Forests

The African rain forests are in a small part of the central region, along the *equator* and beside the western coast. They have much fewer plant and animal species than other rain forests in the world.

*Orchid*

*Hibiscus*

## Exotic Flowers
There are around 18,000 species of orchid and many of these are found in rain forests. Over 60 per cent of the plants in the canopy of the African rain forests are orchids, and many of these have not yet been identified.

The hibiscus is another flourishing rain forest flower. It can grow up to 2 m (6 ft) tall.

*Weaverbird's nest*

## Home Weaving
The West African weaverbird builds the most extraordinary nest, in a kind of trumpet shape. This design is intended to prevent snakes from getting inside. The bird uses its amazing skill of tying knots with its beak and feet to build its complex home.

## THE GIANTS

Gorillas and elephants browse slowly through the forest vegetation eating their favourite leaves, stems and fruit. Find out more on pages 168-171 and pages 174-175

## PARROT PERKS

Senegal parrots migrate from the surrounding grasslands to the rain forests for a change of diet! They are very fond of the fruit and seeds to be found in the forest, and make their nests in unlined tree holes.

*Senegal parrot*

## VELCRO FEET

The day gecko from Madagascar has sticky pads on its toes, like velcro, so it can hold tightly on to branches, even when it is upside-down!

# Asian Rain Forests

The word *jungle* actually comes from the Hindi word *jangal* which means 'forest'. The jungle left in India and Southeast Asia has enormously varied animal and plant life. A great amount of the territory is made up of islands and *archipelagos* (groups of islands) – some huge and some tiny.

## Three-piece Suite

One of the most important *exports* (goods sold to a foreign country) from the Asian rain forests is *rattan*. Rattans are climbing palms whose stems can reach enormous heights and are sometimes over 200 m (660 ft) in length. Rattan canes are made into garden and conservatory furniture. There are over 600 species of rattan – that's a lot of chairs!

## Flying Frogs...

Flying frogs can leap from tree to tree to escape their enemies. They have very large webbed 'hands' and 'feet' which act as parachutes when the creatures are airborne. Wheeeeeee!

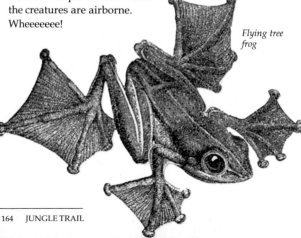

*Flying tree frog*

## ...AND FLYING SNAKES!

The flying snake can travel amazing distances through the air! It can leap over 50 m (164 ft) from one tree to another. It raises its ribs upwards and outwards so its body is almost flat, only to resume its normal shape when it lands. Sneaky, huh?

## FLOWERY SHOES?

There are about 70 species of tropical slipper orchid, most of which grow on the forest floor in the Asian jungle. They are very rare as they can only grow in very specialized habitats. Most of them grow on the ground, although some grow on rocks or trees.

*Tropical slipper orchid*

# Australasian Rain Forests

Millions of years ago, Australia and Antarctica were joined together and the coastal area of this huge *continent* (landmass) was covered with rain forest. Australia then drifted north and became drier, and the present day rain forests are the remains of this ancient jungle. Most of the rain forest lies in New Guinea, to the north of Australia. Many parts are so remote that they have not yet been explored.

### CROAK, CROAK!
White's tree frog lives in the forests, but its habit of popping up in water barrels and lavatories means it is well-known to most Australians!

### SHOW-OFF
The male bird of paradise has the most spectacular plumage, especially designed to hook a mate! As day breaks and sunlight filters through the leaves, these birds swoop through the trees, flashing their fine feathers and calling loudly.

## SHY BEAUTY

One of the world's rarest butterflies, Queen Alexandra's birdwing, lives in a very small part of Papua New Guinea. Little is known about this butterfly other than it is one of the largest. The female, which is bigger than the male, can have a wingspan of up to 28 cm (11 in).

*Queen Alexandra's birdwing*

## CARRIER BAG BABIES

Apart from bats, all the native animals in the Australasian rain forests are *marsupials*. These are animals where the female gives birth to babies which then develop inside her pouch, until they are ready to fend for themselves.

You are probably familiar with kangaroos, but what about the tree kangaroo? These distant relatives of ground kangaroos climb the trees to eat the leaves, yet are still able to hop along the ground.

# ELEPHANTS – GENTLE GIANTS

Elephants of the present and the past have lived just about everywhere, except Australia and Antarctica. They have roamed deserts, rain forests and even glaciers.

## A MIXED RELATIONSHIP?

Elephants and humans have a very mixed relationship. In some countries elephants are seen as useful workers and ceremonial beasts of burden, but in others they are killed for their ivory tusks.

## JUMBO

The African elephant is the largest land animal in the world today. A male elephant, known as a *bull*, can stand 4 m (13 ft) tall and weigh as much as 6,048 kg (13,335 lb). The females, known as *cows*, are smaller.

The Asian elephant is smaller than the African and is very gentle, especially when tamed. A baby Asian elephant can weigh as much as 120 kg (264 lb). Phew!

*Baby Asian elephant*

## DAINTY FEET

Elephants are surprisingly light on their feet for such big creatures. In fact, they walk on tiptoe. Look at this cross section of an elephant's foot and all will become clear!

*Inside an elephant's foot*

*'Heel' cushion*

*Toe bone*

*Tip of toe*

The sole of an elephant's foot looks rather like a dried up river bed with many ridges and cracks. This gives it a good grip when travelling over uneven ground.

## TRUNK CALL

The elephant's trunk is like a nose, an arm and a hand all rolled into one! African elephants even have two 'fingers' at the end of their trunk, enabling them to pick up quite small objects. Such a clever organ gets tired sometimes, so the elephant drapes it across one of its tusks for a rest!

# ELEPHANT LIFE

In elephant society, bulls and cows do not live together. The cows and calves are always in a group led by the *matriarch*, who is usually a grandmother or even a great-grandmother. The bulls spend most of their time alone, or sometimes with a group of other males.

## BABY TALK

Baby elephants must sometimes feel that they live in a world of legs, as the cows always group protectively around them. There is always an aunt or a big sister to help the babies out if they get stuck in mud or caught in low-hanging branches.

## BAD BOYS

The bulls are much more interested in their reputation amongst the other males than in family life. They indulge in great trials of strength to show who is most powerful, but no one ever gets seriously hurt.

## FOOD AND DRINK

Needless to say, such huge animals have huge appetites! The great mound of food shown here is a typical day's food for an elephant in a zoo.

An adult elephant needs to drink about 225 litres
(50 gallons) of water a day.

## All in a Day's Work

Some of the earliest working elephants crossed the Alps
with Hannibal (247-182 BC), the young North African
general who stopped the mighty Roman army in its tracks
with his animal 'tanks'.

Elephants are still used today in wars in Southeast Asian
jungles, as they can move quietly without
leaving any tracks, and soldiers on
their backs have a good view of
the countryside.

Elephants are peacetime workers too. They can pull logs
weighing more than 4 tonnes and lift smaller timbers with
their trunks.

# WHAT IS A PRIMATE?

*P*rimates are a varied group of *mammals* (animals which give birth to live young and feed them with their milk). They include monkeys, apes and humans! Most of them live in trees and their bodies are especially made for this lifestyle.

## OLD WORLD

Old World monkeys live in Asia and Africa and are the largest and most varied group of primates.

The proboscis monkey is an Old World monkey with an enormous drooping nose, which can be as long as 7.6 cm (3 in) in an adult male. It likes to swim, which is unusual for a monkey, and has been known to take a high dive from 15 m (50 ft) into the water!

*Proboscis monkey*

# NEW WORLD

New World monkeys live in the jungles of Central and South America. They are all tree-dwelling and many have *prehensile* tails – that is, a tail that can be used as another arm or leg, for gripping. These monkeys can hang from a branch by the tail only!

Howler monkey – its howls echo around the jungle as it marks its territory

Woolly monkey – very woolly with an extra strong tail

Spider monkey – fruit-eater with a passion for passion fruit!

Capuchin monkey – the most intelligent New World monkey

# UPRIGHT SLEEPER

Baboons have *nonprehensile* tails (no good for grasping) and large red *sitting pads* which help them to sleep sitting up. They are *carnivores* (meat-eaters) and sometimes hunt young gazelles (antelopes) in groups.

# THE GREAT APES

The four great apes – the gorilla, chimpanzee, orang-utan and gibbon – are much larger than monkeys and do not have tails. They are very intelligent and share many characteristics with humans.

CHIMPS

## GENTLE GIANTS

The image many people have of a gorilla is based on the movie *King Kong*. Although an angry male gorilla about to charge is a terrifying sight, he only does this when provoked and if his family is in danger. Gorillas are generally easy-going, gentle creatures who like to sleep, eat and play!

## DINNER TIME

Gorillas are very fussy about their food and only select choice plants. They eat nettles, thistles and wild celery, with bamboo as a special treat. They usually eat sitting down with their huge tummies resting between their knees.

## GORILLA BABIES

Like human babies, baby gorillas are helpless and totally
dependent on their mothers. They are
very small, only 2-3 kg (4-6 lb),
and their fur begins to grow
within days of being
born. At about six
months old they can
romp around with
other 'toddlers'.

*Young gorillas
playing*

## CLOSE RELATIONS

Chimpanzees are the closest apes to humans in
appearance and behaviour. They are highly intelligent
and can use rocks to crack open nuts, and sticks to poke
out delicious insect nests. They spend hours grooming
each other's fur.

Chimpanzees live in large communities of up to 80. When
friends meet, they hoot and hug each other, but rivals eye
each other up and
down. The oldest
chimpanzees are
treated with
considerable respect.

*Baby chimpanzees*

# STRANGER STILL

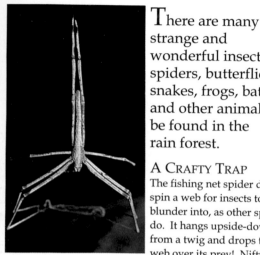

*Fishing net spider*

There are many strange and wonderful insects, spiders, butterflies, snakes, frogs, bats and other animals to be found in the rain forest.

## A CRAFTY TRAP

The fishing net spider doesn't spin a web for insects to blunder into, as other spiders do. It hangs upside-down from a twig and drops the web over its prey! Nifty stuff!

## BLOOMING MARVELLOUS!

The female orchid mantis lurks in the flower head of an orchid looking just like part of the bloom. Down comes an unsuspecting insect and she lashes out with her deadly front legs.

*Lurking orchid mantis*

## ALL LIT UP
Fireflies are not flies but beetles. Their abdominal organs make light to attract other fireflies, not to see where they are going!

## FRUITCASE
Fruit bats have huge eyes and very good vision, but they use their noses and sense of smell to locate supper!

## NIGHT-TIME VISITOR
The tapir is a little-known solitary creature that comes out at night-time. It uses its long snout to rootle for fruits and seeds among the leaves on the forest floor.

*Tapir*

## TWO TO AVOID!
The blue poison dart frog lives on the forest floor and gives off very nasty poisons from its skin.

The cobra is a deadly snake which rears up from the ground with a hiss as it puffs out its hood and injects its victim with a very toxic venom from its front fangs.

*Cobra*

# THE JUNGLE'S BIG CATS

$T$igers are the most powerful cats of all, and can be found from icy Siberia to tropical India. There are lots of other members of the big cat family around the world. Here are a few to get your teeth into.

## THE CLOUDED LEOPARD

The clouded leopard is a beautiful creature, rarely seen and now in danger of extinction. It lives in the forests of Southeast Asia.

## HIDDEN SPOTS

The mysterious-looking black panther is just a leopard with its spots hidden! Mowgli, the boy in Rudyard Kipling's *Jungle Book*, was brought up by the black panther Bagheera.

*Black panther*

## AMERICAN BIG CAT

The jaguar is the only big cat to be found in America. Its name comes from the Amazonian word *yaguara*. Its spots help it blend into its forest surroundings.
It swims in the rivers of the tropical forest where it has been known to kill crocodiles!

## SMALLER KITTIES

There are several smaller wild cats living in forests or jungles on every continent, except Australasia. They are usually solitary hunters and very little is known about them.

*Margay – looks like an ocelot (another type of cat) and feeds on birds*

*Geoffroy's cat – named after its French discoverer; swims and climbs trees to sleep in*

# DEADLY DANGER!

The jungle is full of deadly dangers with both animals and plants kitted out with poisons and killing equipment.

## DON'T PICK THE FLOWERS!

The passion flower's leaves contain toxic chemicals including *cyanide,* so mammals soon learn to avoid it.

Screw pines are tropical plants whose sword-shaped leaves have vicious barbs along the edges.

## FANTASTIC FLUTTERER

The enormous African giant swallowtail butterfly can have a wingspan of up to 250 mm (10 in). It is very poisonous and is completely avoided by all its enemies.

*African giant swallowtail*

## NOT TOO TIGHT!

The boa constrictor grabs its prey with its mouth and then coils itself around the animal's body. Each time the animal breathes out, the snake tightens its grip until the prey is suffocated.

*Boa constrictor dining on a rat*

## MIND YOUR FEET

The giant tiger centipede has vivid stripes across its body warning that it is poisonous.

The tarantula injects its prey with a venom that causes almost immediate paralysis.

*Tarantula*

## WATER FEATURE

The crocodile is the largest of the jungle predators and can reach over 6 m (20 ft) in length. It is capable of incredible bursts of speed and grabs its prey with its frighteningly sharp teeth, holding the creature underwater until it drowns.

*Nile crocodile*

# DOCTOR, DOCTOR

The tribal people of the rain forests know an enormous amount about the plants that grow around their homes. They eat many of them and use others as medicines.

## QUININE

A disease called *malaria,* caused by mosquito bites, can be treated with quinine. This comes from the bark of the South American cinchona tree.

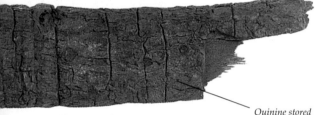

*Quinine stored in bark*

## THE ORDEAL BEAN

The very poisonous seeds of the calabar bean, or *ordeal beans* as they were known, were used to decide a person's guilt. If they survived eating the beans, they were innocent...and very, very lucky! Extracts from the seeds are now used to treat high blood pressure and an eye disease called *glaucoma.*

*Seed case*

*Seed kernel*

*Calabar bean*

## FLOWERING OF HOPE

*Rosy periwinkle*

The rosy periwinkle which grows in Madagascar has helped in the treatment of two kinds of cancer – *Hodgkin's disease* and *leukaemia*.

## YAM, YAM

The yam is eaten as a vegetable, but it also contains chemicals which are used to treat *rheumatic fever* and *rheumatoid arthritis*.

## NATURAL TOOTHBRUSHES

For centuries, tribes people in Africa have used chew sticks to keep their teeth clean. In fact, one tree is called the toothbrush tree! The juices released seem to prevent *bacteria* surviving in the mouth and causing infection.

*Carved handle of chew stick*

## A GOOD TONIC

Guarana plants have *caffeine* in and are made into tonic drinks in Brazil. Strong doses come in handy for getting rid of intestinal worms. Yuck!

# FIGHT FOR LIGHT

Tropical plants battle with each other to reach the light that they need. Growing in the jungle can be tough, but some plants have learned to take short cuts.

## GETTING A LIFT

Climbers and creepers are sneaky plants. They use other plants as their lift up to the light, often killing them in the process by strangling them or blocking out the sun. Some put out tendrils which coil around anything they come in contact with, often in a few minutes!

Another group, including ivy, haul themselves up by means of side prickles, hairs or roots.

*Strong climbing plant climbs up its host*

## HARMLESS HANGERS-ON

*Epiphytes* are tree top plants which cover the branches of their host plants without harming them. Many of them get all the moisture they need by absorbing it from the air, or by collecting rainwater.

*Epiphytes on branches*

## FLOATING FLOWERS

Some water plants are never noticed because they spend all their time underwater. Others, such as water lilies, are obvious because they float on the surface. In some places, the leaves can completely cover the water's surface, depriving the plants below of valuable light.

*Water lily*

# FOOD FOR ALL!

Man-eating plants are only found in science fiction stories, but there are meat-eating plants which feed on insects and small animals. Yum, yum!

## MEAT-EATERS

Venus flytraps are well-known for their insect-trapping habit. Large bristles on the upper surface work like triggers. If one bristle is touched, even by a drop of water, the trap stays open, but if two or more are touched at once, the trap shuts to catch the unsuspecting victim.

*Venus flytrap with supper*

Pitcher plants entice insects with their bright colours and sweet smell, but once victims land on the surface, they quickly slide down to their doom.

## DIY

Mistletoe is only a partial parasite. It does not completely rely on the plant it lives on as its green leaves use the sun's energy to make their own essential food. This is called *photosynthesis*.

*Insects inside pitcher plant*

## HUGE PARASITE

The world's biggest flower is a parasite called a rafflesia. Each flower can weigh up to 7 kg (15 lb) and is about 1 m (3 ft) in diameter. It has a really disgusting smell which attracts flies.

## JUNGLE FOOD

Many fruits, vegetables, nuts and spices that are used nowadays in cooking come from the jungle.

*Cocoa bean*

*Dates*

*Star fruit*

*Pineapple*

*Papaya*

# VERY PRIVATE PEOPLE

Throughout the world there are many tribes of people whose way of life has changed very little over the years. They have respect for the natural world and work with the forces of nature, rather than against them.

## BELIEVE IT OR NOT...

Papua New Guinea has a population of only 4 million people, but it has over 1,000 different languages and dialects. Incredible!

## THE AMAZON BASIN

The Amerindian tribes have lived in the Amazon basin for over 12,000 years. They have a vast knowledge of the plants growing in the jungle around them and use many of them everyday.

## PAINTING BY SEEDS

Body painting is popular in the 143 different tribal groups in Amazonia. The people use the seeds of a plant known as *annatto* in Europe and *achiote* in South America. Every tribe has its own favourite patterns.

*Practising the art of body painting*

## POISONED ARROWS

Tribal people who live in the rain forests use darts tipped with poisons to catch the animals they are after. Different tribes use different plant poisons for this job. Of course, they have to carry their arrows carefully, so they don't end up as their own victims!

*Penan hunter in Borneo*

## ...AND FINALLY!

In the Sundarbans area between India and Bangladesh, forest workers have a simple weapon against an old enemy. Tigers always attack from behind, so face masks are worn on the back of the head! Smart idea!

# Home and Dry!

Rain forest people have no shortage of building materials – tree trunks for walls, palms and leaves for roofing and lianas to bind the whole lot together. Here are some of the ways that they use raw materials in and around their homes.

## Thatched Roofs

In northern Thailand, the tribes people who live on the hills make houses with thatch which reaches far down on all sides, to keep the rain away from the walls. The houses are built on stilts to keep the floors dry.

## The Yam House

Yams are a vital food for the tribes in New Guinea, so special buildings are erected to protect the crop. They must be well ventilated and dry, to stop the yams from going mouldy.

*Chief's yam house*

## A FAMILY AFFAIR

Some tribes house the entire community in one big building while others have separate family units grouped around a clearing in the forest.

## WATERSIDE SETTLEMENTS

New Guinea has such dense jungle vegetation that water travel is the easiest way to get around. Settlements are often built on the riverside, for convenience.

## ESSENTIAL ITEMS

This model of a South American rain forest house shows some of the interior features you could expect to see if you went round for tea.

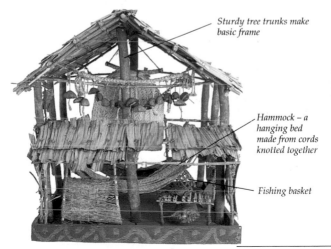

*Sturdy tree trunks make basic frame*

*Hammock – a hanging bed made from cords knotted together*

*Fishing basket*

# To Boldly Go . . .

In the 15th century, the Dutch, English and Portuguese were drawn to the forests of Southeast Asia. At the same time, in South America, the Spanish were looting the Inca and Aztec gold. But it wasn't until the 18th and 19th centuries that explorers began to develop a real scientific interest in the tropical regions.

## ALEXANDER VON HUMBOLDT (1769-1859)

Von Humboldt was a German *naturalist* (a person who studies plants and animals) who had a very keen scientific interest in the natural life of the places he discovered. He explored Venezuela from 1799 onwards, and a woolly monkey from the upper Amazon is named after him!

## DAVID LIVINGSTONE (1813-1873)

David Livingstone was a Scottish missionary who explored unknown territory. He mapped the course of the Zambezi River and parts of the Nile during three expeditions through the African jungle, travelling by river most of the way.

## CHARLES DARWIN (1809-1882)

Best known for his theories on *evolution* (the way all creatures began and developed), Darwin joined an expedition on the ship the Beagle in 1831 to make a journal of the wildlife discovered around the South American coastline.

# HENRY BATES (1825-1892)

In 1848, Bates set off on an expedition to the Amazon.
Over the next 11 years he collected 14,000 specimens
(mostly insects) of which 8,000 were previously unknown.
He kept precise notes in his endless notebooks.

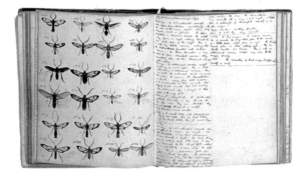

## LONG-DISTANCE PLANTS

Many of the plants found in today's gardens came from
far away, thanks to intrepid *botanists* (people who study
plants) like John Tradescant and his son, and Joseph Pitton
de Tournefort. Azaleas came from the Himalayas,
tulips from Asia and fuchsias
from South America.

# A FUTURE UNDER THREAT

Every minute of every day, about 40 hectares (100 acres) of jungle are destroyed; the trees are cut down, the plants are burned and new roads are made. Modern life interrupts the old tribal ways.

## OVER-COLLECTING
Beautiful, exotic jungle blooms such as orchids attract collectors, but if the collectors overdo it, the plants that they prize will become extinct.

*Yellow slipper orchid*

## HOMELESS
*Felling* (cutting down) trees can make it difficult for some animals, such as orang-utans, to lead a normal life. Their homes and their food sources are often completely wiped out.

*Orang-utan nest*

## IVORY POACHING

There is enormous poverty in some areas of Africa, so people are tempted to hunt elephants for their tusks, because of the huge sums of money offered by illegal ivory dealers. However, they are now more likely to end up in prison than millionaires!

## CATTLE RANCHING

In Central and South America, the number of beef cattle rose from 1 million in 1970 to 5.5 million in 1985. The problem is that after years of grazing, the land becomes completely worn out and useless.

**Acknowledgements:** (KEY: t=top, b=bottom/below, c=centre, l=left, r=right) Peter Griffith, model maker (151c), Museum of Mankind, Royal Museum of Scotland.

**Picture Credits:** Ardea/K Fink: 179c; Heather Angel/Biofotos: 160tl; Camera Press: 171b; Chester Zoo: 170b; Bruce Coleman Ltd/A Compost: 194b; /Luiz Claudio Marigo: 161bl; 173bl; /Rod Williams: 178tr; Colorific!/Ferorelli: 175b; Michael & Patricia Fogden: 154tr; 185t; Robert Harding Picture Library: 188tr; 188bl; 189tr; 190c; E & D Hosking: back cover tr; Hutchison Library: 168tr; /Isabella Tree: 190b; Frank Lane Picture Agency/Silvestris: 150bc; NHPA/Anthony Bannister: 195t; /Kevin Schafer: 183t; Oxford Scientific Films/Roger Brown: 154b; /P Devries: 172b; /A Plumpetre: 175t; Planet Earth Pictures/Mary Clay: front cover clb; 149c; 166c; /Peter Scoones: 160br; Ian Redmond: 169b; 174b; Silvestris: 158bl; Still Pictures/Norbert Wu: 176t; The Wildlife Collection/J Giustina: 173tr; WWF Photolibrary/Peter Jackson: 189bl.

**Additional Photography:** Peter Anderson, Geoff Brightling, Jane Burton, Joanna Cameron, Peter Chadwick, Geoff Dann, Philip Dowell, Frank Greenaway, Colin Keates, Dave King, Andrew McRobb, Karl Shone, Kim Taylor, Jerry Young.

Every effort has been made to trace the copyright holders. Funfax Ltd apologises for any unintentional omissions and would be pleased, in such cases, to add an acknowledgement in further editions.

# MINI MONSTERS

Written by Susan Mayes
Illustrated by Gary Boller

# THE WORLD OF MINI MONSTERS

$D$o things that scuttle, buzz, flutter or slither give you the heebie-jeebies? Do they make you squirm with horror and delight at the same time?

## BEAUTIFUL BUGS AND SLIMY SLUGS

This book reveals a multitude of mini monsters in detailed close-up, for you to study and wonder at. Things that jump and fly and sting and swarm...they're all here. We even reveal the hidden horrors of mini monsters that lurk in your home!

Why do these little beasts look the way they do? Where do they live? What do they eat? How do they protect themselves? Do they have any horrible habits? Just remember...this is their world you're looking into, so what seems odd or slightly nasty to you is really only nature at work!

## INSECT BITS AND PIECES

Many people think that any small creature which creeps and crawls is called an insect; but in fact an insect is a type of creature with special characteristics. Insects have six legs, and their skeleton is on the outside of their body. Weird, huh? They have three parts to their body called the head, the thorax and the abdomen. Look at the dissected jewel beetle on the next page to see what's what.

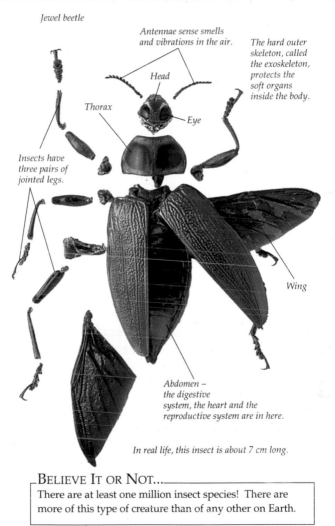

*Jewel beetle*

*Antennae sense smells and vibrations in the air.*

Head

*The hard outer skeleton, called the exoskeleton, protects the soft organs inside the body.*

Thorax

Eye

*Insects have three pairs of jointed legs.*

Wing

*Abdomen – the digestive system, the heart and the reproductive system are in here.*

*In real life, this insect is about 7 cm long.*

BELIEVE IT OR NOT...

There are at least one million insect species! There are more of this type of creature than of any other on Earth.

# THE FIRST MINI MONSTERS

Insects were the first creatures ever to fly. They lived about 300 million years ago, even before dinosaurs! Most of the ancient kinds are extinct now, but many modern creepy crawlies are close relations of the oldies.

## EARLY ARRIVALS

In prehistoric times, there were brightly coloured, scented flowers. These attracted butterflies, bees and other insects which lived in those days. They carried pollen from flower to flower, just as insects do today.

## TRAPPED IN AMBER

We know about insects from long ago because some have been perfectly preserved in amber. This is fossilized resin that oozed from pine trees. Insects attracted by its sweetness became trapped in the sticky stuff, which then hardened and became buried for millions of years.

*This amber necklace is prison to a cricket and spider who met sticky ends about 35 million years ago.*

## ROCKY REMAINS

Some insects became trapped in muddy sediment (grains of sand, soil and plant matter) and became fossilized. Because insects are usually small and delicate, many of them rotted away before fossilization could take place, so there aren't a lot of rocky insect remains around now.

### BELIEVE IT OR NOT...

This fossilized creepy crawly isn't as small as it looks here. It's a gigantic 1.8 m (6 ft) long. That's the size of a tall man! Yikes!

## FANTASTIC FLIERS

Get this! Some ancient dragonflies may have had a wingspan of up to one metre! Most modern dragonflies are much smaller...
thank goodness!

# SPIDERS

Spiders are not insects. They belong to a creepy crawly group called *arachnids*. They have eight legs and two parts to their body. All spiders are carnivorous (they feed on flesh!), but not all of them make webs to catch their prey. Read on if you dare!

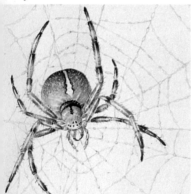

*The common garden spider's complicated web is called an orb web.*

*Web silk is squeezed through nozzles called spinnerets.*

## WONDERFUL WEBS

Some spiders make silk inside their body which they then use to spin a sticky web to catch their prey in. When an unsuspecting creature gets trapped, the spider runs out, wraps it in silk and saves it for meal time.

## SUPER STRENGTH

The silk of some webs is stronger than steel wire of the same thickness.

## BELIEVE IT OR NOT...

There are about 40,000 different species of spider.

## POISONOUS FANGS

Most spiders stun or kill their victims with a bite from
their poisonous fangs. Very few spiders are dangerous to
humans though.

## FISHING NET SPIDER

This crafty hunter spins a stretchy silk net. It hangs
upside-down holding the net in its four front legs, waiting
to drop it over unsuspecting victims.

## TEENY WEENY SPIDERS

Baby spiders are called *spiderlings*. They hatch from eggs
inside a silken cocoon, then cut their way out.

## BIG, HAIRY HORRORS!

Big, hairy scuttlers called tarantulas must be everybody's
spider nightmare, striking fear into the heart of the bravest
people. In reality it's quite a different story. Tarantulas
are shy creatures which live mainly in burrows (and you
thought that only rabbits did that!). However, if you're a
lizard, a mouse or even a bird...watch out!

*Fat feelers
called pedipalps*

*Red-kneed
tarantula*

# BEETLES

Beetles are the largest group of insects. There are around 300,000 different kinds around the world – in freezing cold places, in scorching hot places, in damp and muddy places – there are beetles everywhere.

## BEETLE BUFFET
Beetles eat just about anything. They dine on all kinds of plants and animals, living and dead! They are often thought of as pests because they attack crops, but they do good as well, clearing up dead plants and animals.

## UP, UP AND AWAY!
Beetles have four wings. The front pair are hard and strong. They cover the beetle's back and protect the long, folded wings underneath, which are used for flying.

## BLISTER BEETLES
If the blood of a blister beetle gets on the skin of a person or an animal, it causes painful blisters. An excellent way of saying "leave me alone"!

## WHAT A STINK!
Now don't go upsetting this one. The devil's coach-horse beetle defends itself by arching its tail and squirting foul-smelling liquid from its rear end. NOT a nice habit.

## COLOURFUL CHARACTERS

People often think of beetles as being black, but they come in all sorts of fantastic colours. Green and red are common beetle colours, but they also come in shimmering gold, bright blue and white. Intricate patterns are another special feature of these decorative beasties.

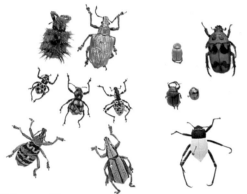

## HEAVY GIANT

An adult goliath beetle can measure as long as 15 cm (6 in). Prepare to be horrified when you check this length out on a ruler.

*Goliath beetle*

# BUGS

The word 'bug' is often used to describe crawling insects, but the truth is that bugs are a particular kind of crawler. They have a long, hollow feeding tube which they use to pierce food and suck up the juices. Delicious! Most bugs eat plant food, but some eat live prey!

## SHIELD BUGS

Many of these bugs have brightly-coloured patterns which look a lot like decorative shields. Shield bugs are also called stink bugs because they ooze a nasty-niffing liquid when in danger. Phewee!

## ASSASSIN BUGS

This delightful creature feeds on other insects. It stabs its victims with its feeding tube and sucks out their juices. Some South American assassin bugs feed on the blood of humans.

*Assassin bug feeding*

## EYE EYE!

A deceptive bug this one! The front of this lantern bug's head looks like an alligator's head. When it flies, it flashes two huge false 'eyes' on its wings. These probably scare off attackers. Well it would, wouldn't it?

*Lantern bug*

## BABY BUGS

Baby bugs look very much like their parents, only they are smaller and have no wings. Aah!

## MIND YOUR TOES!

Giant water bugs are common in the tropics. They are also known as toe-biters, which is a tiny bit worrying! They live underwater and feed on creatures such as snails, small fish or even frogs. So next time you go swimming in the tropics, keep your shoes on!

## SLOWLY DOES IT

The water measurer is a long-legged bug that takes life easy. It moves around slowly on the surface of the water and feeds on insects which are dead or dying.

# ANT ANTICS

Ants belong to a group of insects called *hymenoptera*. They are called 'social' insects because they live in groups. There can be anything from 20 to many thousands in each group, called a *colony*. Their homes are underground nests.

## FANGS A LOT!

Ants have different jaw shapes, depending on what they eat. The fierce-looking bulldog ant below is a *carnivore* (meat-eater). It uses its enormous, spiky jaws, called *mandibles*, for chopping up other insects. Yum yum!

## OKAY BOSS!

Each nest is begun by a single queen ant. She is the only one that lays eggs. The worker ants look after her, search for food and feed her. Big-jawed soldier ants keep enemies out of the nest.

## SMELLY MESSAGES

Ants pass on messages about food, enemies and their nest in two ways. Either they make chemicals called *pheromones*, which other ants can smell, or they make sound signals using vibrations to get the messages across.

## DRIVING THROUGH

Driver ants move their nests from place to place. The whole colony marches along catching all the insects they can find on the way.

## HONEYPOT ANTS

Honeypot ants live in semi-desert areas. In the rainy season, some of the workers are fed with water and nectar until their abdomens are huge and swollen. In the dry season, when food is scarce, the other ants feed off these living larders.

*Honeypot ant*

## CUT AND CARRY

Parasol ants cut pieces off leaves and flowers with their sharp, pointed jaws. They struggle back to the nest with them and use them to grow a kind of fungus, which the ants then eat. Delicious!

*Parasol ants*

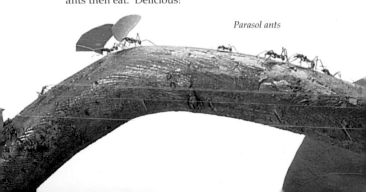

# SNAILS (...AND THE ODD SLUG)

Snails and slugs are called *gastropods*, which means 'belly foot'. Their 'belly' is really a large, flat muscular foot which can slide along. This is made easier by the slime trail which they make to help them slither smoothly.

*Underneath view of a snail*

*Bands of muscle across the foot help push the snail forward.*

## BELIEVE IT OR NOT...

Most slugs and snails are male and female at the same time. The name for this is *hermaphrodite* – but two slugs or two snails still need to mate so that they can lay eggs.

## BABY SNAILS

Most land snails lay eggs like little white pearls in the ground, or under rotting leaves, logs or stones. When the babies hatch out, they already have a tiny curly shell. As a snail grows, the shell grows round and round.

## UH OH!

A snail in danger pulls its feelers in and hides its body inside its shell.

In hot weather, a snail hides in its shell and seals the opening with a plug of slime. Lovely and safe and damp!

DO NOT DISTURB

## TONGUES AND TEETH

Most land snails and freshwater snails are *herbivores* (plant-eaters). Their long tongue, called a *radula*, is covered with tiny sharp teeth that rasp and grate up vegetation.

Now the euglandina is a snail to be reckoned with! It's a meat-eater which uses its long, sharp teeth to tear up other snails. It moves quickly when a meal is nearby and stretches out to grasp its victim. Aagh!

## BELIEVE IT OR NOT...

The giant African snail is a monster muncher. It measures around 23 cm (9 inches) long.

*This is an ordinary garden snail. What a size difference!*

# LOADS OF LEGS

If things with scuttling legs leave you feeling a little peculiar, then these pages are not for you! Introducing some many-legged mini monsters...

## CATERPILLARS
Caterpillars are a bit short on legs compared with a few of the other characters shown here. They have six thin legs at the front of their bodies, some much fatter, sticky legs at the back, and two special ones called *claspers* at the very end.

## WOODLICE
These shy, fourteen-legged creepers like to live where it's quite damp, so underneath logs, stones and pieces of bark are good places to hunt them out.

## CENTIPEDES
The name 'centipede' means 'hundred legs', but most centipedes don't

*Woodlouse*

have that many (although you could spend hours trying to count them!). Centipedes are fierce hunters, with a poisonous bite, so insects and worms must beware when they hear those scuttling legs.

## MILLIPEDES

These many-legged beasties have soft, pale legs hidden underneath their body and a very short pair of feelers at the front. Their name means 'thousand legs', but no millipede really has that many.

*There are four legs in each segment*

*Legs move in a wave-like pattern*

*Despite all these legs, millipedes meander along quite slowly.*

*Millipedes are plant-eaters, so they don't need to rush after food.*

### BELIEVE IT OR NOT...

The leggiest millipede in the world only has 750 legs. 'Thousand legs' my foot!

1. 2. 3. 4...

# LEAPS AND BOUNDS

Legs are important to most creatures.
Their uses include walking, running,
digging, fighting and, of course, jumping.
Here are a few of the mini monsters
whose long legs help them to leap and
bound around.

## LEAPING LOCUST

Look at the legs on this
beastie. It's a locust and it's
getting ready to leap. Its back
legs are folded, ready for the
high jump.

The locust's powerful leg muscles
straighten out its leg joints and
launch it into the air. Its wings
stay closed to keep the body
streamlined, so the locust can
get as high as possible.

When it can go no higher, the
locust opens its wings
as wide as it can and flaps
them to carry it even
further forward.

To help it land safely, the
locust spreads its legs wide,
tilts its hind wings and curves
its front ones. This helps it to
slow down and drop gently to
the ground.

## FROG BEETLE

The frog beetle's back legs are long and strong, like a frog's. It uses them to leap away from enemies, then it uses its wings to fly to complete safety.

## FIT AS A FLEA

Fleas are famous jumpers. They can leap as high as 30 cm (12 in). If you think that this doesn't sound very high, consider the size of a flea. That really is some high jump for a tiny creature.

*Flea*

## HOT AND BOTHERED

The desert cricket uses its strong legs for long leaps, but it also uses them for digging. If it needs to escape from enemies or the raging heat of the midday sun, it digs speedily into the sand. It can bury itself in only a few seconds. Beat that!

*Desert cricket*

# EATING OUT

Mini monsters have different feeding
habits. Some can eat almost anything,
while others have more specialised dietary
requirements. Their feeding parts suit the
sort of food they dine on.

## WEEVILS
Weevils have a long, curved snout called a *rostrum*.
It has tiny jaws at the end for biting small pieces
of plant.

## TONGUE-TIED
Butterflies and moths have a long, tube-shaped mouth
called a *proboscis*. They hover in front of a flower to feed,
stretch out their proboscis and delve inside for the sweet
nectar. When they are not feeding, the proboscis is coiled
up out of the way. Thank goodness for that!

*Just look at the length of this
hawk-moth's tongue!*

WOW!

## TWO SETS OF CHOMPERS
Ground beetles have two pairs of jaws. One huge pair
is for chopping up worms, slugs and other yummy
goodies. A smaller pair is for shovelling the bits into the
beetle's mouth.

## AN IRON GRIP
The praying mantis grips its prey with its front legs and
uses its sharp, strong jaws for slicing it up.

## A Quick Slurp

The darkling beetle lives in the desert. To get a drink, it waits until dew from early morning mist collects on its back. Then it holds its abdomen up so that the water drips down into its mouth. What a performance!

## A Trail of Destruction

Caterpillars chew their way around the edges of a leaf. They grasp it between their legs, stretch out their head, then chew down towards their body. Look at the progress this common mormon caterpillar has made on a leaf. Hungry, or what?

*This is all that's left of the leaf after eight hours.*

# Yucky Habits

If you're about to munch
on a tasty snack while
reading these pages,
a word of warning...
DON'T! Some of
these yucky mini
monster habits
will make you
feel distinctly
peculiar!

## House
## Flies

Do you ever
see flies lurking
around your
kitchen? Well this
is what they are up to.

When a fly smells food, it
lands and tastes it with the taste
buds on its feet. If it fancies the
food, it spreads digestive
juices on it – rather like
vomiting, actually! This
turns solid food mushy, so the fly can dab it up with its
sponge-like mouthparts. That's the last time you leave
food uncovered!

*Spongy mouthpart*

*Taste buds are on the feet*

## Germs Galore!

A mosquito feasts on blood. When it bites someone,
it slurps up some of their blood, plus any germs that
are in it. Then it flies on to someone else and has another
meal, leaking some of the germs from the first person into
the new one. This spreads the germs that cause disease.

## Dung Flies

A dung fly lays its eggs in fresh droppings. When the maggots hatch out, they eat the dung. Apparently, this contains lots of nourishment for them!

YUMMY

## Cave Cockroach

Cockroaches that live in caves banquet on a tasty selection of morsels. They are particularly partial to bat droppings and the remains of dead bats. Other fine food includes mites and fungi.

## Live Food

The weevil-hunting wasp grasps, stings and paralyses weevils, but doesn't kill them. The female puts the weevils in a burrow, and lays her eggs on them. When the larvae hatch, they eat the live weevils' flesh. Ouch!

*The wasp holds the weevil in position with its strong legs.*

# DEADLY BEASTIES

If, by some strange chance, you happen to come across any of the little horrors shown here (fairly unlikely!), the best thing you could do is RUN AWAY! They are DEADLY!

## BLACK WIDOW

The female black widow spider has a bite which can kill a person. She sometimes kills her mate. Nice habit, eh?

## SAHARA SCORPION

Scorpions are eight-legged relatives of spiders. They only sting to protect themselves. The Sahara scorpion is only 7 cm (2.8 in) long, but its sting is strong enough to kill you. So steer clear next time you're in the Sahara desert!

*Sahara scorpion*

## POISONOUS SNAILS

Many seashells you find on the beach are the empty homes of sea snails. The cone shell lurks on coral reefs and stabs its prey with a poisonous dart which paralyses and kills. A number of humans have met a sticky end in this way.

*The geography cone is highly poisonous.*

## PRETTY DEADLY

Just in case you happen to be trekking through the
jungle one day, watch out for these cute, pretty little
frogs. They are called poison dart frogs.
A smear of their poison can
kill a human, so
HANDS OFF!

*This little cutie is
the world's most
poisonous frog.*

## IF YOU'RE A MALE PRAYING MANTIS...

A special warning for YOU. Beware of those crafty
females you're so fond of! If they're hungry, they may
eat males like you while mating.

*The female is bigger
than the male.*

# Flying High

One of the main reasons why insects have survived for millions of years is that they can fly. Their wings help them to escape from danger, find food and places to live.

## What's In a Wing?

An insect's wings are thin and light. (Well, heavy ones wouldn't be very useful, would they?) They are stiffened by a network of veins. The flapping power comes from strong muscles in the insect's middle.

## Getting Warm

Before an insect's wings can move fast enough to fly, the flight muscles need to be warmed up, especially when the weather is cool.

## Mini Helicopters

Hoverflies can move forwards, backwards, sideways, up and down, just like a helicopter. As their name suggests, they can also hover in midair. Very few insects can perform this stunt.

## Gliding By

Some insects have wings specially made for gliding long distances. The African grasshopper has broad hind wings made for this job.

## BEAUTIFUL BUTTERFLIES

Lots of tropical butterflies are big and bright. They avoid hungry enemies by darting in and out of patches of sunlight and dark, shadowy places. This makes them difficult to see.

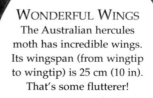

*Australian hercules moth*

## WONDERFUL WINGS

The Australian hercules moth has incredible wings. Its wingspan (from wingtip to wingtip) is 25 cm (10 in). That's some flutterer!

### BELIEVE IT OR NOT...

The fastest ever flier was probably a giant prehistoric dragonfly. These huge insects probably had to fly as fast as 69 km/h (43 mph) just to stay up in the air!

# EYE SPY

Most insects are tiny, but they have more developed senses than most larger animals. They can see and hear things that humans cannot detect.

*Caterpillars are surrounded by their food, so they don't need to look hard to find it. They can make do with simple eyes.*

## SIMPLE EYES

Insects which do not need sharp eyesight have eyes called *simple eyes*. These can probably only see light and shade, and not much more.

## COMPOUND EYES

Now we're talking super-vision here. Beasties with *compound eyes* have excellent eyesight.

Compound eyes are made up of lots of separate sections, called *ommatidia*. The more of these there are, the more sensitive the eye is.

## HUGE EYES

A dragonfly's eyes take up most of its head. This means that it can see in front, above, below and behind, all at the same time. It's no good sneaking up on a dragonfly – it'll see you coming!

*Dragonfly's head*

## LOTS OF EYES

Many insects have simple eyes AND compound eyes.
The wasp and the cicada both have compound eyes and
three simple eyes.

*Simple eyes*

*Wasp*

*Compound eyes*

### INVISIBLE LIGHT

Lots of insects can see ultraviolet light.
This is light from the sun that humans and other
animals can't see.

Some flowers have petals with lines which reflect
ultraviolet light. To an insect, this makes the lines look
like bright runways guiding them right into the middle of
the flower, where all the yummy pollen and nectar is.

### HUNTING SPIDERS

Spiders which hunt for their prey have really sharp
eyesight. Well they should really, because they have eight

eyes to spy what's
happening! This helps
them to stalk their
victims and pounce
on them.

# Touch, Smell and Hearing

Bodies of insects have lots of short hairs connected to the nervous system. These can feel tiny vibrations in the air made by sound and movement. Some hairs can even sense smells and flavours.

## Fringed Feelers

Insects' antennae often have sensory hairs for feeling. The Indian beetle has huge fringed antennae to help it pick up scents in the air. Beetles fan out their antennae when they fly, to help them to smell as much as possible.

The Indian beetle's giant antennae look like antlers.

## Feathered Sensor

A male gypsy moth's big, feathered antennae are so sensitive that they can smell the scent of a female gypsy moth from far away. Moths can also tell different flowers and plants apart by their smells.

## FEELING TOUCHY

Because many insects rely on touch and smell so much, they usually have small eyes, but very long antennae. The longhorn beetle has a fine pair of feelers which are jointed, so they can be moved around.

*A longhorn beetle with its antennae pointing backwards.*

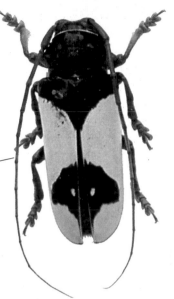

## SEEING IN THE DARK

Insects that live in the dark have to use other ways of 'seeing'. The cave cricket lives in dark caves and feels the world around it with its long antennae.

BELIEVE IT OR NOT...

A cricket hears with its legs. Yes...really! Its ears are a swelling just below the knee on each front leg.

# Doing Battle

Many mini monsters attack and kill the creepy crawlies they feed on. But some beasties fight their own kind to protect their territory and to compete for food and places to mate.

## Battling Bees

Every bee colony has its own scent. If a bee from another colony tries to get into the hive, the others recognize that the intruder smells different and push it out. The intruder may curl up, telling the other bees "I give in".

## The Tale of the Lost Ant

Imagine the scene...your pet cat is basking in the sunshine when an ant crawls on to its fur. Moggy gets up, stretches and wanders to another part of the neighbourhood, where the ant gets off. Far from home, the ant tries to join another colony of ants. MISTAKE! The ants can smell that it's a stranger and kill it. THE END!

## WHO'S BOSS?

Stag beetles compete for the dead wood that they feed and breed on. The males have big jaws which look like antlers, rather like the antlers of a real stag. They use these weapons for wrestling.

When two males meet, they stretch out their antennae to pick up lots of information about each other. Each male takes up a threatening pose to try to frighten off his opponent.

If threats don't work, each beetle tries to grip his rival around the middle, to lift him up and drop him to the ground. Sometimes, the teeth on the jaws of the winning beetle puncture the loser's tough armour.

*Stag beetles*

An injured beetle will probably die, especially if it lands on its back. This can be particularly bad news if there are ants around, because they enjoy a tasty beetle for supper!

# FINDING A MATE

For most creepy crawlies, a female has to mate with a male of her own kind before she can lay eggs. Finding the right mate, avoiding being eaten and laying the eggs in a safe place is full of hazards.

## MOTH MATES

A moth's antennae are so sensitive to smells that it can smell the scent of a mate from far away. The Indian moon moth can smell a mate from a distance of around 11 km (6 3/4 miles) away.

*Indian moon moth*

## CHIRPING GRASSHOPPERS

A grasshopper makes a chirping sound to attract a mate. It does this by rubbing its back leg along its front wing. This makes small teeth on the leg buzz.

## COURTSHIP DANCES

Just to make sure that they have found the right species to mate with, butterflies perform dancing flights. While they dance, they exchange scented chemical signals, called *pheromones*, telling them that the partner they have found is the one for them. Aaah!

## LIGHTING UP

Glow-worms have nothing whatsoever to do with worms.
They are the wingless females of particular kinds of beetle!
At night, the female makes a light near the tip of her
abdomen. This attracts males who come and mate with
her. Some kinds of glow-worm even flash a code
to attract a mate. Smart, eh?

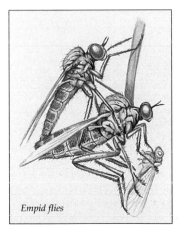

*Empid flies*

## GORGEOUS GIFTS

In some species where
insects feed on other
insects, the male gives
the female a gift of
food when they mate,
so that she doesn't
eat HIM! A tasty
dead insect seems to
do the trick for some
females. Well, they
would be mad to
turn down such a
special present...
wouldn't they?

# ALL CHANGE

For us humans, growing up is quite straightforward compared with growing up for insects. We are born, then we grow until we become adults. But insects go through stages where their body shape changes completely, several times, before they make it to the 'grown-up' stage. This is called *complete metamorphosis* (which means a complete change).

## BUTTERFLIES

A female butterfly lays its eggs on a plant.

The eggs hatch into a squidgy-looking creature called a *larva*. A butterfly larva is called a caterpillar.

*Chrysalis*

*Chrysalis skin splits*

Next, the caterpillar becomes something called a *pupa*, or *chrysalis*. To do this, its caterpillar skin splits to reveal its chrysalis skin underneath. The chrysalis hangs from a branch or under a leaf.

Inside the chrysalis, the butterfly's shape is forming. Many chrysalises look like old leaves. NOT very pretty!

After a few weeks the butterfly emerges from the chrysalis skin. This process takes about 20 minutes of hard work. The beautiful, new creature waits for its wings to harden properly, and then flies off to find its first meal.

## LITTLE BY LITTLE

Some insects don't go through as many stages as others. They hatch from their eggs into babies called *nymphs*, which look like tiny adults.

The nymphs moult their outer skins many times, changing body size a bit each time. This is called *incomplete metamorphosis*. Insects that grow up this way include grasshoppers, cockroaches and dragonflies.

PHEW!
I'M A GROWN-UP
AT LAST.

# STINGING THINGS

If you've ever been stung by a mini monster, you'll know that it's not very pleasant! Here are some beasties with a sting in the tail.

## BEES
Bees are plant-eaters, so the sharp sting in their tail is nothing to do with killing prey for food – it's for scaring off enemies. But give a moment's thought to this poor little buzzer. When it stings something, the sting and part of the body tears away and the bee dies.

## WASPS
These beasties can use their sting several times, so beware! They use them for killing prey and to protect themselves. Wasps do some good though, because they kill creatures that destroy plants and fruit.

## BELIEVE IT OR NOT...
About 40,000 people are killed each year by wasp or bee stings because of allergic reactions.

## THE BIGGEST WASP

The tarantula hawk wasp is the world's biggest wasp. Its wingspan is about 12 cm (5 in). Aagh!

The female captures a big spider and paralyses it with her sting. She then lays an egg on it and pushes it into a small burrow.

When the wasp grub hatches out, it feeds on the living, paralysed spider. Live food... mmm-mmmmm!

*Front wing*

*Hind wing*

*Tarantula hawk wasp*

## BUTTERFLY HUNTER

A type of South American wasp attacks groups of butterflies sitting on the ground and collects them to make a food store for its grubs when they hatch out. After stinging the butterflies, one at a time, it bites their wings off. Nice little creature!

# FALSE ID

Being any sort of small creature can be a dangerous business, so many little beasties have special ways of staying safe. They have sneaky ways of hiding, or they masquerade as something much more frightening.

## CAMOUFLAGE

Some insects have body colouring that matches their background, making them almost impossible to see. This works best of all if they keep still...the slightest fidget and they could become supper to a hungry hunter.

*Can you spot the Indian leaf butterfly? It looks just like an old leaf.*

*Butterfly's head*

*Butterfly's wing*

*Bottom of wing*

Another type of camouflage called *disruptive coloration* disguises the body by breaking its shape up with stripes and areas of colour.

## IN DISGUISE

Many insects mimic (copy) the shapes and colours of things far more dangerous to scare their enemies away.

The hoverfly isn't dangerous, but it looks it because its colouring and pattern is the same as a wasp's. Handy, eh?

The eyed hawk-moth gets its name from the big spots on its hind wings. They look like frightening, staring eyes.

*Hoverfly*

HAHA!

# HOUSEHOLD HORRORS

If you thought that your home was a mini monster-free zone...WRONG! Most homes have some sort of hidden creepy crawly life. Hopefully, yours won't have most of these though.

## COCKROACHES

These beasties are ancient insects. They live almost anywhere and eat just about everything. They can become household pests, eating any food which is left around. Their flattened bodies make it easy for them to hide in cracks, so they are difficult to get rid of.

## BEDBUGS

Now these will have you scratching! Bedbugs are bloodsucking bugs. They mostly live in birds' nests and where bats roost, but they also live IN YOUR HOME! They reproduce quickly in warm conditions, so a nice warm bedroom – your mattress in particular – will make a wonderfully comfortable residence for them.

*Bedbugs in close-up*

*Real size of a bedbug*

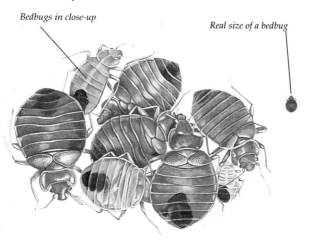

## Houseflies

Every country has houseflies. These excellent fliers love to hang around your home looking for food, and they are not fussy about the quality of it either. Old leftovers will do just fine, thank you!

## Wasps

Wasps often make their nests in the roofs of houses, where it's warm and safe. Ideal for the wasps maybe, but not for the humans they share the house with. Bzzzzzzzzzzz!

## Fleas

Each kind of flea prefers the blood of one sort of animal or bird. The bad news is that fleas can be smuggled into your home on an innocent pet. The good news is that animal fleas have to be very hungry to attack a human.

A flea bite leaves you with an itchy red spot. Beware of madly scratching pets!

## Head Lice

These tiny terrors can live in human hair. They grip on tightly and puncture the skin with their mouthparts, so they can suck up blood. Eeeeek!

## Deathwatch Beetle

These beetles feed on the wood of trees. They are the dreaded enemies of people who live in houses with timbers, as they munch away on the wood. This weakens the framework of the house.

# NESTS

Some insects live on their own (oh, poor things), but others live together in groups, or *societies*. They are called *social insects* and they build nests where they protect each other and bring up their babies. How civilized!

## WASPS

The boss of a wasp colony is the queen. In the spring she begins a new nest made from chewed-up wood. She builds a few cells for her eggs.

The queen builds more paper layers around the cells to make an extra safe and warm home.

Inside, the queen lays a single egg in each cell. When the larvae hatch out, the queen feeds them with tasty morsels of caterpillar.

The first lot of babies grow up and become workers. They gather food for the next lot of larvae. By summer, the nest may have as many as 500 wasps inside. Yikes!

## ANTS

Different kinds of ants build different kinds of nests. Wood ants build enormous ones from the remains of plants. Inside, there is a complicated network of tunnels where all the ants live.

## TERMITES

Termites are social insects that look and live like ants. They have the most complicated insect societies and build huge nests to live in. The nests can last for several years.

*This African termites' nest has umbrella-like layers, but nobody knows why.*

### ___BELIEVE IT OR NOT...___

The tallest termite nests are made by the African termite. They can measure an amazing 12.8 m (42 ft) high. That's as high as seven tall people standing on top of each other!

# MONSTER MONSTERS

Some creepers, slitherers and flutterers are small and sweet-looking, but some are HUGE. Well, that's HUGE when they are sitting next to their small relations. Here are a few of the unbelievably BIG beasties that you really ought to know about.

### THE LONGEST INSECT
Stick insects are the longest insects in the world. African ones can be as long as 40 cm (15 3/4 in).

### THE LONGEST ANTENNAE
The proud owner of the longest antennae is the New Guinea longhorn beetle. Its fantastic feelers are 20 cm (7 1/2 in) long.

### THE LONGEST CENTIPEDE
At 33 cm (13 in) in length, a centipede found on the Andaman Islands in the Bay of Bengal is the longest one on record. It measured almost 4 cm (1 1/2 in) wide.

Yikes! That's a long, skinny scuttler!

### THE LONGEST MILLIPEDE

A kind of millipede from the Seychelles measures as long as 28 cm (11 in).

### THE HEAVIEST INSECT

Goliath beetles can weigh up to 100 g. That's as much as two Funfax books!

### THE LARGEST LAND SNAIL

Imagine this if you can. The largest recorded land snail measured 39.3 cm (15 1/2 in) from tip to toe. What a slime trail that slitherer must have left!

### THE LARGEST DRAGONFLY

A dragonfly from Central and South America measures up to 12 cm (4 3/4 in) across its wings and 19 cm (7 1/2 in) in length.

### THE LARGEST SPIDER

The goliath bird-eating spider is ENORMOUS! One has been found with a leg-span of 28 cm (11 in). Scary, or what?

### THE LARGEST BUTTERFLY

The Queen Alexandra's birdwing butterfly is the largest known butterfly in the world. Its wingspan can measure an incredible 28 cm (11 in). Imagine those wings brushing against your face! Aaaagh!

**Acknowledgements:** (KEY: t=top, b=bottom/below, c=centre, l=left, r=right) Gary Staab (model-maker): back cover tr

**Picture Credits:** American Museum of Natural History/OW Myers: 221c; NHPA/Stephen Dalton: 206b; Oxford Scientific Films/Kathie Atkinson: 208c; /Densey Clyne: 209c; /James Robinson: front cover cl.

**Additional Photography:** Jane Burton, Andy Crawford, Geoff Dann, Angelika Elsebach, Frank Greenaway, Mark Ilcy, Colin Keates, Dave King, Stephen Oliver, Harry Taylor, Jerry Young.

# WEIRD AND WONDERFUL

Written by Susan Mayes

Illustrated by Andrew Peters

# LOOK AT THAT!

Wherever you live, there is probably wildlife of some kind, even if it's only your pet hamster, or a sparrow landing on your windowsill. These creatures are special in their own way, but you should see some of the stunners that are out there in the rest of the world! Here's your chance to ogle some of nature's weirdest and most wonderful wildlife.

Soar, hover and swoop with some of our feathered friends, or admire their drop-dead gorgeous plumage.

Gather your courage and take a peek at some of those awesome creepy crawlies that you love to hate. They look incredible in close-up!

In the wild, eating isn't just for satisfaction; it's a matter of life and death. You should see what some of the world's hungry hunters manage to put away!

*African moon moth*

*Poison-dart frog*

Then there are the architects of the animal world. Some creatures are amazingly skilled builders who construct fancy dwellings for a mate and their offspring.

*Seahorse*

Don't forget the waters of the world. Below the waves there is a vast collection of ugly, weird, big or beautiful sealife.

*Nest*

Stretch up tall and crane your neck to get a better view of some of the terrifically long, lanky creatures to be seen on our planet.

*Macaw*

There are some marvellous animals in places all over the world, from rain forests to frozen wastelands. Delve into this book and discover them for yourself.

# FANTASTIC FEATHERS

Some of our feathered friends have dull, unremarkable plumage, but there are some real stunners, too. We're talking drop-dead gorgeous here!

## FEATHER FEATURES

There are four main types of feathers that make up a bird's plumage: *down feathers, body feathers, tail feathers* and *wing feathers*. They each have a different job.

DOWN FEATHERS – soft, fine feathers next to the skin. They trap a layer of air to keep the bird warm.

BODY FEATHERS – come in a range of shapes and sizes. Some insulate and cover the body, while others are for displaying to mates and enemies.

*African grey parrot down feathers*

TAIL FEATHERS – for steering when flying, for balancing when perching, or just for impressing!

*Peacock tail feathers*

WING FEATHERS – one of the most important parts of a bird's flying gear. They are strong, light and flexible.

*Macaw flight feather*

*Parakeet flight feather*

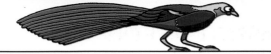

## CACKLING PUNKS

Many of the world's most gorgeous birds live in rain forest tree tops. Lady Ross's turacos live in small noisy groups. They cackle and croak as they run along tree branches, sporting their punk headgear.

*Female eclectus parrot*

## PRETTY POLLY

There are three main types of parrot: *lories, cockatoos* and *parrots.* Not only do they attract attention with their dazzling colours, but they make grating, screeching calls. Male and female parrots usually look alike, but male and female eclectus parrots are completely different.

*Male eclectus parrot*

## SCARLET SPECTACULAR

The swamps of South America are home to flocks of scarlet ibises. The young birds have grey-brown backs for a year, but they become red all over once they reach adulthood.

# FLYING FEATS

$W$hile most birds can fly (there are a few which can't), there are many which can perform amazing feats. Hovering, gliding, swooping, soaring...you name it, they do it!

## SKILFUL HOVERERS

The hummingbird is an excellent hoverer, which makes sipping nectar from flowers dead easy. It's also the only bird which can fly sideways, forwards and backwards.

*Hummingbird's wings hardly seem to move*

## WATCH OUT BELOW!

The peregrine falcon is the world's fastest bird. It *stoops* (dives) to catch other birds at an astonishing 180 kph (112 mph). The helpless victim hardly stands a chance!

BELIEVE IT OR NOT...

The bird with the fastest wingbeat is the horned sungem hummingbird. It beats its wings 90 times a second!

## TOP SEA BIRDS

The frigate bird is a sea bird with a thieving habit. It's a speedy flier which can swoop, dart, soar and hover in pursuit of other sea birds and, more importantly, their food. It steals food directly from their beaks! Bold, or what?

## SOARING HIGH

The Andean condor is the world's heaviest bird of prey. It soars over the mountains looking for dead or sick creatures to feed on. Nice habit!

## ON THE WING

The albatross lives mainly in the Antarctic and has the greatest wingspan of any living bird – up to 3.63 m (12 ft). With the help of this wing power, it can fly up to 500 km (310 miles) a day. Phew!

# SPOTS AND STRIPES

Do you wear dramatic clothes to make you stand out in a crowd? Some creatures sport snappy designs which can have the opposite effect, making them difficult to see in their natural habitat. This is called *camouflage*.

## BLACK AND WHITE

You might think that a zebra's startling stripes make it easy prey for a lion, but when zebras stand together they appear as a mass of black and white patterns. The confused lion finds it really tricky to pick out one victim to chase.

### BELIEVE IT OR NOT...

No two zebras have the same pattern. They recognize each other by their individual designs.

## DAPPLED BABIES

Baby deer, called *fawns*, are helpless when they are born and lie still and quiet in the forest undergrowth. They often have spotted fur, which looks like dappled patches of sunlight to a hungry hunter...not supper at all.

## TIGER TRICKERY

Out in the open, the tiger's black and orange stripes are dramatic and striking, but against a background of grass and shafts of sunlight, they make hiding easy. Good for hunting...grrrr!

## SPOTTED CATS

The jaguar, the ocelot and the leopard are three members of the cat family with splendid spotted coats. Sadly for these sensational creatures, many of them have been hunted for their beautiful fur.

*Jaguar*

*Ocelot*

*Leopard*

*Jaguar*

# ALL CHANGE

Now how about this for weird. There are some extraordinary creatures which can change colour...yes, change colour! This helps them blend in with whichever background they happen to be sitting on, to hide from enemies or to surprise a passing meal. Cool, or what?

## COLOUR-CHANGING CHAMELEONS

If an intruder enters a chameleon's *territory* (the place where it lives), the chameleon has a handy natural response. Its colours become much stronger and more striking, and it puffs up its body to look aggressive and scary.

## BUT HOW?

A chameleon's skin has coloured *pigment* in special cells. The cells containing darker pigment are deeper in the skin. The sight of an intruder triggers a rush of colour to the skin's surface, and...hey presto...a new outfit!

## FLATFISH

Flatfish swim on or near the sea-bed. They are not very active, so their colour-changing and pattern-changing skills are an essential part of their fishy make-up, both for catching dinner and avoiding becoming dinner themselves. They can change to match almost any background.

## BELIEVE IT OR NOT...

The cuttlefish, the champion quick-change artist, changes colour as it swims over different backgrounds... and, weirder still, a shoal of cuttlefish change colour all at the same time! A case of 'all change'!

## MOODY OCTOPUS

The octopus is a shy creature. It spends lots of time lurking in crevices, waiting for food to pass by. If it gets frightened or angry, it changes colour immediately.

*Blue-ringed octopus*

# CURIOUS IN CLOSE-UP

Have you ever been brave enough to take a close peek at a wasp, a housefly or a spider? Curious, aren't they? But they look even curiouser when you look **REALLY** close. Come on now ...be brave!

## FIERCE CHOMPERS

An ant's chompers will have you scuttling! It has strong jaws called *mandibles* which bite and cut up food and enemies.

*Bulldog ant - mandibles have spikes to help grip*

## HAIRY AND SCARY

Uh oh! Introducing one of the scariest creatures around...the tarantula spider. Actually, the tarantula is quite a shy customer, but this doesn't make it look any less frightening, does it?

Even though tarantulas have eight eyes, their eyesight is not good. They rely on their sensitive, hairy legs to warn of danger or a good nosh!

*This tarantula would only bite a person in self-defence – phew!*

*Centipede*

## MANY-LEGGED CREEPER
You can watch a centipede slinking across
the ground, but if you view it in close-up you
can actually count its legs. *Centipede* means
*100 legs*, so here's your chance to
check! 1, 2, 3, 4...

## SUPER SNOUT
A close-up shot of a beetle called a weevil
reveals its long, curved snout called a *rostrum*.
This has tiny jaws at the end for biting up pieces
of leaf and plant.

*Weevil*

## HIDEOUS
## HOUSEFLIES
If you could see a
housefly spreading its
digestive juices on your
leftover food, before it
sucks it up, you would think
twice about leaving anything
around uncovered.

WEIRD & WONDERFUL   257

# LONG AND LANKY

A long neck and long legs can be a great advantage when it comes to feeding. Here are some creatures who benefit from these lanky features.

### GANGLY GIRAFFES

Giraffes are the tallest animals. Their long, long necks make it possible for them to reach the tree tops on the African plains, where they live, to eat leaves that other animals can't get at.

Long legs help the giraffe achieve an average height of 5 m (16 ft). They are also essential for galloping away from *predators* (hunters).

### A GIRAFFE HAS...

- a strange way of fighting other giraffes – they push each other, neck to neck

- an extra large heart to pump blood up to its head

- only seven *vertebrae* (bony segments of the spine) in its neck – each one is 0.3 m (1 ft) long.

## PREHISTORIC LONG NECKS

Dinosaurs called *sauropods* were the prehistoric equivalent of our modern-day giraffe. These peaceful *herbivores* (plant-eaters) could reach the tasty leaves of prehistoric tree tops with the help of an incredibly long neck.

## MEGA BIRD

The ostrich is HUGE. At 90-160 kg (200-353 lb) it is the heaviest bird. It is also the tallest bird at 2.1-2.7 m (7-9 ft). It can run at speeds of up to 72 kph (45 mph), which makes it the fastest two-legged animal. All this is brill, but the ostrich is too heavy to fly. Bad luck!

*Ostrich*

*Marabou stalk*

*Flamingo*

## WONDERFUL WADERS

Long-legged birds such as the flamingo and the stork wade into deep water on their stilt-like legs, to feed on tasty morsels that the shorter-legged birds can't get at.

# Enormous Appetites

In the wild, eating is a serious business; it's a matter of survival. Here are some of the world's hungry hunters...grrrr!

## African Hunting Dogs

African hunting dogs live and hunt in big groups called *packs*. A pack can have up to 30 members, although 90 has been known!

After a kill, the hunters gobble up vast amounts of meat. They return to the dogs that stayed behind and *regurgitate* (vomit) it for them to eat. Yum, yum!

## Greedy Snakes

You might think that slinky snakes are limited to long, thin food. WRONG!

An African egg-eating snake can swallow an egg twice the width of its body. You can see the lump as it goes down whole.

## Believe It or Not...

The pygmy shrew has to eat almost its own weight each day, just to stay alive. Imagine that! Uuugh!

## DEEP-SEA ANGLER

The fearsome deep-sea angler fish lurks in the ocean's darkest depths.

*Before a meal*

Some species of angler fish have a special luminous light which attracts prey. Fish twice the size of it have been found in its stretchy stomach. Gulp!

*After a meal*

## KILLER AT LARGE

Killer whales (or *orcas*) are ferocious creatures which hunt in groups called *pods*. They eat a greater variety of prey than any other marine *mammal* (a warm-blooded animal that is fed on its mother's milk). Their menu includes whales ten times their own size!

*Killer whale*

# BEAKS AND BILLS

A beak (or *bill*) is a vital piece of bird equipment, essential for feeding, *preening* (arranging and cleaning feathers) and nest building. Different beaks are suited to different jobs.

## TAP-TAP-TAP-TAP...

Woodpeckers are known for the loud sounds they make by drumming loudly on dead wood with their beaks. They make all this racket to claim their territory, to make nest holes in trees and to search for grubs to eat.

*Outside of beak made of keratin – the same stuff as your fingernails*

*Toucan*

## BIG AND BRIGHT

The toucan's huge, colourful beak is not as heavy and as cumbersome as it looks. It is light and hollow and makes a delicate tool for picking the bird's favourite foods: passion fruits, berries, other soft fruits and seeds.

## COMBINATION BEAK

A parrot's beak does a combination of jobs. The hooked tip pulls out the soft parts of fruit while the jaws near the base of the beak crack open seeds. Parrots use their feet to hold and turn their chosen snack whilst dining.

*Macaw*

## CURVED PROBE

The curlew is a wading bird with a long, curved beak. It probes deep into the soft mud to pull out worms and molluscs which the shorter-beaked birds cannot reach.

## STRETCHY POUCH

A pelican's bill has a big pouch underneath which can stretch to catch and hold fish. The bill can hold more food than the bird's stomach!

## TEARING AT MEAT

Vultures do the useful job of eating up the remains of dead animals. They use their hooked beak to pull and tear at the carcass. Mmmm!

*Vulture – stretches its long neck to feed inside carcasses*

# Dazzling Displays

During the mating season, many animals have specialized ways of attracting a mate. The males often use the same signals to attract a female as they do to warn off male rivals.

## Hanging Around

Birds of paradise are renowned for their dazzling mating displays. The male blue bird of paradise opens his wings and tips forward until he is hanging upside-down by his feet. Then he opens his tail feathers and fans them out. Hello girls!

## Puffed Up

Anole lizards come from the tropical parts of South and Central America. Their colouring helps them blend into green and brown backgrounds, but when they inflate their brilliant red throat sacs females have no problem in spotting them.

*Anole lizard*

*Male frigate bird*

The male frigate bird also has an inflatable red throat sac. He puffs it out like a huge balloon for hours at a time until he manages to lure a female.

## FEATHERED FAN

The male peacock has a spectacular way of attracting and impressing a female. He spreads out his brilliant tail feathers in an enormous, unmissable shimmering fan. After the mating season, his tail feathers are no longer needed and they drop out.

*Male peacock*

## FIGHTING IT OUT

Male monitor lizards wrestle at the beginning of the mating season, rearing up on their hind legs. They try to push each other to the ground and the first one to manage this wins the female. Butch, or what?

## COURTSHIP DANCE

A pair of western grebes performs a long courtship dance before mating. This includes the nifty manoeuvre of standing up tall and racing across the water. Groovy movers!

# Go Away!

Life is full of danger for wild animals. If they are frightened or threatened, many of them give out signals that tell their enemies, "go away". This is handy because it cuts down the risk of getting into a fight and becoming injured.

## Hair-Raising

A cat with puffed up fur isn't having a bad hair day! It is making itself look extra big and scary, to frighten off an enemy. The addition of an arched back and a hissing sound makes a clear "go away" signal.

## Underwater Porcupine

The porcupine fish can raise its prickles to frighten off attackers, but it can also puff up its body like a balloon. This makes it too big to be swallowed by the average predator. Great trick, fishy!

*Porcupine fish*

## GORILLAS

A yawning gorilla may have more in mind than a quick snooze. If it feels nervous or threatened, a gorilla will give a gaping yawn which shows off its sharp teeth.

## DON'T MESS WITH ME

The Australian frilled lizard makes one of the most spectacular warning displays. It has a large flap of loose skin attached to its neck. When it is frightened, the lizard raises the flap, making a huge ruff-like collar which can be four times the width of its body.

*Australian frilled lizard displaying*

# DESIGNER DWELLINGS

Some creatures are amazingly skilled in the building department. They construct marvellous homes to live in.

## BOWERBIRDS

A male satin bowerbird builds his *bower* (leafy shelter) on the forest floor. He constructs an avenue of twigs and stains them black with charcoal and *saliva* (spit). Then he decorates the area with feathers, stones or flowers, preferably blue. When a female turns up, he wins her over by making noises and holding the brightest objects in his beak.

## WEAVING AND KNOTTING

The West African weaverbird makes an amazing trumpet-shaped nest by weaving and knotting pieces of grass together.

Yes...knotting! It can tie knots in grass using a combination of its beak and feet.

*Chicks live in round part of nest*

*Entrance of funnel makes it difficult for snakes to get in*

## GOOD LUCK

White storks build platform nests in trees or on buildings. The nests have a central hollow lined with stems and grass.

In many parts of Europe, people believe that white storks bring good luck, so they put up platforms on their houses to encourage the birds to build there.

## PAPER THIN

Each spring, a leader of a European wasp colony, called the *queen*, starts a new nest where she lays her eggs. She uses 'paper' which she makes by chewing up wood. She makes individual cells for the eggs and builds protective layers around the outside.

## HOME TO MILLIONS

Insects called termites build wonderful nests which can be home for up to five million! An African termites' nest starts underground but emerges above with the addition of umbrella-shaped layers. The walls are made from tiny pellets of earth stuck together with saliva.

*African termites' nest*

# AMAZING AMPHIBIANS

Amphibians are *vertebrates* (animals that have a backbone). They are cold-blooded, which means that their body temperature changes depending on their surroundings. They mostly live on land, but they breed in the water.

## SPECIAL SKIN

Amphibians *secrete* (release) slimy fluid called *mucus* from their skin to keep it moist and to stop the outer layer from getting damaged.

*Endangered tomato frogs*

## MEAL TIME

Amphibians eat almost any live food that they can swallow. Spiders, snails, slugs, earthworms and insects make tasty meals.

All amphibians eat lots and lots of food when they can get it, so that they can survive when there isn't much food around.

*The ornate horned toad catches other amphibians and mice in its huge mouth.*

## TREE FROGS

Frogs known as *tree frogs* live mainly in trees. They have developed sticky pads on their fingers and toes which help them to hold on to smooth leaf surfaces.

*Bright greenish skin good for hiding in trees*

*Sticky pads*

## POISONOUS FROGS

Poison-dart frogs from Central and South America are amongst the most colourful amphibians. Their bright colours help them defend their territory and warn predators that they are poisonous to eat.

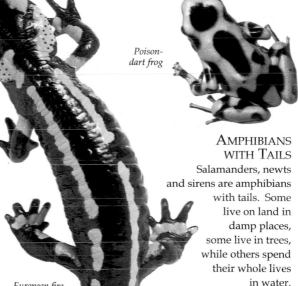

*Poison-dart frog*

## AMPHIBIANS WITH TAILS

Salamanders, newts and sirens are amphibians with tails. Some live on land in damp places, some live in trees, while others spend their whole lives in water.

*European fire salamander*

# TONGUES AND TEETH

Next time you tuck into a plate of food, spare a thought for the world's wildlife who have to catch their every meal. Here are a few creatures which use their super-efficient teeth or tongues at feeding time.

## CHAMELEONS

A chameleon's tongue is the length of its body and tail put together! It is kept bunched up in the creature's mouth until a tasty-looking insect passes by. Then it darts out with lightning speed and catches the meal on its sticky tip.

## PROBING FOR POLLEN

Butterflies and moths use a tongue-like tube called a *proboscis* to feed on flower nectar and other yummy food. When it is not in use, it is coiled up beneath the head, but at feeding time it stretches out to delve for a nourishing meal.

*Extended proboscis*

## CROCODILES

A crocodile lurks in the river, waiting for prey to come along and drink. Then it grabs the animal and pulls it into the water to drown it.

A crocodile's teeth are perfect for gripping food, but they are not as good at slicing and chewing. The creature has to tear off chunks of flesh. Delicious!

## SHARKS

Sharks are always losing their teeth. When the front ones wear out, new ones from a row behind grow in to replace them. Different sharks have different shaped teeth, depending on what they eat.

### BELIEVE IT OR NOT...

A shark can get through thousands of teeth in its lifetime.

# OCEAN ODDITIES

The waters of the world are home to
some really weird-looking creatures.
Feast your eyes on these wonders.

## SEA COWS

Dugongs and manatees are slow, chubby water creatures
with heavy heads and fleshy snouts. These shy and gentle
beasts, which live in warm waters, are often called *sea
cows*. As they are mammals, they have to come up to
the surface to breathe.

There are three species
of manatee: two
live mainly in
freshwater and the
other in the sea.
Sadly, they are
in danger of
becoming *extinct*
(dying out).

*Manatee*

*Dugong*

Dugongs feed
on sea grasses and are
particularly fond of the roots,
which they dig for. They can be
found in herds of several hundred.
Sadly, they are hunted for their meat.

## SEAHORSES

Seahorses are elegant sea creatures. They swim in an upright position by beating their *dorsal fin* (on their back) 20 to 35 times a second. They can be found in corals, sea grasses and seaweeds and hang on to plants with their tails.

*Seahorses can be up to 20 cm (8 in) long*

*Flat, slimy foot crawls over seaweed*

### BELIEVE IT OR NOT...

It is the male seahorse which gives birth, not the female.

## SEA SLUGS

The lettuce slug looks a lot like...yes, a piece of lettuce! It lives on coral reefs and feeds on tiny, tiny plants, called *algae*, which give it its bright green colour.

## COLOURFUL CUCUMBERS

The sea cucumber is another coral reef creature named after salad. It traps small particles of food on its sticky *tentacles* (arms). These are placed inside the mouth and the food is removed.

*Tentacles around mouth*

*Tough skin*

# MORE OCEAN ODDITIES

Here are some more oddities from the oceans for you to ogle. Take a close look and marvel at them.

## MANY-ARMED HUNTER

An octopus hides in a rocky lair during the day and comes out at night to hunt for food, such as crabs. It approaches its prey slowly, then it pounces and wraps its tentacles around the unsuspecting meal.

## GROOVY GEAR

The decorator crab covers itself with pieces of plant and sponge from the sea-bed. The numerous pieces are held in place by tiny bristles.

*Decorator crab*

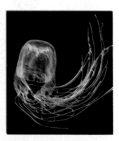

## WOBBLY NASTIES

Jellyfish don't have brains or refined sense organs such as eyes or ears. They are slow movers, so they rely on their nasty stings to keep them safe. The nastiest of these beasties is the box jellyfish which swims near northern Australia and Southeast Asia. A person who is badly stung by one of these can die in four minutes.

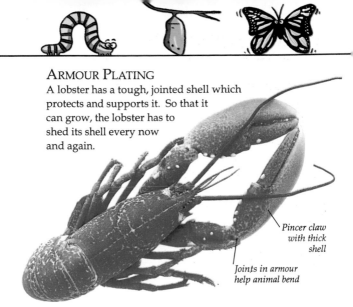

## ARMOUR PLATING

A lobster has a tough, jointed shell which protects and supports it. So that it can grow, the lobster has to shed its shell every now and again.

*Pincer claw
with thick
shell*

*Joints in armour
help animal bend*

## ANEMONES

Animals called anemones use their muscular base to slide along rocks. These flower-like creatures come in lots of beautiful colours, but don't be deceived! Their many tentacles have stinging cells that poison prey, which is then pulled into the mouth.

*Mouth is in
centre of
body*

# FABULOUS FISH

Fish are brilliantly designed for underwater life. There are a mind-boggling 20,000 different *species*, or kinds.

## RAYS

Although rays are flat, they do not actually belong to the family of flatfish. They are the strange relations of sharks. Most lie on their belly near the sea-bed and feed by grinding up fish, shellfish and worms with their flattened teeth.

Blue-spotted ray

## SWIMMING BUTTERFLIES

Butterfly fish have beautiful colours and patterns. You might think that this makes them stand out, but as they live amongst the colours of coral reefs their markings make a good disguise and confuse predators.

*Threadfin butterfly fish*

*Pearl-scaled butterfly fish*

## A SLIMY CUSTOMER

The brilliantly-coloured mandarin fish makes a nasty slime in its skin. This smells and tastes so horrible that it helps keep away germs and big fish that pose a danger.

*Mandarin fish*

## WEDGED IN PLACE

The filefish has a crafty way of keeping out of the grasp of enemies. The first spine on its dorsal fin is serrated, like a file. If the fish is in a sticky situation, it swims into a crevice and locks its dorsal spine in an upright position. This wedges the fish in, making it really tricky for anything to get it out.

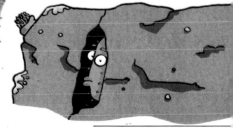

# PRETTY POISONOUS

Some of the world's most beautiful-looking creatures are deadly. Their patterns and colouring advertise their poisonous properties and are an important survival aid, both for the creature itself and for those which hunt it.

## DON'T MESS WITH ME!

The lionfish looks beautiful and elegant, but its striped body does more than just make it look good. The fish's long spines are poisonous and the stripes are a warning to predators to keep away. A hunter that messes with a lionfish will remember not to do the same again...if it survives, that is!

## A LETHAL MEAL

The delicately-spotted puffer fish is eaten in Japan.
The only problem is that the flesh must be prepared by
specially trained chefs as certain parts of the fish's body
contain a deadly poison. Despite expert cooking, mistakes
can be made and people have become seriously ill or even
died after tucking
into a lethal
meal!

*Puffer fish*

## CALL MY BLUFF

The Sinaloan milk snake has striking
coloration which also comes in handy
as a safety device. Luckily, it looks
very like the highly poisonous coral
snake, so many predators are put off
eating this harmless lookalike.

*Sinaloan
milk snake*

## DEADLY FROG

The delightful-looking
poison-dart frog
shown here is not
delightful at
all! It is so
poisonous that
one touch
could kill
a person.

# BUTTERFLIES AND MOTHS

There are at least 150,000 different species of moth but only about 15,000 butterflies. Most butterflies fly by day and many are brightly coloured, while most moths fly by night and are mainly dull coloured.

*Egg*

*Caterpillar*

## A BUTTERFLY IS BORN

A female butterfly lays eggs on a plant. Each egg hatches into a creature called a *larva*. A butterfly larva is called a *caterpillar*.

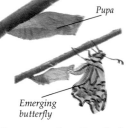

*Pupa*

The caterpillar eats and eats, getting bigger and bigger, so that it has to shed its skin several times. Eventually, it becomes a *pupa,* or *chrysalis.* Inside the pupa, the caterpillar changes into a butterfly.

*Emerging butterfly*

It emerges, then it waits for its wings to expand and harden before flying off.

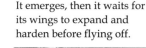

## STUNNING SIGHTS

A butterfly's wings and body are covered in tiny scales (right). The range of colours in the butterfly world is amazing.

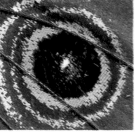

## YUMMY CLOTHES

Clothes moths are a pest because they love to eat wool. They can get into your clothes drawers and make a feast of your favourite jumper.

*Clothes moths*

*Tau emperor moth's antenna*

## NIGHT FLIERS

Many moths have amazing, feathery feelers called *antennae,* which they use for touching and smelling.

## COLOURFUL MOTHS

Some moths are as colourful as butterflies, especially those which live in parts of Africa, Asia, Australia, and South and Central America.

*Jamaican uraniid moth*

### BELIEVE IT OR NOT...

Moths have been around for about 140 million years. Butterflies are mere youngsters in comparison, as they have only been around for about 40 million years.

# POLAR SURVIVORS

The North Pole and the South Pole are amongst the coldest places on earth. The North Pole is surrounded by the frozen Arctic Ocean while the South Pole is surrounded by frozen land called Antarctica. So how do creatures survive in these places?

## ARCTIC FOX

The Arctic fox's winter coat is ideal for freezing cold temperatures. The hairs are hollow and full of air. The air traps warmth from the fox's body, keeping the lucky animal remarkably comfortable.

## AN ICY DIP

Penguins are non-flying birds which are brilliantly adapted to swimming in icy seas. They have layers of fat called *blubber* under their skin, and waterproof feathers which keep them warm on land and in water.

A seal's fur and blubber keep it warm in the Arctic and Antarctic winters, but some types of seal are in danger of overheating in the summertime.

*Small ears don't lose much body heat*

*Eye surface is protected by thin film which keeps out dazzle from snow*

*Hollow hairs trap body warmth*

## POLAR BEARS

The polar bear is the biggest, most powerful hunter in the Arctic. It has an undercoat of thick fur protected by an outer coat of long *guard hairs*. These stick together when the fur gets wet and make a waterproof barrier. Blubber helps to keep the cold out and acts as a food store when there is nothing much around to hunt.

*Non-slip soles grip ice*

# Trunks and Tusks

Imagine having a long nose which has the sensitivity of your fingers, or what about long, long front teeth for fighting. Here are a few of the world's marvellous animals which have a trunk or tusks, or both.

### Elephants

The elephant is the proud owner of both a trunk and tusks. Its trunk can be used for lifting, wrestling, comforting and eating, as well as drawing up water and squirting it over itself, or another elephant!

*Asian elephant*

An elephant uses its ivory tusks as tools and as weapons, but some elephants can do without them, such as the female Asian elephant, which has tiny tusks.

## ELEPHANT SEALS
Male elephant seals have a huge, floppy trunk-like nose. Unlike the elephant's trunk, it isn't very useful, except in the breeding season. Then the seal roars loudly and its incredible nose acts like a loudspeaker.

## WALRUSES
Walruses are amazingly fat relatives of seals. They swim in Arctic waters with the help of four flippers.

A walrus's tusks are actually its upper *canine* teeth. They grow downwards, possibly to as long as 1 m (3 ft), and are used mainly to rake the sea-bed in search of shellfish.

*If necessary, walrus can stab larger prey with its tusks*

*Hard tusk has cavity full of tiny blood vessels*

## NARWHALS
The narwhal is a type of whale. It has two front teeth. In the male the left tooth grows out to become a tusk. This can grow to as long as 3 m (10 ft), which is more than half the length of the animal's body. Wow!

# WONDERFUL WHALES

A whale is a marine mammal. It doesn't take oxygen from the water, like fish; it comes up to the surface regularly to breathe. Female whales give birth to live young. Whales are found in every ocean, and in five of the world's greatest rivers.

## BELIEVE IT OR NOT...

On the day that a baby blue whale is born, it is as big as an elephant. Each day it drinks 200 litres (352 pints) of its mother's milk and puts on an extra 90 kg (200 lb) in weight. Phew!

## BIG BLUE

The blue whale is the biggest animal that has ever lived. It is even larger than the biggest dinosaurs from prehistoric times!

The whale gulps in huge amounts of water containing food, then it filters the water out through huge fringed brushes called *baleen plates* hanging inside its mouth.

*Grooves in throat let it extend when taking huge watery mouthfuls*

## GREY WHALES

In the winter, grey whales stay in the warm waters around northwest Mexico. In the spring, they move north along the coastline, heading for the waters off Alaska where there is plenty to eat. In the autumn, they go south again.

*Grey whale*

## HUMPBACK SONGS

To attract a female, the male humpback whale (below) floats motionless in the water, singing a song for hours on end. Each male sings his own song which develops from year to year.

The humpback has flippers which are much longer than any other whale's. It uses them to slap on the water, making a loud splashing noise. This is called *flippering*.

# ANIMAL FEATS

Here are some fantastic animal feats
for you to memorise. Slip them into
conversations to wow your friends with
your incredible knowledge of the
world's wildlife.

## THE HEAVIEST BLUE WHALE
Not only is the blue whale the biggest creature
that has ever lived, it is also very, very heavy.
The heaviest blue whale recorded was a
female weighing 190 tonnes.

## THE LARGEST LAND ANIMAL
The largest living land animal overall
is the African bush elephant. The
tallest is the giraffe.

## THE NOISIEST LAND ANIMALS
The howling
monkeys of Central
and South America
are the noisiest land
animals in the world.
Once they get going,
they can be heard up
to 16 km (10 miles)
away. Shhhhh!

## THE SMALLEST LAND ANIMALS

The Kitti's hog-nosed bat, also known as the bumblebee bat, has a wingspan of about 160 mm (6.3 in).

The smallest land animal in length is the Etruscan shrew. Its head and body length is 36-52 mm (1.42-2.04 in).

## REGROWTH

The natural sponge *(porifera)* is actually a marine animal. It can regrow lost parts and can even regrow its entire body from a tiny fragment of itself. If it gets broken into tiny pieces, the separate bits can reform into a full-size sponge! Absolutely amazing!

## THE FASTEST LAND ANIMAL

The cheetah is the fastest land animal over a short distance. It can reach a top speed of 96-101 kph (60-63 mph).

**Acknowledgements:** (KEY: a=above, b=bottom/below, c=centre, l=left, r=right, t=top ) Peter Griffiths & David Dunkin, model makers (261tl, cra); Natural History Museum; Parc Zoologique de Paris.

**Picture Credits:** Bryan & Cherry Alexander: 287cra; American Museum of Natural History, New York: 288b; Heather Angel/Biofotos: 258cl; 282br; Bruce Coleman Ltd: 249bl; /E Bauer: 265cr; /Bob & Clara Calhoun: 277br; /John Concatosa: 267tr; /Jeff Foott: 284b; /Charlie Ott: 265bl; /Andrew Purcell: 252b; Robert Harding Picture Library: 281ca; /Global Pictures: 255b; Frank Lane Picture Agency/Eric & David Hosking: front cover tl; 264bl; / F Polking: 269tr; Nature Photographers/MP Harris: 251b; NHPA/Harold Palo: 263bl; Oxford Scientific Films: 250c; /Kathie Atkinson: 256tr; /Mike Britchhead: 283tr; /D Fleetham: 289cb; Planet Earth Pictures: 255c; /Neville Coleman: 276bl; Premaphotos/Preston-Mafham: front cover bl; 257cr; Zefa Pictures: 273b; 291b; /Allstock: 284cr; /S Wayman: 253tr.

**Additional Photography:** Peter Anderson, Geoff Brightling, Jane Burton, Peter Chadwick, Geoff Dann, Philip Dowell, Neil Fletcher, Frank Greenaway, Colin Keates, Dave King, Cyril Laubscher, Mike Linley, Karl Shone, Harry Taylor, Kim Taylor, Jerry Young.

Every effort has been made to trace the copyright holders. Funfax Ltd apologises for any unintentional omissions and would be pleased, in such cases, to add an acknowledgement in further editions.

# AFTER DARK

Written by Fiona Waters

Illustrated by Gary Boller

# OUR WORLD

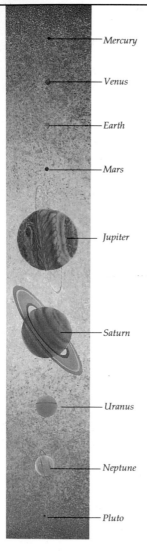

Mercury

Venus

Earth

Mars

Jupiter

Saturn

Uranus

Neptune

Pluto

Everything that exists, including the Earth and the furthest star, is called the *universe*. Scientists think that it exploded into being anything from 15 billion years ago to 20 billion years ago! This giant explosion became known as the big bang.

## WHIRLING AROUND

The Sun, the nine planets that *orbit* (move around) it and their moons are called the *solar system*. The whole thing moves around, together with millions of stars, in a part of space called the *galaxy*.

The planets in our solar system are called Mercury, Venus, Earth, Mars, Jupiter, Saturn, Uranus, Neptune and Pluto.

## NIGHT AND DAY

The Earth spins on its axis (an imaginary line through its
middle), turning once in 24 hours as it orbits the Sun.
This rotation gives us night and day. As the Earth rotates
into the light of the Sun we have sunrise, and as the Earth
continues to rotate away from the light of the Sun we
have sunset.

## LONG JOURNEY

It takes the Earth 365 and a $1/4$ days to circle round the
Sun, which is why there are 365 days in a year! The
quarter doesn't get lost; every fourth year an extra day is
added to February. As the Earth's orbit is not round but
oval we are closer to the Sun at some times than at others.

*The Earth is always tilted at the same angle.*

# THE MOON

The Moon is the closest thing to Earth – that's why we can see it so clearly. There are lots of other objects in the night sky that are bigger than the Moon, but they look tiny because they are so far away.

## MOON MYTHS

In most mythology, the Moon is seen as feminine, but in Europe people used to believe that there was a man in the Moon, put there to make amends for his sins.

When you look at a full Moon it is easy to imagine faces or animal shapes. The Chinese and the Mexicans thought that a hare lived in the Moon.

## MOON MAPS

The first map of the Moon was made by the Italian *astronomer* (a scientist who studies the stars and the planets), Galileo, in 1610. In the 19th century, two men called Johann Heinrich von Mädler and Wilhelm Beer produced amazingly accurate maps. Nowadays, only the areas near the *poles* (the points at the top and the bottom) are as yet unmapped.

## ECLIPSES

Every year a *lunar eclipse* can be seen. This is when the Sun, the Earth and the Moon line up perfectly, and the Earth comes between the Sun and the Moon. The Earth's shadow can be seen crossing the Moon.

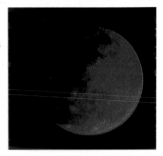

*An eclipse of the Moon – when it passes through shadow cast by the Earth*

As the Moon moves out of the light of the Sun, more and more of it is engulfed in shadow. Sometimes a strange, reddish glow is still visible.

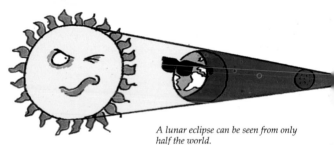

*A lunar eclipse can be seen from only half the world.*

## COLUMBUS THE MAGICIAN

Eclipses can be forecast very accurately. In 1504, the explorer and navigator Christopher Columbus was shipwrecked in Jamaica and found that the islanders were not very welcoming. By predicting an eclipse on 29 February, he was able to wow them and prove that he was not to be trifled with!

# MOON FACT FILE

- The Moon is 384,401 km (238,887 miles) from the Earth.

- The Moon reflects one four-hundred-and-twenty-five-thousandth of the Sun's brightness. (The Sun is the only thing in the solar system which makes light.)

- The surface temperature of the Moon is between –155°C (–247°F) and 105°C (221°F)!

- The time between one new Moon and the next is 29 days, 12 hours and 44 minutes.

- The Moon's *craters* (bowl-shaped holes) were formed between 3,500 and 4,500 million years ago by *meteorites* (space rocks) hitting the surface.

- The same side of the Moon always faces the Earth. It wasn't until the Russian *probe* (vehicle which explores space), Luna 3, sent back photographs of the far side in 1959 that it was seen for the first time.

- The Moon is the Earth's only *satellite* (object which moves around another one). It is about a quarter of the Earth's size.

- The Moon is 4.6 billion years old!

- In 1950, the Moon seemed to turn blue because a huge forest fire in Canada sent up clouds of smoke particles!

# MAN ON THE MOON

On 20 July 1969, the Americans landed their Apollo 11 spacecraft (right) on the Moon. The astronaut Neil Armstrong became the first person to set foot on the Moon's surface.

## SET IN TIME

The Moon's surface has no air and no water, so the footprints left by the first astronauts will remain imprinted for millions of years.

*Astronaut's footprint*

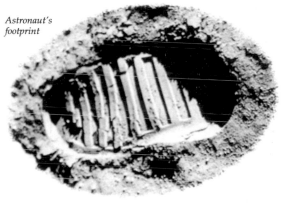

## BELIEVE IT OR NOT...

If the Apollo 11 astronauts had been 'driving' only 1.6 kph (1 mph) too fast, they would have missed the Moon by 1,600 km (1,000 miles)!

# EARLY ASTRONOMERS

The word *astronomy* comes from Greek words meaning 'to arrange the stars'. The Greeks were the first people to catalogue the stars, although others had been studying them for thousands of years before.

## AN EYE ON THE SKY

The earliest astronomers were probably farmers and shepherds who watched the skies for signs of changing weather and shifts in the seasons.

## AZTECS AND INCAS

Two ancient civilizations called the Aztecs and the Incas worshipped the Sun. The Inca kings even believed that they were descended from the Sun god, Inti! They believed in myths about the stars much more than the Europeans did.

*Inca image of the sky or Moon god*

## EARLIEST RECORDS

The earliest astronomical records are clay tablets from a place called Mesopotamia. The calculations were based on years and years of observation.

*Early astronomical records*

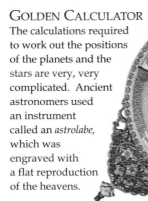

## GOLDEN CALCULATOR

The calculations required
to work out the positions
of the planets and the
stars are very, very
complicated. Ancient
astronomers used
an instrument
called an *astrolabe*,
which was
engraved with
a flat reproduction
of the heavens.

## FURTHER INTO SPACE

Today, astronomers have really complicated instruments
to bring us staggering information about our universe. In
1990, the Hubble Space Telescope (below) was launched
and is now sending back excellent images of things
several billion light-years away.

# THE WORLD OF STARS

When you look at the stars on a clear night you are only seeing about 3,000 of the billion stars in our galaxy. They look tiny, but they are really ENORMOUS!

## THE CONSTELLATIONS

The patterns and shapes that the stars make in the sky are called *constellations*. The top half of the world, called the *northern hemisphere*, sees different constellations from the bottom half, called the *southern hemisphere*.

*Northern hemisphere star map*

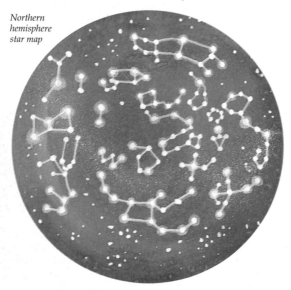

Southern hemisphere star map

## STARS AND MYTHOLOGY

Astronomers group the stars into 88 constellations, each of which has a Latin name and is meant to represent a person or creature from ancient mythology.

*Pattern of stars representing a bull*

## BELIEVE IT OR NOT...

It would take 4.2 light-years for light to reach Earth from the nearest star, Proxima Centauri.

# Stargazing

People have known that curved glass can magnify things since at least 2,000 BC. In the 13th and 14th centuries, the Europeans used lenses to help improve poor sight. In the 17th century, telescopes appeared and people began serious stargazing.

## Mighty Magnifiers

The earliest telescopes were cumbersome affairs. The technology did not exist to make large lenses, so the only solution was to make very long telescopes, which helped magnification.

2.1 m (7 ft) long telescope

Today, multi-mirror telescopes focus on the sky. This telescope (left) in Arizona, USA, is made up of six separate mirrors, each measuring 1.8 m (6 ft) in diameter. Now that's big!

## Caught on Camera

Before the invention of photography, astronomers had to draw everything that they saw through the telescope. Once the camera came along, astronomers could take photographs of the stars instead.

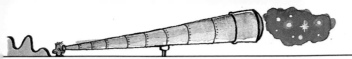

## WATCHING IN COMFORT

In early times, astronomers worked out in the open, so they often got rather wet!

Now, astronomers watch the skies from observatories with dome-shaped roofs.

Some of the greatest early observatories were in the Middle East. The one below was built at Jaipur in Rajasthan, India, in 1726.

## SAILING IN THE DARK

The earliest sailors only had the stars to navigate by. They had no real idea of where they were going and what they would find at the end of their journey.

Later, once sailors understood the movements of the stars and planets, and the relationship between angles and distances, they devised a more accurate system for finding their way around the oceans.

# THEIR NAMES IN STARS

The sky we see at night has changed very little from the sky observed by the earliest astronomers. They would often have seen more clearly with the naked eye than we can now because of pollution and the glare of our streetlights.

## CLAUDIUS PTOLEMAEUS
## (AROUND 100-178 AD)

Known as Ptolemy, he was the source of all that we know about ancient astronomy. He collected the work of the astronomers who had lived before him and his two important books were the leading authority for 1600 years!

## NICOLAUS COPERNICUS
## (1473-1543)

He died the year that he published a book which changed everyone's ideas about the universe. He was one of a number of astronomers who said that the Sun, not the Earth, was the centre of the universe.

## GALILEO GALILEI
## (1564-1642)

Galileo was a brilliant astronomer who had the great misfortune of being born at a time when brilliant scientific thinking was considered dangerous. He was sentenced to what was virtually life imprisonment and was finally pardoned in 1992! A little on the late side!

## TYCHO BRAHE (1546-1601)

He produced the first complete star atlas by remeasuring the 788 stars in Ptolemy's catalogue. He built a huge observatory (right) near Copenhagen in Denmark to continue his studies.

## ISAAC NEWTON (1642-1727)

He was born the year that Galileo died. He invented the first reflecting telescope which got a much better quality image than earlier telescopes. He also laid out the rules of *gravity* (the pulling force that attracts objects to one another) after watching apples fall off a tree in the garden!

## EDMOND HALLEY (1656-1742)

Halley noticed that there had been three very similar descriptions of a comet recorded every 76 years, and he predicted that it would return in 1758. He was right, but he didn't live to take the credit. The comet which now bears his name last returned in 1986.

*Halley's comet*

# TIMEKEEPING

The Earth takes one full day and one full night to spin once on its axis. This period of time is divided into 24 hours; each hour is divided into 60 minutes; each minute is divided into 60 seconds. A year is based on the time it takes the Earth to go around the Sun.

*Sandglass*

## CLOCK STARS

The Ancient Egyptians used 36 'clock stars' to tell the time at night. They used an instrument called a *merkhet* to observe the movement of certain stars, so they could work out the hours.

## SAND CLOCKS

In the Middle Ages, around 1300 AD, the *sandglass* was used to measure the passing of time. The modern equivalent of this is an egg timer! Very down-to-earth!

## SUN CLOCKS

Clocks which use the Sun to tell the time are called *sundials*. The shadow cast by the upright of the sundial falls on to a series of markers. Sundials were used frequently in the past. Some were huge buildings while others were small enough to fit into the pocket.

*Folding sundial*

## TIME AROUND THE WORLD

Because different parts of the Earth face the Sun at different times, their nights and days are different. For instance, when it is midday in London, England, it is night-time in Sydney, Australia, so all the people in the world have to set their clocks to different times. The Earth is divided into 24 *time zones*, one for every hour of the day.

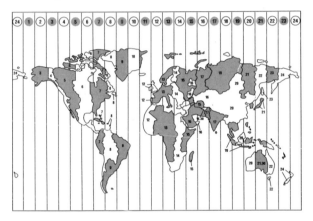

Throughout each zone, the time is the same, but if you cross to the next zone you have to change your watch – put it back an hour going west or forward an hour going east.

# Dark and Light

The polar lands, the Arctic and the Antarctic, can be unfriendly places – cold, windy and dark. In the winter, the Sun doesn't shine at all as it never rises above the horizon. Brrrr!

## The Land of the Midnight Sun

Any land north of the Arctic Circle is called the Land of the Midnight Sun. In the summer, the Sun hardly ever sinks below the horizon and it seems to be day all day and all night! In the winter, the reverse happens and it is almost completely dark all the time.

## Whiteout

The weather condition called a *whiteout* is a real hazard in the Arctic. It happens when snow is thick on the ground and also falling heavily from the sky. It becomes impossible to get your bearings and you just have to wait until the weather changes!

## Winter Pastimes

The Inuit people (or Eskimos) who live in the Arctic are very restricted in their winter activities. There is very little light, so they can't hunt much. Instead, they spend their time carving wood, bone and walrus tusks into beautiful statues of animals, birds and hunting scenes.

## Special Effects

Sometimes, on cold winter nights, the Moon appears to have a halo around it. This is caused by ice crystals high up in the Earth's *atmosphere* (the layer of gases around the planet). They bend the sunlight which is reflected towards Earth by the Moon.

Very rarely, you might see a *moonbow* which is a very faint night-time equivalent of a daytime rainbow.

## Glorious Lights

The *aurora borealis* is a spectacular display of light in the night sky. It is caused by particles from the Sun striking gases in the atmosphere high above the North Pole.

*Aurora borealis*

# SEEING IN THE DARK

There have been endless inventions to make night-time vision easier: some are sensible and some are very bizarre!

## CAT'S EYES

An Englishman, Percy Shaw, invented a road safety device to help guide motorists driving at night. After being saved from crashing on a foggy road by the reflection from the eyes of a cat, he came up with an invention to go in the middle of the road...*cat's eyes*, of course! Clever, huh?

*Beads reflect light from car headlamps*

## LIGHTING THE WAY

Driving at night in the days of early motor cars was hazardous! In the daytime, a man walked in front of the car with a red flag, to warn pedestrians and to make drivers keep their speed down. At night he couldn't be seen, so an oil lamp was carried. Electric lights became standard fixtures on cars in the 1930s.

## DOWN THE LINE

A *laser beam* is a special, intense beam of light which has many different uses. It can measure distances, scan your goods in the supermarket, and it is used in compact disc players.

*Laser beam measuring in a tunnel*

## NIGHT VISION

Soldiers can now use special binoculars that give them enough night vision to see people and equipment moving in the dark.

## INSIDE OUT

Surgeons can use an instrument called an *endoscope* to see inside your body. Light travels along lots of *fibre optic* wires to the tip of the instrument and lights up the darkness. The operator looks into the eyepiece to see inside.

*View inside body*

*Eyepiece*

# LIGHT FANTASTIC

In ancient times, people used to worship the Sun because their lives depended on it rising every day to give warmth, and to help plants grow. Here are some light facts to brighten dark evenings.

## MAN OF MANY PARTS

Leonardo da Vinci (1452-1519) was an artist, engineer and designer, and he left lots of notes on all his investigations, including the study of light. In many of his paintings, he used light and dark to give a dramatic effect.

## PROFILE IN BLACK

Étienne de Silhouette (1709-1767) gave his name to the technique of using shadow images to create pictures. He originally used the idea to make portraits of people that were much cheaper than oil paintings.

## STRAIGHT LINES

Light travels in straight lines. You can see this if a shaft of sunlight comes through a window and lights up dust or water in the air.

*Sunbeam shows light travels in straight lines*

## ENERGETIC

The Sun produces a huge amount of energy every day. In a sunny spot, it can generate 2,000 kilowatt-hours of light energy in a year. This would be enough to boil a kettle non-stop for six weeks!

## GONE IN A FLASH

The first person to attempt to record the speed of light was a Danish astronomer called Olaus Roemer, in 1675. It wasn't until Léon Foucault (1819-1868) did some experiments in the 1800s, that people realised that the speed of light varied depending on what it was travelling through – water or glass, for instance.

## FACE THE LIGHT

Plants grow towards the light as they need the Sun's energy to survive and grow. The French name for the sunflower is *tournesol*, which means 'turn towards the Sun'.

# LIGHTS AND LAMPS

Greek legend says that the god Zeus didn't want humans to have fire, but Prometheus stole it and brought it down to Earth. We commemorate this at the beginning of the Olympic Games, when runners bring a flame from Greece to the stadium.

## FIRE! FIRE!

Fire was vital to early people for keeping warm, frightening off wild animals, roasting meat and hardening spear tips. At first, they probably used accidental fires caused by lightning. Then they discovered that they could make sparks by hitting two stones together or by rubbing two sticks together.

## OIL POWER

Early people realised that the oil from the animals they ate would give out light if it caught fire. The next step was to put some of this oil into a shallow stone to create a primitive lamp.

*Roman clay oil lamp with covered top*

## CANDLES

The first ever candles were made over 2,000 years ago, but they were too expensive for most people. Oil from animals was boiled down to make tallow, which was poured over a wick and left to cool.

Beeswax sheets can be rolled around a wick to make candles. Beeswax candles give off a lovely smell when burning.

## IDEAL MATCH

A short wooden stick, otherwise known as a match, was a marvellous invention. It was tipped with a mixture of chemicals which caught fire if the match was struck against a rough surface.

*Matches and candle*

— *Rough surface*

## ALL LIT UP

After oil lamps, gas was used to provide light. In the 19th century, towns and cities were lit by jets of burning gas. Sounds dangerous!

If you're wondering about electricity, then turn the page!

# What Electricity Can Do

There has always been electricity in our world. Skies can be lit up by lightning (natural electricity), and the animal world has creatures which can make electricity. Scientists have gradually harnessed electrical energy which we now use in countless ways.

## Glow in the Dark

In about 1880, Thomas Edison and Joseph Swan invented the light bulb at almost the same time, without each other knowing. The light comes from a very thin wire called a *carbon filament*, suspended in a glass bulb.

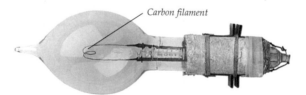

*Carbon filament*

## The Flick of a Switch

In the 1880s, big cities like New York, London and Paris became the first to use electricity for lighting. However, it was years before enough cables were laid to make electric light easily available.

In the early days, electric light seemed miraculous. Many people were deeply suspicious of electricity and worried that it might 'seep out' of the sockets!

## COLOURFUL

Nowadays, there are different kinds of light bulbs with various uses. A *daylight bulb* creates natural daylight. The light comes from a mixture of colours, just like sunlight, and is excellent for doing close work by. *Sodium lamps* are often used for lighting cities. They give off a yellow light.

## NO STARS TO BE SEEN

As with most technical advances, there is a 'down side' to all this light. Light pollution is now a real problem. In some cities, people are not able to see the stars, and the sky always looks bright and yellow at night, not black.

# NIGHT LIFE

Some animals are *nocturnal*. This means that they come out at night and sleep during the day.

## HEDGEHOGS

Most hedgehogs rest during the day and come out at night to hunt for earthworms and insects. They have sensitive whiskers which help them to find their way about.

In northern parts of the world, hedgehogs *hibernate* (sleep all winter) curled up in a tight ball, and only come out when spring arrives.

*Curled up*

*On the move*

## MOLES

Moles are underground creatures with very poor eyesight but excellent hearing. They dig elaborate tunnels below ground, throwing the leftover soil up to the surface where it forms molehills. Moles mainly live on worms. Yum, yum!

## SHREWS

Shrews look like mice but have longer noses and tiny eyes.
The smaller ones have to eat their own weight in food
each 24 hours to survive! They have to hunt during the
night and day to get enough to eat!

## SLUGS

Slugs eat almost everything green in sight, but they in
turn make a very tasty meal for hedgehogs! They mostly
slime their way about at night as they need to keep damp,
and sunshine would dry them out. Most mini-beasts
prefer to move around in the dark.

## FROGS

Frogs prefer night-time foraging. Males do a lot of
croaking at night to attract females!

## WORMS

Earthworms come to the surface at night to
grab leaves to munch on in the safety
of their tunnels during the day.
They also come out in the day
if it is wet. A ready-made
meal for a hungry bird!

# NIGHT BIRDS

Some birds are only seen, or even just heard, at night-time.

## NIGHT TRAVELLERS
Almost half of the world's birds *migrate* (fly to another country) each year to find good weather, food and water, and to nest. They use landmarks, the Sun, the Moon and the stars to find their way. Many travel night and day without food or sleep.

## SECRETIVE SONGSTER
The nightingale is a shy bird that nests in thick shrubs and low bushes. It sings during the day, but its glorious voice is best heard at night when most other birds are asleep. It is a plain little bird to look at, but its song is rich and varied, full of trills and warbles.

## FROG KEBAB
The night heron is often seen standing on one leg by the river bank, absolutely motionless, until it makes a sudden jab and skewers a frog on the end of its beak. Ouch!

*Night heron*

## Hidden From View

The nightjar eats at dusk when the air is full of insects.
During the daytime it stays in its nest, amazingly
camouflaged to look just like a broken twig or branch.

*Spot the nightjar!*

## Noisy Chorus

Starlings have become a great menace
in some cities. Thousands of them
fly in great flocks at dusk to find
places to roost overnight. There
have been different plans to
discourage them, including
bright lights, but the
lights warm up
the cold stone
of the buildings
where they perch,
turning it into comfy
underfloor heating!

*Starling*

# TOO-WHIT, TOO-WHOO!

Owls are very rarely seen during the day, as most of them are night-time hunters. They are powerful and silent as they swoop down on unsuspecting prey.

## SHARP EYES

Most birds of prey have *binocular vision*, which means that both eyes point directly to the front, giving very accurate sight.

Their eyes cannot turn very far in their sockets, but an owl can turn its whole head right round and look to the back. Yikes!

## ODD EARS

Owls have excellent hearing. They can hear the slightest rustle in the undergrowth from an unwary mouse. Some owls have tufts on their heads which look like ears, but these are only feathers.

*Eurasian eagle owl*

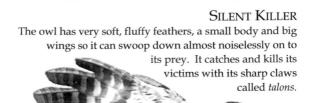

## SILENT KILLER

The owl has very soft, fluffy feathers, a small body and big wings so it can swoop down almost noiselessly on to its prey. It catches and kills its victims with its sharp claws called *talons*.

## LEFTOVERS

Because owls don't have teeth, they eat everything whole. They have to cough up fur, beaks, feet, bones and feathers in a lump called a pellet. Gross!

## WHAT A HOOT!

People used to think that an owl's cry came from evil spirits! This sound actually warns other birds to keep away from the owl's territory, but it can sound very eerie on a dark night.

# The Secretive Badger

Badgers are nocturnal creatures which live in family groups. Their favourite times are dawn and dusk, when the younger ones love to romp and play.

## Badger Portrait

Badgers are stout, heavy animals, with short, thick legs and heavy fur coats. They have strong claws to help them dig. Although they have small eyes and poor eyesight, they have an excellent sense of smell – ideal for hunting out large quantities of earthworms, small animals, fruit and nuts. They can produce a very unpleasant smell to deter their enemies, just like their relations, skunks.

## Happy Families

Each badger family may have as many as fifteen members. There are usually two or three babies called *cubs* which are born in the spring.

## Home Sweet Home

Badgers live in an underground home called a *sett*. This has an elaborate system of tunnels and chambers. Some setts are over 100 years old and have been used by generations of badgers. The sett has many ways in and out, and the badgers keep it very clean. They bring in fresh grass, leaves and moss to make up beds in the larger chambers.

*A sett can have more than 20 entrances and house up to 15 badgers.*

## Personal ID

Badgers have distinctive stripes on their faces. These stripes are useful camouflage when they are stomping through the undergrowth. No two sets of stripes are the same, so they may also help the animals to recognize each other.

# BATS

Bats are the only flying *mammals* (animals which give birth to live young, which they feed with their own milk). There are tiny bats, smaller than butterflies, and others with a wingspan as wide as the height of a man. All bats are night-time creatures.

## ECHO SOUNDER

Bats make their way about in the dark by *echolocation*. This means that they squeak as they fly and the sound bounces off anything in the way. The bat can detect the echo with its ears and can judge what the object is, what size it is and where it is, all within a split second! That's a pretty nifty hunting device.

*A bat's wings need to be kept in good condition for flying.*

## DAY NURSERIES

Female bats all have their babies at the same time. For a few months they set up nurseries in the caves where they live, and look after all the babies together. Most kinds of baby bat can fly in about six weeks.

## FRUIT CASE

The largest bat in the world is the fruit bat, sometimes called the flying fox because of its foxy-looking face. Fruit bats are huge – as much as 1.65 m (5 ft 4 in) from wing tip to wing tip! They fly out at dawn and dusk to feed on fruit, flowers and leaves.

*Fruit bat*

> ### BELIEVE IT OR NOT...
> The tiniest bat is called Kitti's hognosed bat. It is about 3 cm (1 in) long.

## UPSIDE-DOWN DREAMS

Bats sleep upside-down. They don't have a very powerful grip with their hands, but they can hang on with their feet. They often sleep together in great numbers.

## BLOODTHIRSTY

The vampire bat (left) comes out at night in search of animal and bird blood! It is the size of a small mouse and has two very sharp pointed teeth which it uses to scrape a small wound. Its saliva stops the victim's blood from *clotting* (going thick and lumpy). The bat then laps up the flowing blood.

# MOTHS

Some moths are seen during the day but they are mostly night flyers. They have fur on their bodies to keep them warm.

## BEAUTIFUL MOTHS

There are at least 100,000 different kinds of moth compared to around only 15,000 butterflies. Not all moths are drab and dull – some are as gaudy as butterflies, especially those that live in tropical regions.

*Exotic moths*

## DAYTIME CAMOUFLAGE

Most moths hide during the day to escape *predators* (hunters) such as bats. Some have colours which help them to 'disappear' against their chosen background. Others frighten predators away by looking fierce, often with fake eyes on the backs of their wings.

*Startling eye spot*

## MONSTER MOTH

The atlas moth is amongst the biggest moths in the world – even bigger than many birds! Its wingspan can be as great as 30 cm (12 in) and even the caterpillars are twice as long as your middle finger!

*Atlas moth*

## MOTH EARS

Some moths can escape from bats as they have eardrums which can pick up the bats' squeaks. The moth can then duck and dive, or rest on the ground until the danger has passed. Phew!

## TOO BRIGHT

Moths are attracted to bright lights and this is one way that they can be captured for study. They can't tell the difference between candles and electric light bulbs, though, so their curiosity can be fatal.

# Deserts By Night

Deserts are very hot by day and bitterly cold at night. Desert animals have adapted themselves to their harsh surroundings. Many rest during the day to avoid the heat and emerge at night.

## Hot, Hot, Hot!

The ground gecko finds the hot desert sand very uncomfortable. It mainly comes out at night to avoid the problem.

*Ground gecko*

## A Huge Swarm

Locusts are grasshoppers which can cause incredible damage to crops. A swarm of locusts can devour 20,000 tonnes of plants in a day. They have been known to fly in such huge swarms, millions at a time, that they blot out the sun! They rest during the heat of the day but can travel as far as 1 km (about $1/2$ mile) during an evening.

*Locust*

## STING IN THE TAIL

The scorpion is one of the deadliest desert creatures. It uses its sting to kill prey and some have a sting strong enough to kill a person. Don't panic, though; scorpions only do this if they are threatened or stepped on by accident!

During the day, scorpions hide under stones. They can survive without water because they get enough moisture from their food.

## SSSSSNAKES

Most desert snakes hide in sandy burrows during the day and come out to hunt at night. The desert kingsnake has slit-shaped pupils in its eyes which can open wide to help it see more in the dark.

Rattlesnakes warn off their enemies by rattling the hollow segments at the end of their tails.

Rattle

Rattlesnake

# ADAPTABLE NATURE

Here are some more nocturnal animals which have developed ways of coping with their night-time existence.

## BIG EARS

The fennec fox lives in the desert. It is the smallest member of the fox family at only 40 cm (16 in) from nose to tail. Its HUGE ears give off body heat and cool the fox down.

The fox stays in its burrow during the day and hunts lizards and desert creatures called jerboas at night.

Desert hedgehogs have big ears, too!

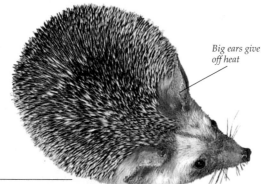

*Big ears give off heat*

## Black Hunter

A panther is a black leopard. It prowls unseen through the forest at night, hunting for food. In the day, it rests in tree branches.

## Furry Feet

Gerbils live in burrows during the day but become very active at night. They have fur on the undersides of their feet to protect them from the burning heat of the desert sand.

## Spiny Mice

Spiny mice come out at night. They have a handy secret weapon! If an enemy grabs a spiny mouse by the tail, that is all it will get! The mouse simply sheds its tail and scuttles off. Wow!

# GLOW IN THE DARK

$M$any animals, fish and plants can glow in the dark...and that's without the aid of an electric torch!

## GLOWING FISH

Many deep-sea fish, such as lantern fish and some angler fish, glow in the dark. Their light is made to send out signals to other fish – predators beware, and mates come on!

*This bit glows*

*Angler fish*

The viper fish is a horrible-looking creature which puts out a glow from its dorsal fin (back fin) and then impales its victim on its big fangs.

*Viper fish and victim*

## WARNING FLASH
Flashlight fish have big lights beneath their eyes which they can flash on and off to warn the rest of the shoal of any approaching danger.

## GLOWING TOADSTOOLS
Plant life can glow too! Some fungi glow in the dark and can be seen as far away as 40 m (over 40 yds).

## FIREFLIES
When thousands of fireflies swarm at night, the skies are all lit up. Each firefly has an amazingly bright glow which is used as a communication signal. Most fireflies are tropical, but there are some European and American varieties.

## GLOWING WATER
Sometimes the sea looks as if it is on fire! This is caused by very tiny sea creatures called *plankton*, which flash as the water is churned up by passing ships or the waves.

*Plankton*

# Night Frights

People have always found night-time frightening. In earliest times, they were fearful that the Sun wouldn't rise again, and many myths arose to explain the strange sounds and sights that could be heard. The superstitious could easily persuade people that witches and ghosts were present!

## Howling Wolf

Wolves howling at night make a chilling sound, but they won't attack humans unless provoked. They howl to communicate with each other.

## Fact or Fiction?

People used to believe that the lights seen over marsh-land were from evil goblins, leading unwary travellers to their doom. The truth is not as dramatic as this! The light occurs naturally, from the gases produced by rotting *vegetation* (plant life).

## COUNT DRACULA

The human vampire Count Dracula, who lives off the blood of the innocent, is entirely the invention of the Irish writer Bram Stoker, who wrote his classic horror story in 1897.

## WITCHES AND WARLOCKS

For hundreds of years, people believed in witches who had evil and strange powers. Women branded as witches were probably early healers, who used herbs and common sense to cure many everyday ailments, and not evil at all!

## BLACK CATS

Superstitious people say that black cats are the companions of witches. They are alleged to have supernatural powers for both good and evil. So treat your moggy with respect!

**Acknowledgements:** (KEY: a=above, b=bottom/below, c=centre, l=left, r=right, t=top) National Maritime Museum, Greenwich, London; Natural History Museum; Noordwijk Space Expo; Science Museum, London.

**Picture Credits:** Allsport/Vandystadt: 316tl; Ancient Art & Architecture Collection: 300bl; Ardea/Adrian Warren: 329bl; EN Arnold: 332c; Bruce Coleman Inc.: 337cr; Bruce Coleman Ltd/Rod Williams: 334b; Ken Day: 314b; Mary Evans Picture Library: 307t; John Hawkins/Eric & David Hosking: 325; Michael Holford: 300cr; Frank Lane Picture Agency/Eric & David Hosking: 321t; NASA: 298; 299tr; 299b; /JPL: front cover tl; National Optical Astro Observatory: 307b; NHPA/JH Carmichael: 337br; /Stephen Dalton: 320br; Oxford Scientific Films/Animals, Animals: 337cl; Planet Earth Pictures/John Eastcott: 322c; /Norbert Wu: 336b; Science Photo Library: 306cr; 311b; /Dr Fred Espenak: 297; /NASA: 301b; /Pekka Parviaimen: 311c; /R Ressmeyer: 319b; /R Ressmeyer, Starlight: 304clb; Tony Stone Images: 318tr; Wild Images/Dutcher Film Productions: 338; Zefa Pictures: 302tl; /Bramaz: 313t; /Gunter Heil: 305.

**Additional Photography:** Jane Burton, Peter Chadwick, Tina Chambers, Frank Greenaway, Colin Keates, Dave King, Cyril Laubscher, Jerry Young.

**Additional Illustrations:** Janos Marffy, Daniel J Pyne.

Every effort has been made to trace the copyright holders. Funfax Ltd apologises for any unintentional omissions and would be pleased, in such cases, to add an acknowledgement in further editions.

# OCEAN EXPLORER

Written by Fiona Waters

Illustrated by Celia Witchard

# WATER, WATER EVERYWHERE

Whenever you dip a toe into the sea, you are connecting with ALL the world's oceans, because the earth's sea water is one continuous mass. Over two-thirds of the entire earth's surface is covered by sea water! Pretty awesome, huh?

## THAT'S SOME STORM!
Today's oceans began to fill up in the last 200 million years of the earth's history. As the early earth cooled, *water vapour* condensed and formed storm clouds, from which rain fell and eventually made oceans.

## WHAT'S WHERE
The five oceans in the world are the Pacific, the Atlantic, the Indian, the Southern and the Arctic. The Arctic is the smallest and its centre is permanently covered by a layer of sea ice. Brrrr!

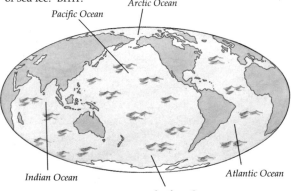

Arctic Ocean

Pacific Ocean

Indian Ocean

Southern Ocean

Atlantic Ocean

The largest ocean is the Pacific Ocean. It covers 165,384,000 sq km (63,855,000 sq miles) – more than one third of the earth!

## WATERY MIND-BOGGLERS

Here are some more mind-boggling ocean figures to
get your head round!

- Total surface area –
  362,000,000 sq km
  (139,800,000 sq miles)

- Average depth –
  3.5 km (2.2 miles)

- Temperature range –
  -2°C to 36°C (28°F
  to 97°F)

- Deepest known point –
  11,033 m (36,198 ft)

- Highest recorded wave –
  34 m (112 ft) from
  trough to crest, recorded
  in 1933

## FACT OR FICTION?

Many early sailors were terrified of creatures that they
believed lived in the oceans. There are many weird and
wonderful stories of strange and sinister monsters coming
up out of the deep.

# LET'S EXPLORE

People have always been fascinated by the sea, both above and below the surface, but it is only fairly recently that we have been able to explore the sea properly. Way back in time, water travel took a while to catch on.

## STAYING AT HOME

Thousands of years ago, people did not travel very far away from their homes. They could make all their own tools, and they could weave and spin cloth or use animal skins for clothes. They also grew crops and kept animals for food.

*Small flint axe*

*Animal skin*

## MOVING ON

Gradually, people realised that they could trade goods and skills with other people, and they began to go further afield.

## WATER TRANSPORT

Early traders were not put
off by little things like
rivers. They simply
invented water transport!

*Indonesian log boat*

*Small mallet for driving
in wooden pegs*

*Tool for fine hollowing*

Early water travel was as
easy as falling off a log...but
people became fed up with wet
clothes, so they hollowed out the
log and sat inside instead! The
first explorers were launched.

### BELIEVE IT OR NOT...

Before the discovery that
the world was round, sailors
used to fear that they would
fall off the edge if they sailed
beyond the horizon.
Whoops!

# A Life on the Ocean Wave

Travelling by water was so convenient
that it soon became commonplace.

## Egyptian Sailors

According to Egyptian priests, the world was a flat
rectangle, and the heavens were held up by massive pillars
at each corner. However, when Queen Hatshepsut sent
ships as far away as the
Indian Ocean...not a pillar
in sight! The priests said
that the pillars must be
further away than they
thought. Sneaky!

*The main body of this
boat is made of papyrus
stalks bunched together.*

The Egyptians' first boats
were made of the stalks
of papyrus plants
bunched together, but
later they used cedar
wood.

## ROMAN ADVENTURERS

The Romans kept their oarsmen up to scratch. A musician played the flute to keep them in time as they rowed.

Without compasses or maps, Roman sailors needed to keep the shore in sight all the time, but the wind could blow them on to the rocks. Sailing was a dangerous business in ancient times!

## ANIMAL TRADE

Roman merchant navy ships were capable of travelling vast distances with huge cargoes on board. Transporting everything from fish sauce to wild animals, working on board could be an eye-opening business.

*Roman merchant ship*

Wild animals were collected from many countries and taken to the Colosseum in Rome. Fancy sharing a cabin with a tiger or a rhinoceros! Putting on a good show was so important to the emperors that they spent vast sums of money on this horrible trade.

# BOLD VOYAGERS

Whether fierce fighters or just plain curious, many bold voyagers took to the seas to discover and claim more of the world for themselves.

## VIKINGS V THE WORLD

For 300 years, from the 8th to 11th centuries, the Vikings took on the world. They were brilliant sailors and their wooden *longships* used to strike terror into hearts wherever they were seen.

## FIERCE BEASTS

The Vikings often carved fierce beasts on the *prow* of their ships to scare their enemies as they landed, and their sails were dyed blood red. Oo-er!

## DRESSED TO KILL

Many of the romantic images of Vikings are wrong. For example, they didn't usually wear horned helmets, but round caps of iron or leather!

Warriors prepared for battle by putting on bearskin cloaks and working themselves up into a fearful frenzy.

## DEAD WEALTHY

The richest Vikings were buried in ships together with their clothes, weapons and furniture. Unfortunately, their servants and even their dogs were killed and also put into the ship, which was then set alight.

## To Boldly Go...

Henry the Navigator (1394-1460), the first of the great ocean voyagers, only sailed a few times himself! He seemed to prefer dry land, but he did finance many of the earliest voyages of exploration.

The first European to sail to India was Vasco da Gama, who was shown the way by an Arab pilot who taught him to use the monsoon winds. Handy, eh!

## The Map Man

Christopher Columbus (1451-1506) discovered the *New World* (America) in 1492, only he was hoping to find Asia! How wrong can you get?

*Christopher Columbus' ship – Santa Maria*

In 1508, the Italian navigator Amerigo Vespucci was made pilot-major of Spain and things improved on the navigating front. All Spanish sea captains had to report back to him so that he could bring his maps up to date.

Before proper maps, sailors had to navigate by the stars. Difficult in the daytime!

# PIRATES

In times past, if pirates appeared over the horizon, the best policy would have been to scarper! Here's why...

## JOLLY ROGER

The feared pirate flag, the Jolly Roger, had many variations. It indicated that the pirates would show no mercy, and walking the plank would be the end for many a victim.

## A BETTER LIFE

Many pirate crews were made up of formerly honest seamen who were fed up with eating maggoty biscuits and sharing their bunks with rats. Well, wouldn't you be?

## BELIEVE IT OR NOT...

One of the most terrifying pirates, Blackbeard, even used to scare his own crew! He stuck burning cords into his hat when he went into battle, and carried six pistols. Fierce, or what!

## FEMALE FIENDS

Not all pirates were men! Several brave women disguised themselves as men and threw themselves into a life of fighting and adventure.

## BURIED TREASURE – DREAMS OR TRUTH?

Pirates used to divide their booty more or less equally, although fights always broke out. One crewman was given a single large diamond instead of several smaller ones. Not happy with this, he smashed his big one into small pieces with a hammer!

'Piece of eight' or Spanish peso

Gold doubloon

Best of all was Spanish gold or silver – a gold *doubloon* was worth about seven weeks' pay. Rich pickings indeed!

## X MARKS THE SPOT

Brimming treasure chests buried according to parchment maps have become almost legendary. William Kidd (c.1645-1701) is supposed to have buried some of his ill-gotten gains near New York. Treasure seekers have tried to find the booty...but the search goes on.

# DISCOVERING SHIPWRECKS

Many thousands of ships lie at the bottom of the ocean – most lost for ever, with their positions unknown. Curious divers have attempted to discover and explore the sunken remains.

## FAMOUS DISASTER

On her maiden voyage, the Titanic was considered unsinkable. But on the night of 14-15 April, 1912, she hit an iceberg and sank with the loss of around 1,500 lives.

## PLANE REMAINS

It isn't just ships that sit on the bottom – aeroplanes can crash into the sea too. There is an area in the Atlantic Ocean called the Bermuda Triangle where many planes and ships have mysteriously disappeared.

## DISTINCTLY DAFT DIVING DEVICES

Some of the earliest diving equipment seems to have come from the world of fantasy, such as this primitive diving suit. Other inventions were more sensible, like the early diving bell. Four people could sit on the sea-bed in it for 90 minutes.

*Dangerous, primitive diving suit*

## SERIOUSLY HEAVY!

The most important parts of
early diving suits were the
very heavy metal helmet
and the lead-soled boots.
You couldn't run far
wearing that lot!

*Lead-soled diving boots
and diving helmet from
around 1840*

## FREE-FLOATING

A Frenchman, Jacques Cousteau, invented the aqualung in
1943. This was a huge advance – for the first time ever, a
diver could go as deep as 30 m (98 ft) without being
attached to a ship.

# DIVE, DIVE, DIVE!

The first submarines made underwater travel possible. They also became important as wartime fighting machines.

## BELIEVE IT OR NOT...

A submarine was used in 1776, during the American War of Independence! Called the Turtle, it was made of wood and held one man. Scary!

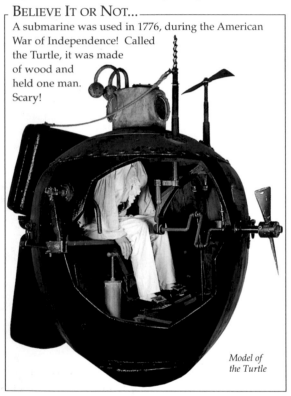

*Model of the Turtle*

## BOTTOM CRAWLER

An underwater vehicle which could drive on the sea-bed was invented in 1894. It could go to depths of 6 m (20 ft), and the diver could get out and wander around.

## LONG-DISTANCE TRAVEL

Modern submarines can run on nuclear power and are able to travel great distances before needing to refuel or surface. They have very sophisticated sonar systems to locate other vessels.

HMS Dreadnought was Britain's first nuclear-powered submarine and carried an 88-person crew underwater for weeks at a time. Its design was based on the shape of a whale!

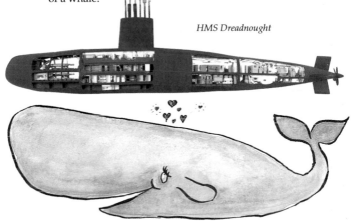

*HMS Dreadnought*

## BIG AND FAST

The Russians have the biggest and the fastest submarines in the world. The Typhoon type measures 170 m (558 ft) and the Alpha can probably exceed 42 knots when submerged.

No, a *knot* isn't just something you tie in a piece of string! It's the unit of speed used by ships and aircraft. One knot equals one nautical mile per hour.

Today's nuclear-powered submarines can carry high-powered torpedoes to fire at enemy vessels and are the most powerful weapon carriers ever.

# SUBMERGED

$P$eople have been rocketed into space to explore what's out there, but the ocean depths are just as mysterious, with hidden places that remain undiscovered.

## SUBMERSIBLES

*Submersibles* are like miniature submarines and are used for underwater exploration. They cannot travel far and have to be raised and lowered by a vessel on the water's surface.

*The French submersible, Nautile*

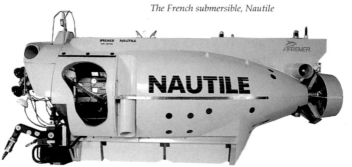

On deep dives, a submersible becomes very cold inside. The pressure outside is so enormous that the curved portholes, made of special glass, actually flatten!

## SNORKELLING

If you don't fancy going quite so deep, how about snorkelling? It's dead simple. The snorkel, which is a tube with a mouthpiece attached, sticks out above the water. You just breathe normally, flap your flippers and off you go!

## Who Goes There?

Apart from all those snorkellers, submersibles and submarines, what else is wandering around the oceans? It all depends on how deep you go! The ocean is divided into zones, starting from the surface:

Sunlit zone: 0-200 m (0-660 ft) – lots of animals and plants

Twilight zone: 200-1,000 m (660-3,300 ft) – no more plants, but diving whales and octopuses!

Dark zone: 1,000-4,000 m (3,300-13,120 ft) – the weirdoes – angler fish and gulper eels...yuck!

Abyss: 4,000-6,000 m (13,120-19,700 ft) – very, very cold and very, very dark! Hot water bottles needed!

Trenches: Over 6,000 m (19,700 ft) – sea cucumbers... and no, these creatures won't make nice sandwiches!

## Trenches

A *trench* is a deep valley on the ocean floor.
The Mariana Trench, the deepest ever at 11,033 m (36,198 ft), could hold 28 Empire State Buildings standing on top of each other. That's some elevator ride!

### Believe It or Not...

It would take 25 years for a dead shrimp to sink to the bottom of a deep trench. It CERTAINLY wouldn't be nice to eat by then!

# GOING DOWN

There are some pretty weird creatures living in the dark depths of the world's oceans. They have developed in ways which help them to hunt and survive in the blackness.

*Deep-sea hatchet*

## THE TWILIGHT ZONE

Things are pretty strange down here! Many fish have rows of lights on their undersides, to camouflage them against spots of light showing through from the world above. Seriously weird!

A deep-sea hatchet (not the kind you find in a tool box!), has huge eyes to help it spot its prey in the darkness.

Some species of angler fish have a light at the end of a fin on their head which attracts an instant meal. Next time you go fishing, try this technique!

## THE DARKEST DEPTHS

You would expect the fish here to keep bumping into each other! They are mostly black and the water is black too...and very, very cold. Brrrr...

Deep-sea fish, such as the angler fish, have huge mouths and stretchy stomachs, and have been found with fish twice their own size inside them, swallowed whole. Greedy guts!

*Deep-sea angler fish before a meal*

*Deep-sea angler fish after a meal*

# Nowhere Else to go!

The bottom of the ocean is not a nice place to be. It is very dark and cold, and covered in ooze – yuck! The few animals around have extra long legs, like the sea spider whose legs are 80 cm (2 ft) across. NOT one to find in the bath!

*Deep-sea cucumber*

...And there are cucumbers on legs! Totally weird.

## Deep-sea Earthquakes

Earthquakes on the sea-bed cause tidal waves above called *tsunamis*. Once they hit the coast they cause terrible devastation.

The highest tsunami ever recorded was about 85 m (279 ft) tall and the fastest was travelling at 900 kph (559 mph). Phew!

## On the Move

The ocean bed is constantly changing as the giant *plates* which make up the earth's surface shift about. *Lava* (hot, liquid rock) spouts up from the *crust* (the earth's outer layer) to form new ocean floor, and plates slide under each other.

## SMOKERS

*Smokers* are like huge chimneys on the ocean floor. They spew out clouds of fantastically hot water – up to 400°C (752°F).

Smokers are home to a number of creatures. Tube worms up to 3 m (10 ft) long lurk around, together with giant clams. Whenever a vent stops producing water, the local wildlife has to set up home somewhere else.

*Smoker*

*Tube worm*

# HOME SWEET HOME

The sea-bed is home to many plants and creatures. Here are a few of them...

## MOVING HOME
The hermit crab steals other shells to live in. As it grows bigger, it has to find a larger shell to move into. It pulls its body out of the old shell and slips quickly into its new home.

*This hermit crab is out of its shell – a vulnerable moment.*

## WEEDY!
The sargassum fish lurks in clumps of sargassum seaweed. Frilly bits on its head and body make a crafty disguise, so predators can't spot it. Nifty, fishy!

## D.I.Y.
Carrier shells are sea snails which stick bits of pebble, broken shells and even glass on to their own shells. It's not just decoration – it makes it jolly difficult for predators to get inside with that lot in the way!

## STUCK FAST

*Sugar kelp*

Seaweeds are not weeds at all, but nutritious plants. They don't usually have roots – they hold on to rocks with root-like anchors called *holdfasts*. They can have a real tug of war with the waves!

*Bladderwrack*

## SEAWEED AND CHIPS

*Carragheen*

Some people eat seaweed cooked like a vegetable. Eat up your greens? Double yuck!

*Dulse*

## BELIEVE IT OR NOT...

In California there is a giant seaweed called kelp that can grow 1 m (3 ft) in a day, and reaches over 100 m (328 ft) in length.

## HERE IS THE WEATHER FORECAST...

If you live near the sea, you can hang a piece of seaweed outside the back door and you will always know when you need an umbrella! If it is sunny, the seaweed will dry up, but when rain is coming, it will swell up again and feel damp.

# She Sells Sea Shells

Whatever the shape or size of a shell that you find on the beach, it has been made by an animal, and it has grown outwards from the middle. The coil shapes made in this way can help you work out the age of the shell, a bit like the rings on a tree.

*Cross-section of a nautilus shell*

## Snap!

The biggest shells of all are giant clams and they can weigh over 250 kg ($^1/_4$ tonne). They can be used as baths, but make sure you don't fall asleep! Living clams are capable of trapping divers by their arms or legs.

## Alive, Alive-O

Birds and sea otters eat the contents of shells...and so do humans! Scallops, mussels, clams and oysters are all delicious – and very good for you, as they are very low in calories but rich in protein. Yum, yum!

*Oysters*

*Venus clams*

*Scallops*

*Mussels*

## TRUE GRIT

Next time you look at your granny's pearls, remember that a pearl comes from a very irritated creature! Whenever a tiny piece of grit becomes stuck in its shell, the animal will try to soothe the irritation by covering it with layers of *nacre*, a shelly material, and a pearl is born. Aah!

*Black-lipped oyster*

## NOT WHAT THEY SEEM

Tusk shells are nothing to do with elephants! They are shells which live with their heads always buried in the sand.

The slit-worm shell looks as if it has become unravelled! It can't move much, so it usually fixes itself to a rock.

## COLLECTING SHELLS

If you have a collection of shells, make sure you store them in a box or drawer as they fade if they stay in the light for too long. Make sure you wash them out first, otherwise the pong will be too much!

*Slit-worm shell*

# HARD CASES

Many sea creatures have hard cases and outer skeletons to protect their soft innards. Crabs and lobsters are hard-cased creatures, and so are beautiful coral reefs. Eh? Find out more...

## DRY BONES
In warm, clear tropical waters, coral reefs cover huge areas. Coral actually has minute algae living within it, and together they make a hard, bony skeleton.

## THE BIGGEST CORAL REEF
Australia's Great Barrier Reef is the biggest coral reef in the world at over 2,000 km (1,250 miles) long. Millions of things live there, from fish to giant clams.

## HOW DOES YOUR GARDEN GROW?
The reefs look like gardens with plants and fronds everywhere. Some things that look like plants are actually animals! The lettuce slug breathes through its skin, which looks like a leaf. Salad, anyone?

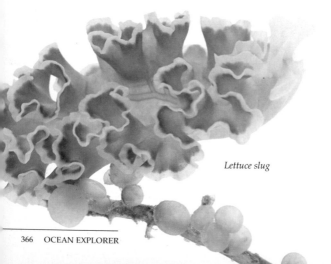

*Lettuce slug*

## ARMOUR-PLATING

Crabs and lobsters belong to a group of creatures called *crustaceans*. They have jointed shells, rather like the armour worn by medieval knights, to help them move.

### BELIEVE IT OR NOT...

Because of the way a lobster's segments are joined together, it can only swim forwards or backwards. It cannot twist from side to side.

## ANCIENT CREATURES

Trilobites were ancient sea creatures with jointed limbs and an outer skeleton. They lived over 510 million years ago.

*Trilobite fossil*

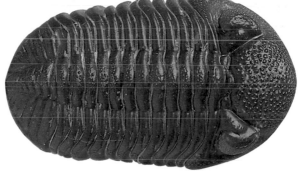

## OWN GOAL?

Crabs sometimes use their small, jointed legs to kick food into their mouths! They use their main pincers to break food down into bite-size pieces.

# Heavyweights and Horses

Now you know about fish and shell creatures, but there are some other amazing sea creatures that you shouldn't miss out on.

## Biggest and Fiercest!

• Lobsters have been known to live for 50 years and can weigh 20 kg (44 lb).

• The largest crab is the Japanese spider crab, whose legs can reach an awesome 3.7 m (12 ft).

*Lobster*

• The mantis shrimp can bash its way out of a fish tank with one hefty blow! Yikes!

## Turtles

Turtles can glide through the water. They come ashore to lay their eggs in the sand, but sadly, only one in a hundred of the babies will survive.

*Mantis shrimp*

## Deep Diver

The deepest diving turtle can go down to 1,200 m (3,937 ft).

## SEA HORSES

Sea horses won't win many races! These elegant creatures get their name because of their horse-like shape, but there the similarity ends.

Sea horses live in seaweed or corals, as they don't like being out in the open water. They swim upright, moving along as waves pass down the *dorsal fin* (on their back).

*Sea horse*

Curiously, it is the sea horse father who carries the eggs inside a special pouch, until they are fully developed.

## URCHINS

Sea urchins are covered in spines which they use to move around. They can be beautiful colours and strange shapes, but they are very painful if you stand on one!

*Sea urchin*

# TEEMING MASSES

The oceans are teeming with teeny-tiny critters that you can't even see. The most prolific plants in the oceans, if seen under a microscope, look more like tiny fish! These little plants have a very large name – *phytoplankton*, usually shortened to plankton.

## FOOD CHAIN PHENOMENON

Phytoplankton have an importance way beyond their size, as they are at the bottom of the *food chain*. Here's how it works:

Phytoplankton are eaten by *zooplankton* (swarms of tiny animals) – which are eaten by small fish (like herring) – which are eaten by bigger fish (like dogfish) – which are eaten by even bigger fish or dolphins.

*Zooplankton*

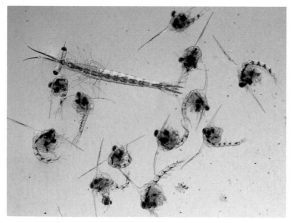

Some huge ocean animals, such as whale sharks and blue whales, cut all that out and just eat the zooplankton!

## ALL DRESSED UP

There are many beautiful fish, but looking good isn't
their intention. They are dressed to kill, or to avoid being
killed. Their bright colours either camouflage them or
warn off intruders or predators.

*Mandarin fish*

The mandarin fish looks like an upside-down bird
with its low-slung fins.

The royal gramma fish lives in underwater caves.
Its bright colouring probably helps to scare its
competitors as it chases them away.

*Royal gramma*

# SERIOUSLY WEIRD

Now that you have been introduced to some members of the sea creature family, meet some of their weirder relatives.

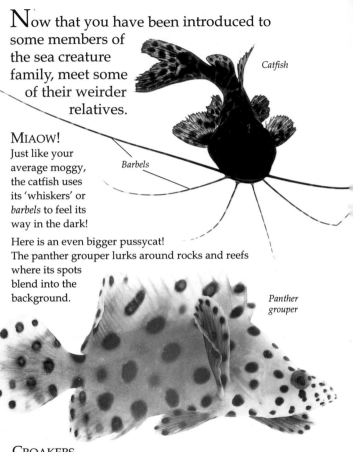

*Catfish*

*Barbels*

*Panther grouper*

## MIAOW!
Just like your average moggy, the catfish uses its 'whiskers' or *barbels* to feel its way in the dark!

Here is an even bigger pussycat! The panther grouper lurks around rocks and reefs where its spots blend into the background.

## CROAKERS
Drumfish, or *croakers* as they are sometimes called, can communicate over long distances. They make drumming and knocking sounds which carry far underwater. Once they get closer, they can recognize each other's striped pattern.

## BLOW-UP FISH

The porcupine fish looks rather like an underwater hedgehog. One moment it looks quite ordinary...the next, WOW! It blows up to three times its normal size!

*This porcupine fish would make a prickly mouthful.*

## SPLAT!

Rather like a water cannon, the archer fish squirts water at its prey, knocking it over to provide instant supper!

## WATERY GLIDERS

Flying fish? Yes, really. They leap out of the water and skim along the surface by spreading out their side fins like wings.

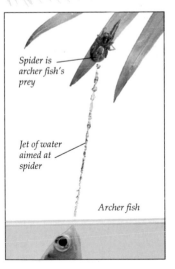

*Spider is archer fish's prey*

*Jet of water aimed at spider*

*Archer fish*

# SCARY AND DEADLY

Here are some dodgy customers that you would do well to avoid. Some just look scary, but others are downright deadly.

## DEAD NASTY

The lionfish, scorpionfish or dragonfish (to use three of its names), is lovely to look at but deadly to touch. It has spines on its back and under its tail, all tipped with a deadly venom. Ouch!

*Lionfish*

## A STING IN THE TAIL

The stingray looks gorgeous with its huge 'wings', but beware! It hides in the sand, then cruises out to lash at its prey (or any passing human) with its thin tail, and then injects venom with its sting.

The electric ray can deliver shocks of over 200 volts to finish off its victims!

## JET-PROPELLED

The squid uses jet propulsion to power
through the water in the same way
that a jet plane uses air to fly.
Its body is streamlined to
reduce drag, and if
attacked it can
zoom off!

*Squid*

## SUPER SQUID

The giant Atlantic squid
is the largest of all
*invertebrate* animals (those
without backbones). It can grow
to more than 15 m (50 ft) in total,
and weigh in at 2 tonnes. Gross!

To go with its huge size, the giant squid
has HUGE eyes. Each one is more
than 40 cm (15.7 in) in diameter.

## FLOATING GNASHERS?

The scallop has eyes around the edge of its shell to detect
passing fish. When swimming, it looks like a set of false
teeth grinning!

*Swimming scallop*

# LEGS AND EGGS

Here are some more fishy facts for you to digest.

## AN ARM AND A LEG
The octopus sneaks up behind its prey, then pounces and wraps seven of its tentacles tightly round its victim, while keeping the one remaining tentacle anchored to the surface of a rock.

Another cunning octopus trick is to change colour within a second to hide from enemies. It can also squirt ink into the water while it makes good its escape.

## MONSTER AHOY!
The kraken was a legendary sea monster with huge eyes and many tentacles, reputed to come up from the deep. Help!

## TRAFFIC LIGHT TENTACLES
The beadlet anemone can be red, amber or green. Fully grown, it can have about 200 tentacles! 1, 2, 3, 4...

## A GIANT FLOWER?
The largest anemones grow in tropical waters and can be more than 1 m (3 ft) across. Pretty big, huh?

*Giant green anemone*

## EGG CASES

The female dogfish (which doesn't bark!) lays its eggs in an egg case called a *mermaid's purse*. You may find a dried-up, empty one washed up on the beach.

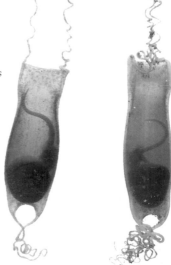

*Egg cases with dogfish growing inside*

---

### BELIEVE IT OR NOT...

Genuine black *caviar* is fish eggs which come from the beluga sturgeon. It costs hundreds of pounds just for a teaspoonful and tastes very salty. DON'T ask for it for breakfast!

## STANDING AROUND

The tripod fish is a bottom-of-the-sea dweller. It props itself up on two stilt-like fins and just stands around waiting for action!

# Ocean Olympics

Dolphins love each other's company. They jump and splash about in large groups called *schools*. They are great show-offs and do all kinds of somersaults, backflips and acrobatics.

### Fangs a Lot!
The shape of their beaks makes dolphins look as if they have a permanent grin on their faces! Those with long beaks can have as many as 260 teeth.

### High Powered
Some dolphins can move at very fast swimming speeds. They do this by leaping out of the water whenever they need to breathe, rather than swimming along at the surface. This is known as *porpoising*...but porpoises don't do it! Confusing, isn't it?

### River Cruise
Some dolphins never venture into the ocean. They are called river dolphins and they are much smaller than their sea-going cousins. They don't show off as much either, and usually only poke a beak above water!

## CLICKETY-CLICK
Dolphins communicate with each other when swimming with a series of whistles and clicks. The sounds come from the nose, below the blow hole.

*Bottlenose dolphin*

## ON PORPOISE
Porpoises are small relations of dolphins. Not much is really known about them as they are very shy, solitary creatures. Sadly, they are in decline as many drown when caught in fishing nets.

*Porpoise*

## OPEN WIDE
The easiest way to tell a dolphin from a porpoise is to take them to the dentist together. Dolphins have cone-shaped teeth while porpoises' are spade-shaped.

# SHARK AT BAY

The mere mention of a shark has swimmers heading for the beach. Aaagh! Here are fearsome facts for you to get your teeth into.

## WHAT BIG TEETH YOU'VE GOT!
A shark never runs out of teeth! When its gnashers break or fall out, they are replaced by new ones from the row behind. During its life, thousands of its teeth will be replaced.

## FOSSIL FANG
The massive fang shown here is the fossil tooth of a megalodon, an ancestor of the shark which probably lived 15 million years ago.

*This megalodon fossil tooth is shown at only half its actual size.*

## BAD REPUTATION
In spite of their awesome reputation, only a few sharks are a danger to humans. There are only about 100 shark attacks a year and about 25 of these are fatal.

## GENTLE GIANTS
At over 12 m (40 ft) long, the whale shark is the largest fish in the world. It is so gentle that it will let divers hitch a lift by hanging on to its fins. It feeds on plankton and its teeth are no bigger than a match head. Aah...sweet!

*Whale shark is so big that it provides living space for large numbers of remoras (shark sucker fish)*

## CRUISING ALONG

Sharks swim gracefully through the water by swishing their tails from side to side, but they can't hover or swim backwards. They normally glide along at about 3 kph (1.8 mph), but when on the attack they rev up to about 25 kph (15 mph).

## UNFAIR ADVANTAGE

Sharks have the same five senses as humans – sight, hearing, smell, touch and taste – but they also have a sixth sense which lets them pick up signals given out by their prey. Very handy!

## GREAT, WHITE AND FAMOUS

The most famous and most awesome shark is the great white. Over 6 m (20 ft) long, it can eat a seal whole. Gulp!

*Great white shark*

# A WHALE OF A TIME

Whales are not fish, but mammals, because they give birth to live babies which they feed with their own milk. Prepare to be wowed by some wonderful whale info...

## GIANT SIEVE

Whales eat by filtering small fish called *krill* through giant fringed 'brushes' called *baleen*, hanging inside their mouths.

Years ago, ladies used to wear very tight corsets stiffened with baleen. Ouch!

## GINORMOUS!

The blue whale is the biggest animal that has ever lived. The largest living animal on land, a bull elephant, could stand on the blue whale's tongue!

## BELIEVE IT OR NOT...

A baby whale is already the size of an elephant when it is born, and at six months it measures 16 m (53 ft) long! It cannot filter food from the water at first, and relies on the milk from its mum. It guzzles about 100 litres (175 pints) every day!

*Mother whale and her baby*

## BEACHED

A whale's weight is supported by the water. If it gets stranded on the beach, its internal organs are crushed by the weight of its own body, and it dies.

## SPLASHING AROUND

Whales may communicate by leaping out of the water and coming down with a huge splash that can be heard many kilometres away. This is called *breaching*.

## LOVE SONGS

A lovesick male humpback whale will sing a haunting song for hours to attract a female.

## SLAPSTICK

Humpback whales slap their flippers on the surface of the water to make a loud splash. This is called *flippering*.

*Humpback whale*

## TAILPRINTS

Each humpback whale has a distinctive pattern on its tail. A bit like a human fingerprint, no two are the same.

# OCEAN PRODUCTS

Many things are harvested from the sea besides fish. Here are some of them.

## PIPED ASHORE

Oil and gas are hidden deep below the ocean's surface in rocks on the sea-bed. Oil and gas platforms, with their *flare stacks* burning brightly, are a constant reminder of the danger when working with highly flammable ingredients. The oil and gas are sent ashore in special pipelines from the rigs.

## NEIGHBOURS

An oil platform is like a small village. There can be as many as 400 people on board, living and working together. Some are *riggers*, who operate the drill. There are *geologists* (people who study the earth's structure) and scientists on board too. Probably most important of all are the cooks and cleaners who have to look after everyone!

*Platforms like this are built in sections on shore.*

## BATH TIME

Did you know that when you use a natural sponge you are washing yourself with a soft skeleton? Harvested sponges are covered in soft, slimy stuff – living tissue! The sponge you use in the bath is the bit left behind.

## BLOWING IN THE WIND

The slate pencil sea urchin is protected by short, blunt spines that were once used to write on slate boards in school. Now they are collected to make wind chimes.

## SEA SALT

When sea water evaporates, it leaves behind a crystal crust which you then put on your chips – salt! Salt is commercially produced in big, shallow pans.

## WHALE PRODUCTS

The poor old whale produces this lot!

*Whale meat extract used in margarine*

*Ground-up whale meat used in pet food*

*Whale liver used for its vitamin A*

*Sperm oil once used as a lubricant in cars*

# Oceans in Peril

The world's oceans are full of many wonders, but they hold dangers too – man-made ones. Here are some of the things which humans are guilty of doing.

### Rubbish Dump
When a ship spills oil on the sea, the immediate disaster is obvious as dead and dying fish and sea birds are washed ashore, but underwater the damage can be even worse. The tiny, settling grains of sand and rock become toxic and can't support any form of life.

### Poison Dump
Many poisons and pesticides are illegally dumped at sea. People can choose not to swim in polluted sea, but whales and dolphins can't read notices!

### Rubbishy Beaches
A tremendous amount of rubbish finds its way on to beaches. Some of it will eventually disintegrate or be covered over, but some plastics are virtually indestructible.

## WORST OF FRIENDS?

Dolphins and tuna swim together. When the fishing nets
are put down to catch the tuna, the poor dolphins become
tangled up too, and they drown.

## EXOTIC ORNAMENTS

Souvenir hunters collect exotic shells because they are so
beautiful, and can be made into ornaments and jewellery.
People often don't know that their gift or souvenir has
been taken from a living animal.

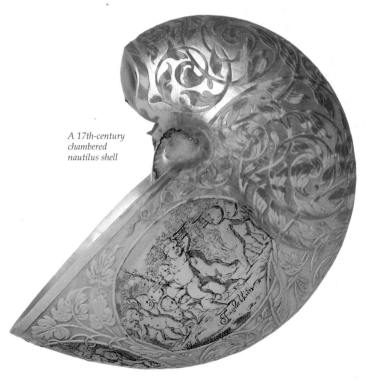

*A 17th-century
chambered
nautilus shell*

**Acknowledgements:** (KEY: b=bottom, c=centre, l=left, r=right, t=top) British Museum; Exeter Maritime Museum; Museum of London; National Maritime Museum, Greenwich, London; Science Museum, London.

**Picture Credits:** Ardea London Ltd/F. Gohier: 383b; Bruce Coleman Ltd/Bob & Clara Calhoun: 376br; Jacana/F. Gohier: 383t; The National Maritime Museum, Greenwich, London: 352; Natural History Museum, London: 379b; 382b; Oxford Scientific Films/Max Gibbs: front cover tl; Planet Earth Pictures/Doc White: 378;/Keith Scholey: 386;/Marty Snyderman: 380b; Popperfoto/T Heyerdahl: 346; Tony Stone Images: 343t; Trustees of the British Museum: 348.

**Additional Photography:** Tina Chambers, Andreas von Einsiedel, Steve Gorton, Frank Greenaway, Charles Howson, Colin Keates, Dave King, Ray Moller, James Stevenson, Harry Taylor, Kim Taylor.

Every effort has been made to trace the copyright holders. Funfax Ltd apologises for any unintentional omissions and would be pleased, in such cases, to add an acknowledgement in further editions.

# SUPER STRUCTURES

Written by Fiona Waters
Illustrated by Celia Witchard

# WONDERS OF THE WORLD

Early people found that caves made handy shelters, but there weren't always caves available, so they turned to making huts instead. Little did those early builders know what they were starting! The world is now full of fantastic constructions of all shapes and sizes. They have been made for lots of different uses, including living, burial and worship.

## THE ORIGINAL SEVEN WONDERS

Ancient and medieval scholars made a list of the seven most wondrous structures in the ancient world. All of them, apart from the pyramids at Giza, have vanished or are in ruins.

- THE TEMPLE OF ARTEMIS – This marble temple was built in about 350 BC. Only one of the original 127 columns remains.

- THE MAUSOLEUM AT HALICARNASSUS – This vast marble tomb was built in about 350 BC. The foundations can still be seen and some of the statues are in London's British Museum.

- PHAROS LIGHTHOUSE AT ALEXANDRIA – This was built in about 297 BC. At night, a fire burned and was reflected by bronze mirrors, to give light.

- THE PYRAMIDS OF GIZA, EGYPT – These pyramids were built between about 2,575 and 2,465 BC. The pyramid of Cheops (King Khufu) may have taken 100,000 men about 20 years to build!

- THE COLOSSUS OF RHODES – This bronze statue of Helios, the sun god, stood at the entrance to Rhodes harbour, Greece. It was more than 35 m (110 ft) high.

- THE STATUE OF ZEUS AT OLYMPIA, GREECE – This magnificent statue of Zeus, the king of the gods, measured 12 m (40 ft) and was made of ivory and gold.

- THE HANGING GARDENS OF BABYLON – The king of Babylon built these astounding terraced gardens for one of his wives.

# ROCKY DWELLINGS

$E$arly people called *hunter-gatherers* lived by hunting animals and gathering wild plants. They were *nomadic*, which means that they were always on the move, and they used caves as protection from the weather and wild animals.

## ROCK TEMPLE

At Ellura, in India, there are 34 temples carved into the rocky cliff. Although they are not dwellings as such, worshippers may have spent much of their time here.

*Carved pillars inside the Ellura temples.*

Inside, the rock has been carved into lots of decorative statues and columns, and in places it has been cut right through to let the sunlight in.

## CAVE DWELLERS TODAY

Cave dwellers are called *troglodytes*. In Spain, there is a whole community of these people who apparently think that their caves are more comfy than anything modern architecture can provide!

## MULTIPURPOSE

In France, cave homes were carved out of the soft limestone in the Loire Valley. They are now used as all sorts of things, including restaurants, hotels, wine cellars and even a zoo!

## DUG IN THE DESERT

The people of Matmata in Tunisia, North Africa, live in cave-like homes which they dig in the desert ground. These underground dwellings are perfect for desert life because they keep out the heat in the day and the cold at night. (Desert nights can be chilly. Brrrr!)

# BUILDING PYRAMIDS

The Egyptian pyramids were built around 4,500 years ago. Each one is a tomb, built by a *pharaoh* (king) as a final resting place for his body. There are more than 80 in Egypt itself, and there are another 100 further south in the Sudan.

## EARLY PYRAMIDS

The first Egyptian pyramids had stepped sides. These may have been seen as a stairway for the dead king to climb, to reach the gods and the stars.

The step pyramid of King Djoser was the first pyramid. It was made of six rectangular structures, one on top of the other.

## BELIEVE IT OR NOT...

King Djoser's pyramid was only part of a large complex which included a court where the king ran a course in front of crowds to prove his fitness. Show-off!

*King Djoser's pyramid*

## TRUE PYRAMIDS

Smooth pyramid shapes developed during the reign of King Sneferu (2,575-2,551 BC). The smooth outer facing was achieved with fine limestone and granite.

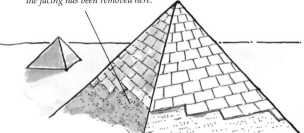

*Some of the fine limestone facing is left; the facing has been removed here.*

## HARD WORK

The Ancient Egyptians didn't have giant cranes like modern construction workers. They probably had to shift heavy stone blocks by dragging along earthen ramps built along the sides of the pyramid.

*The Egyptians used sledges to move heavy objects. This may have been how they moved blocks for making pyramids.*

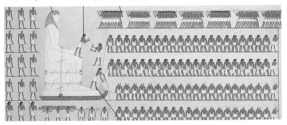

## INTRUDERS

Pharaohs were buried with lots of goodies, ready for the *afterlife*, which they believed came after death. Sadly, every known pyramid had been looted by 1,000 BC, by tomb robbers who were after all the riches.

# GREAT PYRAMIDS AND OTHERS

The great pyramids at Giza are probably the most famous pyramids of all. Even the Egyptians thought of them as ancient wonders. These incredible structures were an inspiration to *architects* (people who design buildings) for many centuries to come.

## BELIEVE IT OR NOT...

It took 100,000 men 20 years to build the Great Pyramid, but they probably didn't mind as they believed that they were helping their pharaoh on his journey to everlasting life.

## GIZA'S GREATS

The great pyramids of Giza are massive. The biggest was built for King Khufu, around 2,550 BC. At 147 m (481 ft) tall, it was made of about 2,300,000 blocks of limestone. Each block weighed about 2.5 tonnes! Heavy or what?

The smallest pyramid was built for King Menkaura and is only 66 m (218 ft) high – the baby of the group.

## AFTER DEATH

After a pharaoh died, he was *mummified* (preserved). The *mummy* was taken to a temple next to the pyramid where priests performed sacred rites on it, before it was laid to rest in the pyramid. This was a posh, lengthy affair.

*Mummy case*

## COPY CATS

Many centuries later, the Mayan people in Central America also built pyramids. These had steps outside and a flat top with an *altar*. This was where thousands of unfortunate people became victims of ritual sacrifices.

## PYRAMIDS LIVE ON

*Trans-America Building*

Modern pyramids include the Luxor Hotel in Las Vegas, San Francisco's TransAmerica building and the entrance to the Musée du Louvre in Paris.

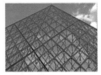

*Musée du Louvre*

*The Luxor Hotel*

# CASTLES

The first castles were built around the 9th and 10th centuries. A castle was the strong, safe home of a lord who ruled the surrounding land from his impressive accommodation. As the years went by, castles became stronger to protect the lords and their staff from marauding enemies.

## A GUIDED TOUR

Castles came in different shapes and sizes depending on where they were to be built, how much money was available and the likelihood of being attacked. Here is a basic guide to what was where in an average castle.

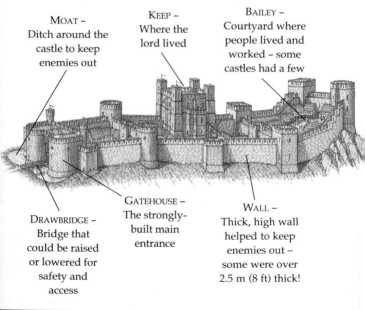

MOAT –
Ditch around the castle to keep enemies out

KEEP –
Where the lord lived

BAILEY –
Courtyard where people lived and worked – some castles had a few

DRAWBRIDGE –
Bridge that could be raised or lowered for safety and access

GATEHOUSE –
The strongly-built main entrance

WALL –
Thick, high wall helped to keep enemies out – some were over 2.5 m (8 ft) thick!

## INSIDERS

Here are some of the castle characters you might have met if you went visiting in ye olden days.

The lord and his family were the castle VIPs. Everyone else was there to serve them.

The page was a young servant.

The priest looked after the worship side of things and was the lord's secretary.

The fool provided the entertainment.

A host of other staff helped to run the castle and its *estates* (land owned by the lord).

## SHOW-OFFS

Needless to say, castles were a symbol of power. Rich families began to show off and competed to build taller and taller towers on their castles. In San Gimignano, in Italy, rival families built 72 castles in the same town! Only 14 of these have survived.

# Castle Collection

Castles varied from place to place and from country to country. Here is a small collection of castles from around the world. Imagine what it must have been like to live in one of them. (Dream on!)

## WALLS FOR SAFETY

In the 13th century, it became common to build castles with rings of stone walls, one inside the other, to make it trickier for the enemy to get in. Castles built like this were called *concentric castles*.

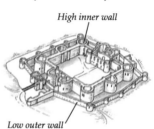

*High inner wall*

*Low outer wall*

*Caerphilly Castle, Wales – a concentric castle*

## IN SPAIN

*El Real de Manzanares*

Spain was ruled by people called Moors, from North Africa, until almost 1500. A Spanish castle called el Real de Manzanares (a bit of a mouthful) is a good example of the Moorish style. It has lots of square shapes and decoration.

## IN JAPAN

Japanese castles had a style all of their own. In the 16th and 17th centuries, when European castles were low in the popularity ratings, Japanese castles were in their heyday. The one shown here sports fine roofs – a status symbol in Japan.

*Himeji Castle*

## FAIRY-TALE CASTLES

Some castles look like the fantasy homes of fairy-tale princes and princesses. With their numerous towers and turrets, they rise high above the surrounding landscape. A magical, awesome sight!

*Neuschwanstein Castle in Germany*

# TOWERING ABOVE

People have been building towers for thousands of years and for different reasons. One of the most common reasons is to adorn religious buildings and give them a look of importance and beauty.

## MINARETS AND BELL TOWERS

Islamic places of worship, called *mosques*, have ornate towers called *minarets*. At certain times each day, an official person called a *muezzin* climbs up and calls people to prayer.

Bell towers are another way of summoning people to worship. The 1,000-year-old *campanile* (bell tower) of St Mark's Basilica in Venice did its job faithfully until it collapsed dramatically in 1902. Whoops!

*Minaret*

*Bell tower of St Mark's Basilica collapsing*

## DOMES AND SPIRES

Domes also help to draw attention to buildings of importance. Russia's St Basil's Cathedral has some pretty impressive onion-shaped domes.

*Patterned domes of St Basil's Cathedral, Moscow*

Decorative spires reaching towards the heavens were a popular addition to religious buildings.

*The Leaning Tower of Pisa, in Italy*

## LEANING TOWERS

The Leaning Tower of Pisa in Italy, was built in 1173 as a bell tower for the cathedral. It leans 5 m (16.4 ft) to one side because of the gradual *subsidence* (sinking) of the ground. Yikes!

# WEIRD BUILDING SITES

Choosing the right site for building on is a serious business. The land must be suitable and the finished thing must be easy to get to. However, some pretty weird places have been chosen for some of the world's buildings.

## BUILDINGS ON WATER?

Venice, in Italy, was built on over 100 islands and mud flats in a *lagoon* (a mass of water cut off from the sea). The buildings stand on massive *piles* (columns), mostly made of wood, which are driven deep into the sand and clay under the water.

*The houses in Venice are connected by narrow streets, around 100 canals and over 400 bridges.*

*Marshland houses are connected by a series of raised paths or roads called causeways.*

## MARSHLAND HOUSES

In some parts of America, people live on marshlands because the soil is rich for farming. In North Carolina, the ground has been built up above the water level and a town constructed on top.

## BUILT ON STILTS

In New Guinea, an island in the Pacific, coastal houses are built above the water on pillars. This saves land which is precious, because it is used for other things. It also makes it easier for people to get to the sea for fishing.

*Each pillar is made from a whole tree trunk.*

## NO WAY OUT

Some places are designed to make getting in or out difficult, not easy! Alcatraz, an island off San Francisco, was home to one of the grimmest prisons in the world until 1963. The birds were the only inhabitants of the island that could leave easily.

The island is made of rock and has no natural earth of its own, so soil had to be shipped from another island to make garden plots for the prison guards.

*Alcatraz is still an intimidating sight on the horizon.*

# SPECIAL REQUIREMENTS

Architects have to make sure that the buildings they design suit their uses. For instance, it's no good building a railway station without any space for the platforms, or a theatre without changing rooms!

## INDUSTRIAL TIMES

In the 18th and 19th centuries, first Britain, then Western Europe and the United States were transformed into *industrial* countries, making all sorts of things from raw materials. This time became known as the *Industrial Revolution* and it brought special building requirements with it.

*Factories were built to a very grand scale, to house huge pieces of machinery.*

Lots of people moved to cities to work, and houses had to be built especially for them. In England, the workers lived in long, straight streets of houses.

*Terraced houses*

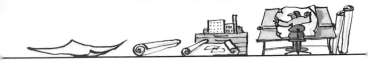

## PENGUIN PROBLEMS

In a new penguin pool designed for London Zoo in the 1930s, slanting concrete ramps made it easier for the penguins to get in and out of the water.

## BUILT TO CATCH THE WIND

Windmills do their work by using wind power. Their uses include grinding corn, crushing seeds and driving sawmills. In Holland they have been used to drain the land, to make it good for farming.

Modern windmills called *wind turbines* use wind power to make electricity. These graceful structures are built where they can catch plenty of strong gusts.

*Sails are mounted on a cap which can be turned to face the wind.*

*Cap*

*Sail*

*Wind turbines*

# THE FORBIDDEN CITY

 In China, during a period called the *Ming Dynasty* (1368-1644), the Emperor Yung-lo ordered the old capital city to be rebuilt. It became known as Peking, also called Beijing. The central part was called the Forbidden City.

## THREE-ZONE CITY

Peking had three zones. The outer zone had houses, shops and government buildings. Inside this was the Imperial City with lakes and gardens. At the centre was the new palace which was so big that it was like a city itself. Only the emperor's family, court and people on business were allowed in. Ordinary people couldn't enter the city, which is why it was called the Forbidden City.

*Plan showing Peking's zones*

## BELIEVE IT OR NOT...

Almost 1,000 buildings form the Forbidden City, including halls, temples, workshops, stables and a library. There was a throne for the emperor in the middle of each hall.

## Colour and Decoration

Colour was very important. Pillars and walls were red, platforms were white and the roof tiles were yellow. Yellow was a colour only used on buildings for the emperor.

The underside and edges of the Imperial Palace's roof were decorated with carvings of dragons and other creatures from Chinese mythology.

## The Last Emperor

The last emperor of China was a two-year-old boy called Pu-yi, who came to the throne in 1908. He hardly ever went outside the walls of the Imperial Palace until 1924, when he was forced to give up his title and leave the Forbidden City for ever.

# ROMAN WONDERS

The Romans were powerful – very powerful! They ruled over a vast empire that stretched from Britain to Asia and Africa. They had vast numbers of people to construct their huge public buildings, including temples, markets, *basilicas* (where courts were held and business was done) and places of entertainment.

*Roman arches were semicircular*

## THE ROMAN STYLE

The Romans adapted the style of Greek buildings and added domes, *vaults* (arched roofs or ceilings) and large arches. An arch is a strong shape which made it possible to construct bigger buildings.

## THE PANTHEON

The Pantheon is a circular temple in Rome. It was first built in 27 BC, but was rebuilt by the Emperor Hadrian in 120-124 AD. Its huge dome was built by pouring concrete over a temporary wooden framework. Yes...concrete! The Romans also used this handy stuff.

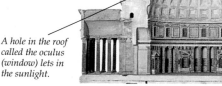

*A hole in the roof called the oculus (window) lets in the sunlight.*

## THE COLOSSEUM

An ideal day out in Roman times would be to go to the Colosseum. This was an *amphitheatre* – a big building used for entertainment and sport. The main purpose of this engineering masterpiece was to provide a place where trained fighters called *gladiators* could fight each other to the death. Gruesome!

## COLOSSEUM FACTS

- The *arena* (where the action took place) was 189 m (620 ft) across and could hold over 50,000 spectators.

- The arena was covered with sand – to soak up the blood!

- The crowd could be protected from the sun by a huge canopy suspended from 240 poles around the top storey.

- There were 80 entrances. The spectators had numbered tickets to show which door they should use.

- A huge chandelier was hung above the arena to provide light for night-time games.

# PLACES OF WORSHIP

Throughout time, people have worshipped their gods in specially constructed buildings. These are very different from country to country because of different beliefs, traditions and building styles.

## A GRAND TEMPLE

Usually, an Egyptian temple was built to honour the gods, but Rameses II built a temple at Abu Simbel to celebrate his own reign (1279-1213 BC). The whole thing was carved out of the cliffs above the River Nile.

*The front is decorated with four vast statues of the king himself.*

## STONE CIRCLE

Stonehenge is a massive prehistoric circle of stones in England. It was constructed around 2,800 BC. The siting of the circle is thought to have had religious meaning for the *Neolithic* people who built it, because its position lets the sun shine through and rise above certain stones.

*Some stones were transported more than 216 km (134 miles).*

## Mud Mosques

Mud is used as a building material in hot, dry places. In northern parts of Africa, huge mosques have been built using mud bricks baked hard in the sun. These can even withstand heavy rainfall, as long as the sun comes out to dry them soon afterwards!

*Pieces of wood support structure – also handy as scaffolding for doing repairs*

## Totem Poles

North American Indians made *totem poles* (carved or painted poles). They were symbols representing each family, with their crest – a bear, eagle or wolf, for instance. Some were memorials to dead relatives.

## Three-tiered Temple

Beijing's stunning Temple of Heaven has three roofs covered with blue glazed tiles. The largest of these beautiful roofs is supported by 12 pillars, each made from a single tree trunk.

# AZTECS AND INCAS

In the 16th century, Spanish explorers reached Central and Southern America and found two ancient and mighty civilizations – the Aztecs and the Incas. Both peoples built spectacular cities and temples, where they worshipped the sun.

## THE GREAT AZTEC TEMPLE

The temple at the Aztec capital, Tenochtitlan, was the centre of the Aztec world. Each ruler tried to make a bigger and better temple. It was here that gruesome human sacrifices took place.

*Reclining figure called a chacmool held container for hearts and blood of victims*

*Decorative skull panel*

## ONE-WAY TRAFFIC
The Incas lived in highland or coastal areas and built their cities high in the mountains. These cities had to be built wherever the rugged landscape allowed. One of the most remote is Machu Picchu. There are 143 buildings – 80 are houses and the rest are ceremonial buildings, such as temples.

## BIG HEAD
Much of what we know about the Aztecs and the Incas comes from studying their buildings and the bits and pieces which they left behind.

One puzzle is the huge rock heads that have been found. They weigh over 20 tonnes and stand over 1.5 m (5 ft) tall. They could be portraits of rulers or chiefs.

## ON THE TERRACES
Inca farmers built terraces on the hillsides to make more land for growing crops. The terraces also helped to stop the wind and rain from wearing away the soil.

# BURIAL PLACES

Ever since ancient times, many peoples have wanted to protect their dead and send them on to an afterlife, complete with riches to ensure everlasting peace. Tombs became more and more elaborate through the ages and could sometimes take a lifetime to construct!

## MEGALITHS

*Megaliths* is the name given to a group of ancient monuments consisting of huge slabs of stone. Early people used megaliths as burial chambers, to store human remains.

## THE TAJ MAHAL

One of the most famous and most lavish tombs is the Taj Mahal in India. It was built in the 17th century by the

Emperor Shah Jehan, for his wife. He wanted her resting place to be more beautiful than any other building. The white marble walls are inlaid with semiprecious stones. Divine!

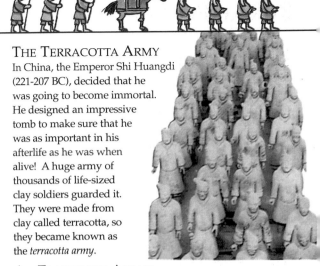

## THE TERRACOTTA ARMY

In China, the Emperor Shi Huangdi (221-207 BC), decided that he was going to become immortal. He designed an impressive tomb to make sure that he was as important in his afterlife as he was when alive! A huge army of thousands of life-sized clay soldiers guarded it. They were made from clay called terracotta, so they became known as the *terracotta army*.

## AN ELABORATE AFFAIR

The temple of Angkor Wat was built in Cambodia in the 12th century. It is an elaborate affair, surrounded by moats and courtyards. It is famous for the huge cone-shaped tower at each corner. Believe it or not, it was only discovered in 1860!

## THE SPHINX

In Egypt, the statue of a sphinx guards King Khafre's tomb at Giza. It has the body of a lion and the head of King Khafre. It was carved from limestone rock and is the biggest free-standing sculpture to survive from ancient times.

*King Khafre's tomb at Giza*

# BUILDING BRIDGES

When hunters first ventured from their villages, they found that obstacles such as rivers got in the way. The answer? Put a log across and walk safely over. Hey presto – the first bridges! Today, huge bridges are built to carry people, trains and roads.

## BRIDGES OF VENICE

In Venice, Italy, there are two world famous bridges. The Rialto Bridge crosses the Grand Canal and is the geographical centre of the city. There is a shop in each of its archways.

*The Rialto Bridge*

The Bridge of Sighs, built in 1600, was where prisoners on their way to trial or execution had their last view of the outside world.

## GOLDEN GATE BRIDGE

The longest span of the Golden Gate Bridge in San Francisco, California, measures 1,280 m (4,200 ft). It is called a *suspension bridge* and hangs from long steel cables attached to tall towers.

The cables are made from thousands of steel wires bound tightly together.

*The Golden Gate Bridge*

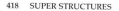

## HEAD FOR HEIGHTS?

One of the world's scariest bridges is in Spain. This tiny crossing perches precariously high above a mountain chasm which is some 180 m (590 ft) deep. Heeeelp!

## SIDE BY SIDE

The Forth Rail Bridge near Edinburgh, Scotland, was the first major steel-built bridge in the world. The sections are held together by 8 million rivets and balance on huge piers embedded in the river. This type of bridge is called a *cantilever bridge*.

## BELIEVE IT OR NOT...

No sooner has the Forth Bridge been painted from end to end than it has to be done all over again! Phew!

## GLASS BRIDGES

In San Francisco's financial district, the twin towers of the First Interstate Center skyscrapers are joined together by glass sky-bridges. Don't drop anything heavy!

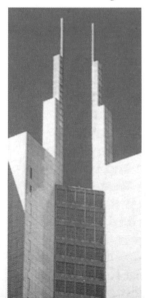

# NATURAL MATERIALS

The earliest buildings were made of natural materials including wood, stone and grass. When people learned to bake clay, bricks appeared on the scene and things began to look up for many builders. Today, buildings are a mixture of natural and man-made materials.

## SNOWMEN

In the Arctic, the Inuit people build temporary shelters called *igloos* from blocks of snow. Apparently, these can be remarkably cosy inside!

## MUD

In Syria, Asia, mud houses were made in the shape of old-fashioned beehives. The layers of mud were built up one at a time, with each layer drying before the next one was added.

## EARLY CONCRETE

The Romans made concrete by mixing volcanic earth with rubble and bricks. This made a really tough material which is still used today, although the recipe has changed slightly since those early times!

*Ovens in Pompeii, Italy – made of concrete*

## LOCAL TRADITIONS

All around the world, people still live in very traditional houses which have been built in the same style for hundreds of years.

*Zulus in South Africa live in kraals – groups of dome-shaped, grass-covered houses with low openings at the front.*

*The Masai people in Kenya live in long, low houses made from bent branches covered with cow dung. Phewee!*

*In Switzerland, wooden chalets are built with steeply-sloping roofs to prevent too much snow from piling up on them.*

*Mongolian nomads live in yurts – willow-framed tents covered in felt and canvas.*

*In Bolivia, South America, Aymara Indians make their houses from woven reeds.*

*In New Mexico, the houses are built with bricks made from sun-baked mud, called adobe.*

# Added Extras

Constructing fine buildings is all very well, but without one or two vital additions such as windows and staircases, moving around them could be a bit of a problem.

## Letting in Light

The earliest windows were holes cut into the wall to let light in and let smoke and smells out. If it was cold or wet, the gap was plugged with an animal skin or a piece of wood.

In hot countries, people built very tiny windows to keep the sun out. They did the same in cold countries, but for a different reason – to keep the snow out!

*Small windows in India, where it is hot*

## Stained Glass

As glass became more common, windows became bigger, and by the 14th century they were vast. By mixing different chemicals into hot, melted glass it was possible to colour it, and the stained glass window was born.

*Stained glass in
Chartres Cathedral, France*

## Super-modern

In the Institut du Monde Arabe, in Paris, the entire south side of the building is made up of metal screens, each containing small 'windows' which open and close depending on how much light there is. Futuristic or what?

## Long Flight

Steps are one thing, but the Spanish Steps in Rome are in a class all of their own. They link the church with the *piazza* (square) below, but it takes a lot of puff to reach the top! Their curves and terraces make them a huge tourist attraction.

## In Time

Some buildings are designed especially to tell you the time. The clock tower on London's Houses of Parliament holds a 14-tonne bell, known as Big Ben, whose chimes are broadcast daily on the radio.

The gold and blue clock face on the clock tower in Venice's Piazza San Marco shows the phases of the moon and the zodiac.

# WALLS, CEILINGS & ROOFS

Walls and roofs are absolute essentials for most buildings...but why be dull? Here are some of the world's fine examples for you to marvel at.

## ROOF-TOP WONDER

Until the invention of flying machines, only birds could see some of the world's beautiful roof-tops. The roof of the Stephansdom in Vienna, shown below, is covered with over a quarter of a million glazed tiles. It had to be restored after it was damaged in World War II.

Just take a look at these stunning tiled roofs from around the world.

*France*

*Nevada, USA*

*Germany*

# A Long Job

Between 1508 and 1512, Italian artist Michelangelo painted the ceiling of the Vatican Palace's Sistine Chapel. He didn't just slap a bit of paint around...oh no! He painted elaborate Bible scenes, and it took him four years lying on especially designed scaffolding to do it!

# Flimsy Walls

Traditional buildings in Japan are made on wooden frames with overhanging roofs. The floor area is divided into rooms by using movable screens covered in paper.

# The Biggest Wall

A bit of a cheat, this one! The Great Wall of China has nothing to do with buildings. It was constructed in the 3rd century BC by the emperor, to help defend his lands. It stretches for over 2,400 km (1,500 miles) and can be seen from space. That's some building project!

# Scraping the Sky

When building space in some big cities became difficult to find, there seemed to be an obvious answer – build upwards! *Skyscrapers* was the name given to those tall buildings which towered over the city below.

## The First Skyscrapers

In the 19th century, people began constructing buildings that had iron and steel frames, and really tall buildings started to appear. The first skyscraper was built in 1883 and was ten storeys high.

## A Head For Heights

Most of the construction workers in New York employed to work on the early skyscrapers were Mohawk Indians. Only a handful of men were hired at first, and they taught their relatives to 'walk the high steel'.

## Building Regulations

As buildings became taller, the streets below became darker, so regulations were made to stop cities becoming gloomy places. When a building reached 38 m (125 ft) high, the next part had to be stepped back, and at the thirtieth storey it had to be stepped back again. The end result was a building that looked a lot like a tiered wedding cake!

## THE FLATIRON BUILDING

The Flatiron Building in New York got its name because it was the shape of an old-fashioned flat iron. When it was built in 1902 it was the world's tallest building and most people thought it would fall down! Wrong!

*The Flatiron building*

## THE EMPIRE STATE BUILDING

The Empire State Building in New York was the tallest building in the world for around forty years. There are some awesome facts attached to this mighty construction.

- It has 73 lifts and more than 6,000 windows!

- It has been struck by lightning many times – once nine times in 20 minutes.

- The top floor sways up to 1 m (3 ft) in strong winds!

- Because of strange wind currents that move around the building, snow blows up, instead of falling down outside the windows!

# SPECTACULAR SPECTACLES

$A$round the turn of the 19th century, things really began to change on the architecture scene. People had a fresh look at what they could do with traditional ideas and the result was some pretty amazing buildings.

*Her torch was to be used as a lighthouse but the light was too weak.*

## WELCOME TO THE NEW LAND!

For over a hundred years, a very spectacular lady has welcomed travellers to New York. She is the Statue of Liberty – a gift from the people of France to the people of the United States. She stands in the entrance to the harbour.

• She weighs 204 tonnes and is 93 m (305 ft) tall from the base to the tip of her torch.

• Her face is 3 m (10 ft) from ear to ear, and her nose is over 1 m (3 ft) long!

• There is a door at her foot leading inside and 354 steps up to the observation platform in her crown.

• The seven spikes of her crown represent the seven seas and seven continents of the world.

## EIFFEL TOWER

Paris's famous Eiffel Tower was originally built as the entrance to the Paris Exhibition of 1889. At the time it was not liked by everyone and was described as 'the shame of Paris', but now it is one of the world's great tourist attractions. How wrong can you be! It is made up of 18,038 wrought iron pieces and on a hot day it becomes slightly taller as it expands!

## THE REAL MASTERPIECE?

The Guggenheim Museum in New York houses one of the world's best modern art collections, but the building itself is a work of art, too. It looks like a giant shell and at dusk it is lit up with purple light. It was designed so that people start at the top of the building and walk down in a great spiral to look at the pictures.

*The museum was designed by Frank Lloyd Wright.*

# INTO THE FUTURE

 $N$ew building materials and improved techniques have led to exciting designs. Some seem to soar through the air, defying gravity.

## MUSICAL SHELLS

The Sydney Opera House is one of the world's most spectacular buildings. Under the shells that form the roof there are four main halls, two main restaurants, and 60 dressing rooms! The building is surrounded on three sides by water and the roof is covered with over a million gleaming tiles.

## OUTSIDE PLUMBING

The Pompidou Centre in Paris looks like an inside-out building! The architects decided to put the lifts, escalators, air and water ducts and even the steel 'skeleton' on the outside.

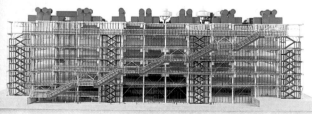

## ALL-ROUND EXPERIENCE

Paris is also home to another remarkable modern building. La Géode is a huge cinema with a 1,000 sq m (11,000 sq ft) dome-shaped screen which creates amazing visual and sound effects.

## GIANT SAUCER

Brazil's capital, Brasilia, has many modern buildings. The giant 'saucer' of its Chamber of Deputies is a reversed dome.

*The dome reflects sunlight.*

## OUT OF THIS WORLD

The ingenious architect Antonio Gaudí designed many fantastic buildings for his native city of Barcelona, in Spain. The buildings are full of curves and many of them are decorated with stunning mosaics.

# WHAT NEXT?

So where do we go from here? There are some ultra-modern buildings scattered around the world, and there are plans underway to build more. Some of these ideas may seem like dreams at the moment, but fantasy can become reality!

## SEALED IN

Biosphere II is a building in Arizona, USA, constructed as an experiment. Scientists wanted to explore ways that people could survive on other planets, so the glass and steel building had to be completely sealed and have its own artificial *atmosphere* (air and climate). The idea was that people inside could survive without anything from the outside world.

## FLY INTO THE FUTURE

How about this for a building project – a sophisticated airport in Japan, constructed on an artificially-built island in Osaka Bay, Japan. The terminal had to be made strong enough to withstand earthquakes and typhoon winds, and large enough to take millions of passengers a year.

## COMING SOON...

- The Millennium Tower in Tokyo will be 767 m (2,515 ft) tall.

- Computers will control devices to protect buildings from earthquakes.

- Construction materials will be more ecologically friendly and recycled where possible.

*The TransAmerica building has been designed to withstand earthquakes.*

- Solar power will be used for heating and lighting.

*This is what the house of the future might look like.*

- Then, of course, there will be cities in outer space. Awesome! The Russians already have a space station called *Mir* in orbit around the Earth. The US is leading an international space station project called *Freedom*.

*Mir space station*

# RECORD BREAKERS

We've come a long way from the days when the first people were holed up in draughty caves. Look around and you will see all sorts of wondrous architectural designs. From the longest to the highest, here is a selection of some really super structures.

The tallest habitable building is the twin Petronas Towers in Kuala Lumpur, Malaysia. Including their spires, the towers are 452 m (1,482 ft) high.

The longest ship canal in the world, the Suez Canal, links the Red Sea with the Mediterranean and is around 160 km (100 miles) long!

The biggest castle in the world is Prague Castle in the Czech Republic, which covers 8 hectares (20 acres).

The largest railway station in the world is the Grand Central Terminal in New York, USA, which has 44 platforms.

The biggest shopping centre in the world is the West Edmonton Mall in Alberta, Canada, which is as big as 90 American football fields!

The longest road tunnel in the world is the St Gotthard Tunnel in Switzerland, which is 16.3 km (10.1 miles) long.

The world city with the most skyscrapers is New York City, USA. It has 131 skyscrapers.

The highest city in the world is Wenchuan, China, at 5,099 m (16,730 ft) above sea level.

The Great Canal of China which runs from Beijing to Hangzhou was built during the 1200s and is still in use today!

The Great Pyramid at Giza, Egypt, may now seem small, but it held the record for being the tallest structure for over 4,000 years!

The largest sports stadium in the world is the Strahov Stadium in Prague, Czech Republic, which can hold 240,000 people.

The country with the longest rail network is the USA, with 240,000 km (149,129 miles) of track.

**Acknowledgements:** (KEY: a=above, b=bottom/below, c=centre, l=left, r=right, t=top) British Museum; Gordon Models (back cover tr); Sir John Soane's Museum, London.

**Picture Credits:** Adams Picture Library: 426br; 435; Bryan & Cherry Alexander: 420c; Ancient Art & Architecture Collection: 396c; Arcaid/Prisma Parc Guell: 431b; Christopher Branfield: front cover tr; Corinthian capital, British Museum: back cover tl; Britstock-IFA: 399b; J Allan Cash Photolibrary: back cover cl; 402br; Courtesy Chinese Cultural Embassy: 417tr; Colorific!/Blackstock/P S Mecca: 426cl; Michael Copsey: 412b; Comstock/George Gerster: 425bl; Culver Pictures Inc.: 427br; Michael Dent: 404cr; Chris Donaghue The Oxford Picture Library: 423crb; ESO/Meylan: 433b; ET Archive/V&A Museum: 425cr; Edifice/Darley: 407tl; /Jackson:403tr; /P Lewis: 406cr; Chris Fairclough Colour Library: 408tl; Sonia Halliday Photographs/Jane Taylor: 409c; Robert Harding Picture Library: 397bl; 397br; 424bc; 430tl; 433cr; /Gascoigne: 392cr; /Peter Scholey: 409t; /Adina Tovy: back cover bl; 413br; Michael Holford: 400bl; Angelo Hornek: 420b; Hutchison Library: front cover br;1; 394; 411; 416bl; The Image Bank/Bernard van Berg: 424bl; /Michael Coyne: 405tr; /David Gould: 406b; INAH: 414c; James H Morris: 421tl; 422cl; Kansai International Airport Company Ltd: 432b; MacQuitty International Photo Collection: 393b; Magnum Photos/David Hurn: 432c; Panos Pictures: 413tr; Pictor International: 404bl; Nick Saunders/Barbara Heller: 414b; Scala/Vatican Museum: 425t; Tony Morrison, South American Pictures: 415b; Tony Stone Images: 402tl; 407bl; 413bl; /Charlie Waite: 424br; The Venice in Peril Fund: 402bl; Werner Forman Archive/Anthropology Museum, Veracruz: 415cl; Michael Zabé: 397c; Zefa Pictures: 401br; 433cl; /Rosenfeld: back cover bc; 431t.

**Additional Photography:** Max Alexander, Geoff Brightling, Geoff Dann, Mike Dunning, Peter Hayman, John Heseltine, Dave King, Neil Lukas, Andrew McKinney, Michael Moran, Robert O'Dea, Stephen Oliver, John Parker, Tim Ridley, Kim Sayer, Karl Shone, Peter Wilson.

**Additional Illustrations:** David Ashby, Joanna Cameron, William Donahue, Paolo Donati, Andrew Nash.

Every effort has been made to trace the copyright holders. Funfax Ltd apologises for any unintentional omissions and would be pleased, in such cases, to add an acknowledgement in further editions.

# LIVING IN HISTORY

Written by Fiona MacKeith

Illustrated by Robin Edmonds
and John Cooper

# TIME DETECTIVES

Here's your chance to become a time traveller. Zoom through the centuries and find out about the very first people...or perhaps you would prefer to see medieval life through the eyes of a knight's visor. You can even discover how North American *shamans* (medicine men) treated illness.

People who study remains from the past, called *archaeologists,* have been able to piece together tiny fragments to give us marvellous insights into the places, peoples and lifestyles of vanished times. Here are some examples to whet your appetite.

## A REAL GIANT

Barnum Brown, fossil collector, discovered the fossilized bones of a dinosaur in Montana, USA, in 1902. He spent three years *excavating* them (digging them up) and the beastie became known as Tyrannosaurus rex, or T. rex for short!

*Model of T. rex*

## BOG PEOPLE

The amazingly preserved
remains of humans have
been found in peat bogs.
They may either have
been the victims
of sacrifices
or muggings.
The people who dig
up the remains have to
be careful not to crush or
damage the delicate bodies.

*Well-preserved body from
Northern European peat bog*

## A RIGHT ROYAL CEMETERY

In Ancient Egypt, the *pharaohs* (kings) had enormous
pyramids built to house their bodies in the *afterlife* (life
after death). The pyramids at Giza have been around for
over 4,500 years.

## WHAT A WAY TO GO

When the volcano
Vesuvius, in Italy, erupted
on 24 August, 79 AD,
thousands of people were
covered in volcanic ash
and mud. This cooled,
forming a solid rock case
around the bodies.
Although the bodies
decayed, they left
perfect moulds of the
people's shapes.

*Plaster poured in hollow
reveals dead person's shape*

# Early People

About ten million years ago in Africa, early apes were adapting to their ever changing surroundings. Many scientists believe that these apes developed into early humans over a period of several million years.

## Hello Granny!

In 1974, in Ethiopia, Africa, the fossil skeleton of an early *australopithecine* was found. That incredibly long word means that she (it was a female) could walk upright and had a bigger brain than her ape-like ancestors. Scientists named her Lucy and think that she is between one and four million years old.

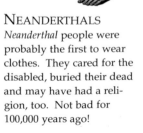

*Model of Lucy*

*Neanderthal people*

## Neanderthals

*Neanderthal* people were probably the first to wear clothes. They cared for the disabled, buried their dead and may have had a religion, too. Not bad for 100,000 years ago!

## TREASURES IN DEATH

Ancient people have always treated their dead with respect. When the simple grave of a young girl was excavated in the Holy Land, she was found buried with her animal-shaped feeding bottle.

### BELIEVE IT OR NOT...

During the Bronze Age, they had a very nasty little habit of beheading human sacrifices at funerals. Yuck!

## DEAD SEA SCROLLS

In 1947, in a place called Qumran, a shepherd boy nipped into a local cave for a bit of peace and quiet. What a surprise when he made the historic discovery of the ancient Hebrew manuscripts now called the *Dead Sea Scrolls*, the oldest known versions of the Bible's Old Testament.

*Caves where Dead Sea Scrolls were found*

*Dead Sea Scrolls were stored in pottery jars*

# AZTECS AND INCAS

The Aztecs and the Incas were important and powerful civilizations. The Aztecs were a wandering people who settled in Mexico in the 13th century. The Incas' great empire was centred on Peru.

## GOING TO WAR

The Aztecs believed that their gods needed human sacrifices to keep the sun in motion, so they had to go to war with their neighbours to keep up the fast food supply of human bits and pieces!

## CHOCOLATE

Aztecs be blessed! They gave us that unbelievably mouth-watering experience – chocolate! They made a pretty fine chocolate drink using cocoa sweetened with honey and flavoured with vanilla. Mmmm...delicious!

*Aztec warrior figure*

## BELIEVE IT OR NOT...

You might think that your teacher can overdo the discipline from time to time, but at least they don't shave your head when you fail a test – a daily occurrence in Aztec times!

## A WOMAN'S PLACE

Aztec women were ahead of their time. They could own property and even get a divorce.

## Inca City

The Incas built a beautiful and dramatic city called Machu Picchu on a high plain between two mountain peaks. It was a natural fortress as it was protected by steep slopes and high mountains.

*The remains of Machu Picchu*

## Sending Messages

The Inca emperor used relay runners to carry messages. Each runner used to blow on a conch shell to let the other runners know that he was on his way. The runners covered vast distances each day.

### Believe It or Not...

We may never have had the muscovy duck if it wasn't for the Incas, who domesticated them. Quack, quack!

## Pan-pipes

Ever heard the haunting sound of pan-pipes? Well the Incas made them from the quills of a bird of prey called the condor.

*Pan-pipes*

# THE ANCIENT GREEKS

The civilization of Ancient Greece was made up of mainland Greece and many small islands scattered in the Aegean and Adriatic Seas.

*Greek drinking cup*

The Greeks were brilliant in the areas of literature, the arts, politics and sport, to name a few.

## POWER TO THE PEOPLE

In early times, rich landowners called *tyrants* controlled the poor, until the poor took control and gained power and freedom. This new form of government was called *democracy*.

## GREEK DRAMA

The Greeks were very fond of watching plays, but did you know that all the actors were male, some taking female parts? Women were probably not allowed to go to the theatre at all!

## OLYMPIC GAMES

The most important Greek athletics festival was held at Olympia every four years – the Olympic Games. Wars were sometimes suspended to allow people to travel to and from the Games in safety. The Olympics are still held today.

## A FAMOUS TALE

A famous Greek poet called Homer told the tale of how the Greek army captured the city of Troy.

The Greeks built a giant wooden horse which they left outside the city. The Trojans pulled the beast into their city, little knowing that it was full of Greek soldiers who crept out and opened the gates for the rest of the army. Sneaky or what?

*Modern replica of Trojan horse*

# GREEK GODS

The Ancient Greeks worshipped lots of different gods and goddesses, who they thought were a lot like humans: they fell in love, married, argued and had children, to mention just a few similarities.

*Zeus*

## HOME SWEET HOME
Mount Olympus, the highest mountain in Greece, was thought to be the home of the gods.

## ZEUS
Zeus was the king of the gods. He is usually shown as a man of great power and dignity. He sometimes carries a thunderbolt, his symbol.

## DIONYSOS
Dionysos was the god of wine, fruitfulness and vegetation.

## APOLLO
The god Apollo is linked with the sun, with light, with healing and medicine. He was the brother of Artemis, the goddess of the hunt.

## APHRODITE

The goddess of love and beauty, Aphrodite, was born from the sea foam. Although she was married to Hephaistos (the lame god), she fell in love with Ares, the god of war.

*Aphrodite*

## ATHENA

The goddess of wisdom and warfare was called Athena. She watched over the arts, literature and philosophy.

## DEMETER AND PERSEPHONE

This mother and daughter team were goddesses of the grain.

## GREEK TEMPLES

Religion was the most important thing in Greek life, so it isn't surprising that the temples were the biggest and most beautiful buildings of all. They were made of limestone or marble, with wooden roofs and ceilings.

*Temple of the Parthenon, dedicated to Athena*

# LIFE IN ANCIENT ROME

So legend has it, Rome was founded by twin brothers, Romulus and Remus, in 753 BC. Unfortunately, the brothers had a dreadful quarrel and Remus died... so Rome it was, after Romulus!

*In legend, the infant twins were abandoned, but a she-wolf saved them by suckling them.*

*Coins depicting Roman emperors:*

*Caligula 37-41 AD*

*Claudius 41-54 AD*

*Nero 54-68 AD*

## HEADS YOU LOSE

The Romans didn't have newspapers or TV, so coins were used to advertise the emperor and his deeds. All the power seems to have been a bit much for some of them. Caligula went mad and was murdered, and Nero couldn't take the strain either; he went mad and killed himself!

## The Colosseum

The Romans were mighty good builders. Just look at the Colosseum, the greatest of all *amphitheatres* (big buildings used for entertainment and sport). It held about 50,000 people, all of which could get out in three minutes through the 80 *vomitora* (exits).

*Inside the Colosseum*

*Outside the Colosseum*

## Blood and Guts

There was plenty of gory entertainment to be had at the amphitheatre. The spectators enjoyed watching wild animals attacking defenceless criminals.

At around midday, all the dead bodies were removed and fresh sand was spread around, ready for a nice fresh start with the arrival of the gladiators in the afternoon. The gladiators fought each other to the death.

# MORE ROMAN LIFE

Here are some down-to-earth facts about ordinary life in everyday Rome for you to devour.

## ROMAN WOMEN

Women had to fight for their rights in Roman times! It was thought that it wasn't worth educating girls beyond the *primary* standard. The best way to get ahead was to be a *widow* (a woman whose husband has died). Widows enjoyed plenty of independence, especially if they were wealthy!

## BATH TIME

Most families didn't have bathroom facilities, so they went to the huge public baths instead. These weren't just places for getting clean. The men went after a day at work to exercise, chat, play games and meet friends. The women had separate baths, or they went in the morning.

*Roman baths at Bath, England*

## KEEPING CLEAN

Forget the soap – the Romans rubbed oil all over themselves and then scraped off the sweat, dirt and oil in one go.

## ROMAN TOILETS

Going to the public toilets could be quite a social event for the Romans, as they used multi-seater loos! Instead of toilet paper, they used sponges on sticks! A water channel under the seats carried the sewage away.

*Oil flask*

*Strigil – for scraping skin clean*

*Roman multi-seater toilet*

## ANCIENT WRITING

Throughout the Roman Empire, Latin was the language which was used for all-important dealings and business. The Romans introduced the Latin alphabet to northern Europe and it is still used there today.

# THE ANCIENT EGYPTIANS

The Ancient Egyptian civilization lasted for many centuries, from about 3,000-300 BC. The Egyptians were well-known for their amazing pyramid-building skills, but here are some other facts that you may not be so familiar with.

## JUST TAKING A NAP

Before the Egyptians became experts in *mummification* (preserving bodies), they arranged a dead body in a sleeping position and buried it in sand. This absorbed all the water from the body and preserved it. Then the person's spirit could recognize it and inhabit it again in the afterlife. Very handy!

*Preserved body of a 5,000-year-old man*

## STORAGE JARS

Once the Egyptians developed the art of mummifying bodies, there was no stopping them. Even beloved pets and other creatures were mummified. The mummy's vital organs had to be removed, dried out and then stored in jars.

*Canopic jars – for storing organs in*

## TUTANKHAMUN

Tutankhamun is probably the most famous pharaoh. He was laid to rest with a solid gold mask weighing over 10.2 kg (22.5 lb). Myth has it that he laid a curse on all who entered his tomb.

## A GRITTY PROBLEM

There was nothing that the Egyptians liked better than a good party. Eating could have been a little tricky for some Egyptians, though. Grit got into the flour when the bread was made and this wore their teeth away. Ouch!

*Tutankhamun's mummy mask*

## LOOKING GOOD

The Egyptians wore wigs made from human hair and stuck them in place with beeswax. Some tied cones of scented animal fat to their wigs! In the words of one top ten Egyptian hit song, 'Put myrrh on your head and dress up in beautiful clothes'!

*Courtiers with cones of animal fat on their head*

# THE VIKINGS

Vikings were brave warriors and explorers from Norway, Sweden and Denmark. For 300 years, from the 8th to the 11th centuries, they took the world by storm with their daring raids.

## WHERE THEY WENT

Thanks to the Vikings' excellent seafaring skills and their sensational ships, they could take other people completely by surprise. The brown parts on this map show where the Vikings had settlements.

## VIKING ATTIRE

Viking warriors didn't wear uniforms. Each soldier had to supply his own clothes and weapons. The more important Vikings got to wear iron helmets, while the poorer ones had to make do with leather caps. Not ideal in a battle situation!

*Iron helmet*

## HOME LIFE

Vikings who made it to Iceland had to make do with the building materials that they found. Because timber was scarce, the walls and roofs of the houses were often made from turf. Wood panelling helped to keep out the cold and damp.

*End view of Viking house with turf roof*

## THAT'S IT FOLKS!

When it came to dying, the Vikings didn't believe in leaving anything to chance and were buried with everything they would need in the next world. The wealthiest were buried in boats crammed full of belongings. Even servants were killed and sent off to the next world with their masters! The ships were then often set alight in a blazing *funeral pyre*, or covered with mounds of earth.

*Re-enactment of a Viking funeral pyre*

# MEDIEVAL LIFE

*Medieval* times were also called the *Middle Ages*. This was roughly the time between the 5th century to the end of the 15th century...so that's quite a bit of history!

## REVOLTING PEASANTS

Medieval peasants had a tough time. After a lethal plague called the *Black Death* wiped out thousands of people, the survivors in England had to work extra hard and pay extra taxes. They got fed up with this and in 1381 they marched to London, led by a chap called Wat Tyler, to complain to the king about their treatment.

*Rat – plague spreader*

## WHAT A STINK!

Peasants didn't wash their outer clothes. It's a good job that they kept big fires going because the woodsmoke acted as a deodorant and kept the pong down a bit!

## BREATH FRESHENER

Medieval toothpaste was made from ingredients such as ground up oyster and whelk shells. And if you had a touch of bad breath, well you just sweetened it with honey, coriander and cumin seeds. Simple!

## FARMING

In medieval Europe, more than 90 per cent of the population lived and worked on the land. They often used a *three field system* where two fields were sown with crops in one year and the third field was left to recover, so it would be good for growing things the next year. If a harvest failed, it could mean that a whole village starved.

*Stained glass shows farmer sowing seeds*

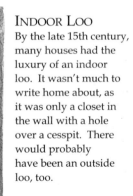

## INDOOR LOO

By the late 15th century, many houses had the luxury of an indoor loo. It wasn't much to write home about, as it was only a closet in the wall with a hole over a cesspit. There would probably have been an outside loo, too.

*The 'smallest room'*

# Life in a Castle

A castle was a private fortress, owned by a nobleman or a baron. It was also a home and a community with lots of staff to look after the day-to-day running of the place.

### Enemies Beware

Castles were incredibly strong buildings with walls as thick as 4 m (13 ft). Marauding enemies were always a danger. They sometimes tried to tunnel under the walls, but bowls of water put on the ground were a good early warning, as the vibrations made the water ripple.

If you think that's sneaky, what about *murder holes!* These holes in the roof could be used to rain down scalding water, hot sand or other horrible bits and pieces on the heads of the intruders.

## FOOD GLORIOUS FOOD

The main hall was where people ate, slept and carried out business. Breakfast consisted of bread soaked in ale or watered-down wine. The main meal was eaten at about ten or eleven o'clock in the morning. Then there were various suppers in the evening.

## AN EARLY START

When as young as seven years old, a boy from a noble family might be sent to a castle to become a *page* and learn good manners. Girls were often sent to a castle to learn the arts of sewing, home-making and how to behave correctly, especially in front of the gentlemen.

## FIT FOR FIGHTING

Lords were also knights. They could be called to fight for their king at any time. Taking part in *tournaments*, where they entered team games or single combat, kept them in practice.

*16th-century knight's helmet*

## BELIEVE IT OR NOT...

Pigs were bred for the meat that they provided, but they were also trained as retrievers, like modern dogs. They were used when poaching!

# KNIGHTS

Who were knights? They were warriors who fought on horseback and date back to 800 AD. When we talk about knights today, we probably mean the 11th-century knights in armour.

## SUITS OF ARMOUR

Early armour was made from *chain mail* and was easy to slip on over the head. But a suit of armour was a weighty business. By the time all the gear was in place, it could weigh up to 25 kg (55 lbs) and was pretty hot!

*Getting kitted out*

*Fully dressed*

## BEST BEHAVIOUR

When knights weren't fighting, they traditionally behaved in a courteous way and they had their own knightly code of conduct. It placed special emphasis on showing excellent manners towards women. Knights who displayed these qualities were known as *chivalrous*.

## JOUSTING

It must have been a scary sight to see a knight charging towards you on horseback! The knight's aim was to shove his opponent off his horse with a single blow of his *lance*. Jousting required special armour, but it was so heavy that the knight could hardly move in it!

## MRS KNIGHT

A knight's lady was expected to run the castle's domestic affairs and have children. When a knight married, all his wife's goods became his, so knights were often on the lookout for a rich partner!

## JAPANESE KNIGHTS

Japan had its own kind of knight called a *samurai*. A samurai had to be prepared to fight to the death for his supreme lord, called the *overlord*. In samurai families, Japanese women were sometimes trained to fight as well.

*Japanese armour*

# FARMING

Farming began more than 10,000 years ago in Turkey and the Middle East. People discovered that certain grasses had seeds which could be eaten and also planted to grow new crops.

## GRINDING GRAIN

Early farmers ground their grain into flour. They did this with a *stone quern* (hand mill) which was simple to use but must have been very time consuming. The grain was placed on the flat surface, then the lump of stone was used to grind the grain down.

## FARMING TOWNS

Farming made a lot of wealth. Towns with hundreds of houses were built and most of the people worked on the land, growing cereals and fruits and raising livestock. Other people made clothes, pottery and tools which they traded with farmers for food.

*Part of an early Turkish town – most of its people farmed*

## HARVEST

Everyone helped to gather in the crops. The women, children and men all worked together to cut the wheat with *sickles*, being careful not to shake loose any of the precious grain. Then the wheat was tied into bundles and taken to the barn once it had ripened. Finally, the whole harvest was *threshed* (beaten) to loosen the grains.

## TITHES

Villagers had to give the priest a tenth, or a *tithe*, of everything that they produced – anything from crops to eggs! This made the church very wealthy.

## ANIMAL POWER

Animals have been used to pull ploughs since early times. Even camels and llamas have been used in some countries.

In 18th-century Europe, horses became the main method of pulling new farm machinery, such as ploughs. This century, tractors have taken their place, although poorer countries still use animal power.

*Horses at work*

*Modern tractor*

CASE INTERNATIONAL 7110

# SAILING

People the world over have always wanted to explore and claim new lands. In the earliest days, one way to get there was by boat.

## EGYPTIAN IDEAS

The Egyptians thought that the world was flat and that the heavens were supported by four massive pillars. However, when Egyptian sailors were sent out by Queen Hatshepsut in 1490 BC and reached as far as the Indian Ocean, the Egyptian priests said that the supports were further away than they thought!

## AROUND THE WORLD

Ferdinand Magellan is said to have been the first to sail around the world. Well, his ship might have, but he didn't! Only one of his five ships returned after the gruelling three-year voyage, and Magellan was not on board!

*Ferdinand Magellan*

## BELIEVE IT OR NOT...

In 1492, Christopher Columbus discovered the New World (America). The only thing was, he set off in search of Asia!

## HARD TACK

Sailors often spent many months away from home. They lived in cramped, dirty conditions. After the first few days, the fresh fruit and vegetables ran out and they had to live on *hard tack* – horrible rock-hard biscuits which often became infested with maggots.

## RATS

Very often, a ship's *hold* (where the cargo is stored) was infested with rats. The fleas that lived on the rats were responsible for spreading the *Black Death*, or *bubonic plague*, which reached Europe in the mid-14th century. It killed about one-third of the total European population.

## PIRACY

Pirates sailed the seas, attacking and robbing treasure-laden ships. They were bold brutes who showed no mercy to their victims.

Many of the crew were once-honest seamen who got fed up with the life of maggoty biscuits and rats, and joined the pirate ranks.

# SOLDIERS

A soldier is trained for battle. It's an unfortunate fact of life, but there have been battles since time began!

## GREEK SOLDIERS

Greek soldiers were called *hoplites*. They had to pay for their own armour and equipment, and for this reason only men from wealthy families could be hoplites.

*Hoplite*

## BELIEVE IT OR NOT...

If you were in the French infantry during the Napoleonic period, you stood a good chance of being shot by your comrades from behind. They weren't as skilled as they might have been in loading and aiming their guns!

## QUICK MARCH

Soldiers are trained to take the same sized paces so that they will all move at the same speed. To this day, a *pacing stick* is used in the British army to make sure that this happens.

## MARKS OF RANK

Badges of rank make it easy to recognize another soldier's status. The North American Plains Indian used to wear an elaborate feather headdress to mark him out as a cut above the rest.

## GRUB UP!

During the Crimean War (1853-56), the British soldiers were served such awful grub that a great chef, Alexis Soyer, was sent out to the battle front to try to spice things up a bit.

## WOUNDS AND DEATH

During the Crimean War, the sick and wounded lay dying in the rat-infested corridors of Scutari Hospital in Turkey. But when Florence Nightingale (nicknamed *the lady with the lamp*) arrived in 1854, she soon got things shipshape and cut the death rate to 2.3 per cent within six months. Good old Florrie!

# COWBOYS

Cowboys were horsemen who raised and herded cattle on the plains of North and South America. Sometimes, authorities and citizens thought that these people were wild and dangerous, but they became national heroes.

## COWBOY GEAR

Dressed for the practical, tough, outdoor life, the cowboy had essential items of clothing and equipment.

Cowboys rarely took off their one-piece underwear called *long johns*. They didn't need to, because they had a convenience flap at the back for going to the loo!

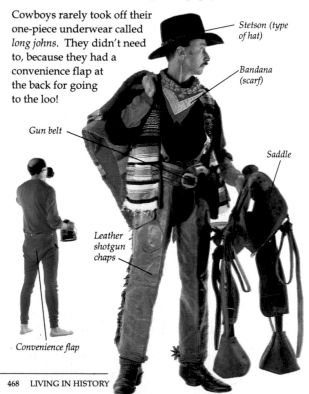

Stetson (type of hat)

Bandana (scarf)

Gun belt

Saddle

Leather shotgun chaps

Convenience flap

A cowboy's boots had high heels to stop them from slipping through the stirrups. They could be dug into the ground, too.

The spiky bits, called *spurs,* on the back were used to dig at the horse's sides to make it move. This wasn't as cruel as it sounds because the whole point of spurs was to penetrate the horse's thickly matted hair, so that it could feel the prod.

*Spur*

## DIFFERENT NAMES

Cowboys had different names depending on where they came from: *gaucho* in Argentina, *llanero* in Venezuela and *huaso* in Chile. They all did the same kind of job though, and loved their independent way of life.

*Gaucho's clothes*

*Poncho*

*Panuelo (knotted scarf)*

*Bombachas (trousers)*

### BELIEVE IT OR NOT...
A cowboy sat on his saddle for up to 15 hours a day! Ouch!

# NORTH AMERICAN INDIANS

By 1500, there were more than 300 tribes of North American Indians. Large numbers lived east of the Mississippi, in California, and in the Northwest. Their way of life centred around their hunting and artistic skills.

The Indians' world was changing all the time: they had to move around because of droughts and fighting between tribes, and the animals they hunted became extinct. Over the next 400 years, Europeans brought changes that caused the downfall of the Indian way of life.

## INDIAN GEAR

The Dakota Indians were the lords of the North American plains by the mid-1800s. They terrorized their Indian enemies. Here, you can see the ceremonial dress of a Dakota elder (senior member of tribe).

*Shirt made from mountain sheepskin*

*Eagle feather headdress*

*Beaded moccasins (shoes)*

## PEACE-PIPE

The Menominee Indians believed that smoking increased their wisdom. At important discussions or ceremonies a pipe called the *calumet* was passed around. Because these get-togethers often happened at the end of fighting, the pipe became known as the *peace-pipe*.

*Sacred Menominee calumet*

## THE FAMILY HOME

The *tipi* was a traditional Indian family home. It was made from a cone of long poles covered with buffalo hides and decorated with traditional painted designs. There was space inside for a family, their bedding and their belongings.

*Tipi*

## INVASION

When white settlers arrived, things began to go badly for the Indians. The settlers brought diseases which the Indians couldn't fight against, they claimed all the richest land and broke agreements about land ownership. The free-roaming Indians were herded on to *reservations* – areas of land set aside where they had to live.

# Cars, Boats and Planes

Where would we be without transport? Sitting at home, probably! Here are just a few fascinating facts about historical ways of getting about.

## The Automobile

The *automobile,* or car, was invented in 1885 when the *Benz Velo* went on sale to the public. It had a top speed of 20 mph (32 kph)! Built at the pioneering factories of Karl Benz in Germany, it was the first car to sell in large numbers.

*Benz Velo*

## Henry Ford

Car maker Henry Ford could be said to have put America on the road. By 1930, over 15 million of his Model T Fords had been made on his car assembly lines and sold.

*Model T Ford*

## BALLOONS AND AIRSHIPS

The first people who successfully took to the skies went up in a hot-air balloon in 1783.

By the 1920s, enormous airships were ferrying people across the Atlantic Ocean. Tragedy struck one called the Hindenburg in 1937, when it went up in flames.

## THE WRIGHT BROTHERS

In December 1903, the inventor brothers Orville and Wilbur Wright took to the air in their powered plane. It flew unsteadily for 37 m (121 ft) and then came down to land safely. This was a historic first powered flight.

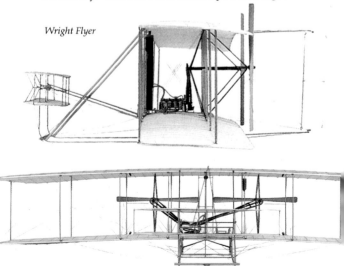

*Wright Flyer*

# Daft Inventions

Through the ages, those clever inventor people have come up with some pretty nifty bits and pieces to change our lives, but some have been a little on the odd side!

## What, No Hands!

In the early days of motoring, long before indicators were invented, a weird and wonderful cable-operated hand device was developed which clipped on to the car door. It was operated from a knob on the dashboard, so that the driver could give hand signals. It even lit up at night!

*Cable-operated hand*

## Warm Toes

John Logie Baird might have introduced television (which he did in 1926), but try as he might, he couldn't get his self-warming socks to work!

## A Stitch in Time
Isaac Singer built the first practical sewing machine in 1851.

## Food Fact
The tin opener wasn't invented until 44 years after the arrival of tinned food! Handy!

## Fast Flush
A kind of flushing toilet was being used by the rich way back in 1596, but toilet paper wasn't invented until 1857. Hmmm!

## Before the Bike
Before the bicycle, people used a machine called a *hobby horse* to get around. Constructed of a wooden beam over

two spoked wheels, the rider sat on the plank and pushed the ground with their feet...and went very slowly. Uh oh!

## Filling the Cavities
For those of you with a thing about the dentist, the first dental drill was a clockwork wind-up affair which kept going for a full two minutes. Agony!

*Harrington's clockwork dental drill*

# RELIGION

There are literally hundreds and hundreds of religions around the world. Some go back thousands of years while others are modern-day. Here are one or two facts about a very few of them.

## CHRISTIANITY

Christians believe that Jesus Christ is the Son of God. Their symbol of the cross stands for the cross on which Jesus was crucified. Christianity began in Jerusalem, in Israel. Today, there are over 20,000 different branches of Christianity because of disagreements over ways to practise the faith.

*A dove – symbolizes the Holy Spirit*

*The cross – symbol of the Christian religion*

## BUDDHISM

The Buddhist faith began in India. Today, it has spread throughout most of Southeast Asia. It is based on the teachings of an Indian prince who lived a life of meditation and preaching and became known as Buddha.

The symbol of Buddhism is an eight-spoked wheel.

## ISLAM

The Islamic faith is based on belief in one God – Allah – and it began in Mecca, in Saudi Arabia. People who follow Islam are called Muslims. The religion is based on the teachings of the prophet Muhammad, Allah's main messenger.

The Muslim's symbol is a star and a crescent moon.

## JUDAISM

Followers of Judaism are called Jews. Judaism began in the *Promised Land*, in Israel. The Jews believe in one God, who revealed the Law to his people. Their symbol is the Star of David.

*This case shows the Star of David. A tiny parchment scroll with biblical texts is enclosed.*

## HINDUISM

Most Hindus believe in many gods, but they all believe that when a person dies their soul is reborn again in another body. Hinduism began in India and is spread throughout much of Southeast Asia. Their symbol is a sacred sound, OM.

## SIKHISM

Sikhism is based on the worship of one God and on the cycle of rebirth. It began in north India and today has spread to Britain and North America. Its symbol is a design of weapons.

*Sikh symbol – steel ring, a two-edged sword and crossed, curved swords*

# CLOTHES

Clothes have been worn for many thousands of years. The first people made clothes to protect themselves from the cold, the heat and the rain. Since those early times, clothes have become much more than basic essentials; they are fashion items.

## A COVER-UP

In the *Renaissance* (14th-17th centuries), the man about town was a very fashionable sight in his *doublet*. He wore a *codpiece* over his well...his more intimate bits! Often highly decorated, it used to cover up the flap opening in his tights!

## WIGS GALORE

During the 18th century, wealthy men and women wore extremely tall, white powdered wigs. The only trouble was that they ran the risk of being set alight by chandelier candles!

## NAME TAPES

The Ancient Egyptians were the first to use name tapes. As all their linen clothes looked the same, they needed a way to identify what belonged to whom.

### STEEL HOOPS

In 1856, ladies probably gave a huge sigh of relief. Instead of wearing up to six petticoats to achieve the perfect figure, they used a flexible frame called a *crinoline*. It was made of steel hoops and either one or two petticoats could be slipped over the top.

*Crinoline*

## ALL GATHERED IN

Since time began, women have been pulled, padded and lifted, but there can have been little worse than the rigid, immovable *corsets* of the 1880s which caused fainting attacks, broken ribs and displaced organs!

# MEDICINE

From earliest times, plants and herbs have been used as medicines. Prehistoric people used *catmint* for colds and *rue* for headaches, whilst the Incas used *urine* (wee) for treating fever! Since then, there have been many developments in the field of medicine.

## MEDICINE MEN

The native North American *shaman* was a man or woman believed to be able to harness the supernatural forces of the spirit world. Shamans used dramatic ceremonies to help sick people reject their illness by mind power.

## FALSE TEETH

The first well-fitting false teeth were made in 1774. They had springs to keep them in place!

*Wooden wand held by shaman during healing ceremony*

*Coiled spring*

*Porcelain teeth*

## SURGERY

Before the 1800s, surgery was very often more threatening than the problem which needed treating! Luckily, the 19th century saw the discovery of new surgical equipment, *anaesthetics* and *antiseptics*. This was a far cry from the Middle Ages when surgery was often performed by barbers! Uh oh!

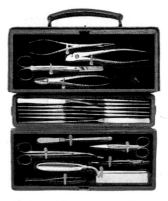

*Steel surgical instruments could stand high-temperature sterilization.*

## PENICILLIN

In 1928, British scientist Alexander Fleming discovered the bacteria-killing properties of a substance made by a mould (fungus) called Penicillium. He called his discovery penicillin, and millions of people worldwide owe their lives to it.

## NEW LIMBS

Replacement limbs were made in the 17th century. The artificial hand shown here was made of iron.

*17th-century iron hand*

# Food

Nowadays, foods from different countries are available in other parts of the world, but it hasn't always been that way. At one time, you could only get food from the place where you lived. Explorers and traders helped to take new foods to the countries that they visited and this livened up the local diets no end!

## Believe It or Not...

A delicacy that the Romans couldn't resist was dormouse cooked in honey and poppy seed!

## Bog Man's Stomach

The 2,000-year-old body of a man was found preserved in a peat bog near Grauballe, Denmark. His stomach revealed millions of intestinal worms' eggs which would have lived in poorly-cooked meat, so we know that he was a meat-eater. His tum also contained his last meal – vegetable soup and muesli. Yuck!

*The body found near Grauballe*

## VIKING MEALS

Viking settlers on the Atlantic islands enjoyed poached gulls' eggs. The gulls didn't do much better though, as they got roasted as a quick snack! Roast horse was also on the menu. The Vikings stewed their meat in huge pots, or *cauldrons*, made of iron. In times of famine, the Vikings sometimes killed their old people and children so they wouldn't have to feed them!

*Viking cauldron*

## PIRATES AHOY

When pirates could get it, they usually lived on turtle meat. If shipwrecked or stuck in calm seas they were even known to eat their satchels! They left the recipe:

Slice the leather into pieces, then soak and beat and rub between stones to tenderise. Scrape off the hair, and roast or grill. Cut into small pieces and serve with lots of water.

## TABLE MANNERS

During medieval times, an aspiring young lord might be given a few table tips which included: don't remove your hat as lice will drop into the grub...and don't pick your nose! Well!

**Acknowledgements:** American Museum of Natural History, New York; Barleylands Farm Museum; British Museum; Graham High, Centaur Studios (model-makers); Museum of Mankind; National Maritime Museum, Greenwich, London; Norfolk Rural Life Museum; Pitt Rivers Museum; Science Museum, London; University of Trondheim, Norway; Viking Ship Museum, Oslo, Norway; Walsall Leather Museum; Weald and Downland Open Air Museum.

**Picture Credits:** (KEY: a=above, b=bottom/below, c=centre, l=left, r=right, t=top) Ancient Art & Architecture Collection: 450; 461b; Bruce Coleman Ltd: 476cl; DAS Photo: 455b; Forhistorisk Museum, Moesgard: 482; Sonia Halliday Photographs: front cover c; 445; 457tc; Robert Harding Picture Library: 453tr; 453b; Michael Holford: 437; 447tl; Hutchison Library: 441b; INAH: 442cr; Simon James: 449tr; 451br; Jewish Museum, London: 477t; Scala: 446; 448t; Syndication International: 464br; Trip/Helene Rogers: 477bl; Universitets Oldsaksamling, Oslo: 454; Worthing Museum & Art Gallery: front cover bc; Zefa/Neville Presho: 443tl; /Konrad Helbig: 447b.

**Additional Photography:** Peter Anderson, Jane Burton, Geoff Brightling, Andy Crawford, Geoff Dann, Mike Dunning, David Exton, Lynton Gardiner, Christi Graham, Dave King, Richard Leeney, John Lepine, Liz McAulay, Nick Nichols, James Stevenson, Clive Streeter.

**Models:** John Denslow, Andrew Nash.

Every effort has been made to trace the copyright holders. Funfax Ltd apologises for any unintentional omissions and would be pleased, in such cases, to add an acknowledgement in further editions.

# TRAVEL THROUGH TIME

Written by Susan Mayes

Illustrated by Colin H. Paine

# ON THE MOVE

Imagine having to walk EVERYWHERE! For thousands of years people hardly travelled more than a mile or two from where they were born. If they did venture out, then they went on foot. Tough, eh?

Here are a few of the brilliant ideas which have made a difference to the way we get from A to B.

*Stone-Age hunter carrying his kill*

## THE FIRST BOATS

The very first form of water transport was probably a simple raft or float. Then came the hollow boat shape – probably a hollowed-out log. Exciting stuff! This marvellous invention was to be the ancestor of all bobbing boats and seafaring ships.

## THE WHEEL

The wheel was invented more than 5,000 years ago. It is probably the most important invention ever, because it was vital for the development of transport, among other things. Let's hear it for the wheel!

## THE STEAM ENGINE

In 1712, a clever chap called Thomas Newcomen invented the first really useful steam engine. It provided power for factories and mines. Later, more powerful steam engines were used to power locomotives and ships.

*A 1925 internal-combustion engine*

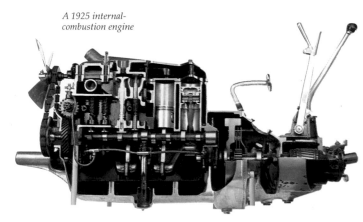

## THE INTERNAL-COMBUSTION ENGINE

A bit of a mouthful this one, but worth getting your tongue around just to impress your friends! The first workable internal-combustion engine was built c1860 by Etienne Lenoir. After improvements by other inventors including Nikolaus Otto, the engine burned fuel to make power and it was used in vehicles such as cars and planes.

# SETTING SAIL

Once people discovered the art of boat making, things began to hot up on the travel scene.

## SENSATIONAL SAILS

The Ancient Egyptians probably made the first sailing boats, around 3100 BC. They used a square sail which caught the wind and sent them boating up the River Nile. On the return trip, they had to paddle or drift with the current.

*Egyptian sailing boat (model)*

Papyrus (reed-like plants) grew in abundance on the banks of the River Nile. The Egyptians used bundles of papyrus reeds to make their boats. The sails of early boats were also made of papyrus, linen being used later on.

## WOODEN WONDERS

Around 2700 BC, the clever old Egyptians began building wooden sailing ships which could go out to sea. They sailed along the coasts of the Mediterranean to trade with nearby countries. They sold their wares in exchange for exciting new things such as ivory, greyhounds and cinnamon spice.

## JOURNEY WITH A DIFFERENCE

Some Egyptian ships were built for ceremonial use only. A huge barge was made for King Khufu in about 2600 BC. When he died, he was buried in the Great Pyramid at Giza. His barge was taken apart and buried nearby, ready to help him on his journey to the afterlife.

## TRIANGULAR SAILS

Things really got going in 200 BC when triangular lateen sails were invented. These sails allowed boats to travel against the wind, as well as with it. Nifty, eh?

*Ship with lateen rigging (model)*

## MAGNIFICENT WARSHIPS

The Greeks and Romans built magnificent warships called *galleys*. The *trireme* was a Greek version of the galley which had three rows of oars on each side. These huge vessels were rowed by 170 oarsmen.

# Horses + Wheels = Chariots

Travelling on land began to head in
the right direction when someone came
up with the idea of putting horses
and wheels together. What a simply
marvellous thought!

## Horses
About 5,000 years ago, people learned to ride on
horseback. What a development! It was a more personal
way of getting around, ideal for hunting and fighting, too.

## More About the Wheel
By 2000 BC, wooden wheels with sections cut out were
being used. They were much lighter than the solid disc
wheels. As time went on, more of the wheel became cut
away, until spoked wheels were being made. (Not to be
sneezed at! We use spoked wheels today!)

## Chariots Appear
Combine a couple of harnessed horses with a few wheels
and what do you get? Chariots, of course; although it was
probably a little more complicated than that. The four-
wheeled chariot came first, swiftly followed by the two-
wheeled version.

*The two-wheeler was faster than the
four-wheeler. It was very handy for
wartime attacks.*

## FUN AND GAMES

Chariots were good for getting around, but they also turned out to be heaps of FUN! Chariot racing soon made it into the Olympic Games, which began in Ancient Greece. 40 chariots started the 14 km (9 mile) race, but only a few finished.

*The prize went to the owner of the winning chariot, not the driver. Humph!*

## BELIEVE IT OR NOT...

The children of wealthy Romans had toy chariots. They were probably pulled by dogs, geese or goats. (Er...put that rabbit down!)

# ROAMING ROMANS

The Ancient Romans became rich and powerful people. This was because they didn't let little things like the sea or vast distances over land stop them from travelling. They found new and better ways of getting to other countries where they traded and ruled.

## ROMANS ABROAD

The *corbita* was a type of big Roman merchant ship. It could hold up to 1,000 tons of cargo which included spices, gems, wine, silk and animals. Some of these ships sailed as far as India to trade and to find out about other countries.

## ROMAN ROADS

The Romans needed an easy way to travel across their enormous empire, so they came up with the idea of roads. The Roman army built new roads as they conquered new lands. They made them as straight as possible, so they could get to places quickly. No hanging around, thank you!

Oops! Sorry, sir, we got a bit carried away!

## ROADS IN TOWN

Town roads had high pavements on either side. There were big stepping stones in the roads so that people could get across without getting messy when the roads were wet and muddy. Very sensible!

## ROMAN LITTER

The roads in the city of Rome got so jam-packed with traffic that carts were banned during the daytime. The only way that the rich Romans could get around without the effort of walking was by *litter*. This was a covered seat suspended between two poles and carried by slaves.

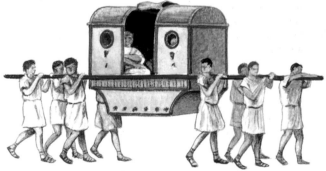

## HORSE-DRAWN COACHES

Many Romans got from one place to another in horse-drawn coaches. Each coach took passengers who travelled inside and on top. Needless to say, journeys could be uncomfortable and slow.

# INTREPID EXPLORERS

Many brave people made it their life's work to travel the world, to discover what was out there. They endured tortuous trips across land and sea in the name of exploration.

## THE VIKINGS

From the 8th century to the 11th century, the Vikings travelled the world in search of land, slaves, gold and silver. They left their homes in Norway, Sweden and Denmark, and sailed to Constantinople (now Istanbul), Iceland and Greenland, among other places.

## MARCO POLO

Marco Polo was born in Venice, Italy, in 1254. He was the first person to travel the whole length of a trading route called the *Silk Road*. The road was about 7,000 km (4,300 miles) long and was very dangerous.

*Long caravans of camels travelled the Silk Road because they could survive the harsh conditions.*

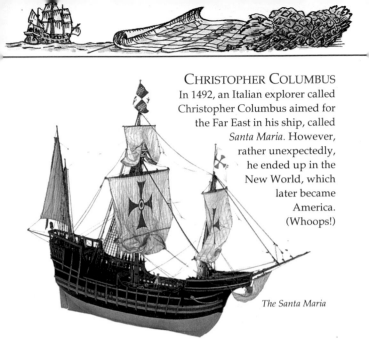

## CHRISTOPHER COLUMBUS

In 1492, an Italian explorer called Christopher Columbus aimed for the Far East in his ship, called *Santa Maria*. However, rather unexpectedly, he ended up in the New World, which later became America. (Whoops!)

*The Santa Maria*

Columbus' crew were frightened of sailing off the edge of the world because they believed it was flat (eh?), so he lied about how far they had travelled each day. Very wise!

### BELIEVE IT OR NOT...

On his arrival in the New World, Columbus discovered the pineapple. He had never seen anything like it back home in Europe. (A little gem of exploration info for your collection!)

# THE AGE OF SAIL

Explorers such as Columbus were in at
the beginning of the exciting *Age of Sail*.
For the next three hundred years, the
sailing ship made it possible to travel the
continents. But life on board ship had its
ups and downs...

## TRADING SHIPS

After the explorers had done their bit, the trading ships
zipped off around the world. These vessels became
home to many men (and a woman or two) who worked
on board.

## HANGING AROUND

To start with, sailors had to sleep on deck.
(Uncomfortable, or what?) Luckily, 16th-century
sailors discovered the hammock in the West Indies.

## FOOD AT SEA

As there were no refrigerators, keeping food on a ship was
tricky. Anything fresh rotted quickly, and meat had to be
salted and stored
in barrels.

*Biscuits were really
hard and maggot-
infested. Yuck!*

*This Biscuit was given
Miss Blacket at
Berwick on Tuesday
13 April 1784
Berwick*

## GROG

On board ship, water quickly became undrinkable, so beer was often carried as the main drink. However, a beverage called *grog* was probably most popular of all, as it kept much longer than beer. It was a mixture of one quarter rum and three-quarters water. Hic!

*The cat-o'-nine-tails*

## SCURVY

Without plenty of vitamin C, from fresh fruit or vegetables, sailors developed a nasty disease called *scurvy*. Luckily, it was discovered that eating limes (packed with natural vitamin C) improved things no end. Slurp!

## PAINFUL PUNISHMENT

Wayward sailors received a flogging with a cruel-looking whip called a *cat-o'-nine-tails*. It had nine lengths of knotted cord attached to a handle. The worse a sailor's crime was, the more strokes he was given.

# COACHES AND CARRIAGES

Throughout the world, the horse was invaluable for getting around. One, two or four could be used to pull people-carriers.

## POSH FOUR-WHEELERS

Before 1560, even royalty had to travel in bumpy, basic carriages. But Queen Elizabeth I of England started a new trend by having her own state coach.

*Queen Elizabeth I's coach was luxury in its time.*

## BUMP OR BOUNCE

A clever chap called Obadiah Elliot came up with the idea of using springs in horse-drawn carriages. Travelling became a bouncy affair, rather than a bumpy one. Boing!

## CONVOYS

In the 1800s, once they had reached America, European
families travelled to the west in canvas-covered wagons
called *prairie schooners*. Convoys of 100 or more wagons
trekked across the prairies
on a gruelling five
month trip.

*Prairie schooner*

## LAST JOURNEY

If you died in 18th-century England, you could at least
be sure that your final journey would be a posh, comfy one.
A dead-smart funeral hearse, pulled by a pair of horses,
would take you to your final resting place. How reassuring!

## AN ELEGANT RIDE

An elegant horse-drawn carriage called a *phaeton* was
popular in the early 19th century. Young gents liked to
be seen dashing around town in this trendy status symbol.

## TRAMS

Horse-drawn trams ran on metal rails embedded in the
street. Later, trams were powered by electricity, instead
of nags.

# TRAIN TRAVEL

Before locomotives were built, humans or horses pulled loaded wagons along tracks. They probably breathed a sigh of relief when mechanised rail travel arrived!

## THE STEAM LOCOMOTIVE
The world's first steam locomotive was built by Richard Trevithick. In 1804, it pulled a train carrying 70 people a distance of 16 km (10 miles). Well...it was a start!

## AMERICAN RAILROADS
The coming of the railway made a huge impact on the USA. By 1869, people could cross the huge continent from east to west, by rail. Yee ha!

## HOORAH FOR THE STEPHENSONS!
The Englishman, George Stephenson, and his son Robert set up a locomotive works in 1823. They began to build steam locomotives for other countries around the world. A clever plan, chaps!

*George Stephenson invented the famous Rocket locomotive.*

## ALL ROUND IMPROVEMENTS

Gradually, passenger trains were improved. Heating was installed and corridors were added. This made getting to the loo and the restaurant car a lot easier. Oh joy!

## LUXURY TRAVEL

With the introduction of first-class dining facilities, plus the creation of sleeping cars, the wealthy began to have a whale of a time on the railways.

### BELIEVE IT OR NOT...

Britain's Queen Victoria travelled in a specially built royal train. It had a bedroom, a day room and a little bathroom (plus loo). Everything was finished to the highest standards. Lucky old Queeny!

# Runaway Trains

Although steam trains still operate in some parts of the world, diesel and electric power are used much more widely.

## Diesel Engines

The diesel engine was invented by Rudolph Diesel in 1892. It generated electricity which could be used to turn the wheels of a train. The first diesel-electric locomotive ran in 1923.

## Electric Trains

Trains powered by electricity are faster, quieter and cleaner than diesel or steam trains. On the first practical electric railway, trains nipped along at an impressive 6.5 kph (4 mph)!

## Top Speed

A French high-speed electric train called the *TGV* is the fastest train in the world. It runs on a special track at an average speed of 212 kph (131.7 mph). In trials, one TGV set a world speed record of 515.5 kph (320 mph). Zzzzzooooooooom!

## UNDERGROUND TRAVEL

London had the first electric underground railway
system. It was so successful that other cities around the
world copied the idea. Paris, Tokyo, Moscow and
Washington are some of the cities with undergrounds
of their very own.

## SENSATIONAL NEW SYSTEMS

Railways just keep on developing! Here are a couple
of the hi-tech ways you can get around in some parts
of the world:

*Maglev* trains hover above a metal track and are
pulled along by magnets. Try the system in
Birmingham, England.

Channel Tunnel trains run between England and
France, under the English Channel. An ideal alternative
to seasickness. Uuugh!

# ON YOUR BIKE

In the days before the car was developed, cycling was the 'in' leisure activity. Not only was it an excellent way of seeing the countryside, but it kept you fit at the same time. Marvellous!

## BEFORE THE BICYCLE

The *running machine* (or *hobby horse* as it was known) was an early ancestor of the bicycle. It had no pedals and no steering. (Ooh-er!) The rider sat on a wooden seat, leaned over and took huge strides to make the machine move forward. Aaaaaaaah... CRASH!

Handlebars

Bar for leaning on

Seat

## AIRY TYRES

Air-filled (*pneumatic*) tyres were invented in 1845, but they did not become popular until 1888. There must have been numerous numb bottoms from all that jolting. Ouch!

## THANK GOODNESS FOR GEARS!

Cycling uphill was horrendously hard work until gears were invented. These effort-saving devices made the wheels turn at different speeds, while the cyclist pedalled along happily.

## THE PENNY-FARTHING

The *penny-farthing* bicycle arrived in the 1870s. It had a

huge 1.5 m (5 ft) tall front wheel. One turn of this took the cyclist a long way...unless they stopped suddenly, that is. If this happened, the cyclist was catapulted over the handlebars. Wheeeeeeee...

## SAFE AT LAST

John Starley proved to be a bit of a star when he invented the *safety bicycle*. It had two wheels of the same size and a saddle in between. Much safer, thanks John!

## CYCLE RICKSHAW

In many cities in Asia, vehicles which look like a cross between a bicycle and a pram are used as taxis. The *cycle rickshaw* looks like a comfy alternative to the bike.

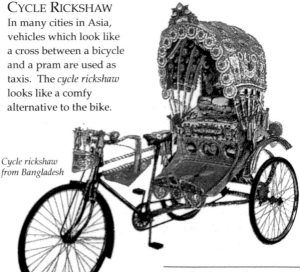

*Cycle rickshaw from Bangladesh*

# New-Style Ships

Early ships were all made of wood, but from the late 1600s iron parts were added for strength. From 1840, some ships were made completely of iron.

## Ironclads

Ships protected with iron are called *ironclads*. The first ironclads had a hull protected by iron armour plates, but later versions got rid of the wood altogether. Iron ships were not only stronger than wooden ones, but they were lighter, too. Amazing!

## Shipbuilding Yards

Ships are built in enormous shipbuilding yards on riversides. Armies of workers including plumbers, electricians, riveters and blacksmiths are employed to put a ship together.

## Champagne Reception

When a new ship is launched, it is traditional to smash a bottle of champagne over her bow. Yes fellas, that's HER...ships are known as 'she'.

## LUXURY LINERS

The 1920s and 1930s were the golden age of luxury ships, called *liners*. They were floating hotels which carried large numbers of passengers across the Atlantic and the Pacific. Ah...what a life!

## TITANIC TRAGEDY

Passengers on the liner, the *Titanic*, did not have the trip they were hoping for. Although the ship was proclaimed to be unsinkable, she hit an iceberg on 14 April 1912 and sank – it was her maiden voyage! Only 700 of the 2,200 passengers managed to escape in lifeboats.

Modern ships carry lifeboats for everyone on board, and all passengers have to do lifeboat drills. Good idea!

## SPEEDY CATAMARANS

The *catamaran* is a modern, speedy, seagoing people-carrier. It is powered by water jets and can go as fast as 42 knots (78 kph/48 mph).

*Catamaran*

# Up, Up, and Away

From very early on, people have had a peculiar urge to fly like a bird. (Weird, huh?) There were numerous attempts at imitating our feathered friends, but these mostly ended in disastrous free falls. Heeeeeeelp!

## The Leaping Monk

In the second century, a monk from Malmesbury decided to have a go at flying. He jumped from a tower with wings on his hands and feet. He didn't fly, but he did manage to break his legs. Surprise, surprise!

## Leonardo's Studies

The brilliant Italian painter, sculptor, architect and engineer, Leonardo da Vinci, was a bit of an all-rounder. In 1505, this talented bloke started a study of flight and made drawings of flying machines.

*Model of a wacky flying machine called an **ornithopter**, based on drawings by Leonardo da Vinci.*

## BALLOONING SENSATION
The first successful form of air transport was nothing like a bird. On 21 November 1783, the French brothers Etienne and Joseph Montgolfier caused a sensation when their enormous hot-air balloon carried two passengers 9 km (5.5 miles) across Paris. Way-hay!

## AIRSHIPS
Balloons were a jolly good idea, but they were at the mercy of the wind. In 1852, Henri Giffard came up with a steerable, cigar-shaped balloon powered by a steam engine. *Airships*, as they were known, became the first large aircraft and carried people across the Atlantic.

## ENORMOUS DISASTER
A German company called Zeppelin were big in the world of airships, but then disaster struck. In 1937, their enormous 245 m (800 ft) airship, the *Hindenburg*, burst into flames and burned to nothing. Tragedies like this, caused by the flammable hydrogen gas, led to the virtual demise of airships. (Just as well, really!)

*The Hindenburg*

# EARLY AUTOMOBILES

The beginning of the age of the automobile (or the car to you) was an exciting time. Inventors came up with new and better designs all the time. This is how they made a start in the race for the road...

## ARRIVAL OF THE CAR

In 1862, the Belgian inventor Etienne Lenoir took his latest invention out for a spin in a forest near Paris. It was an engine (invented by him) mounted between the wheels of an old horse cart. A historical moment in the history of motoring!

## BRILLIANT BENZ

In 1885, the German car maker Karl Benz sold his first car to the general public. The *Benz Velo* was the first of his cars to sell in large numbers...130, actually!

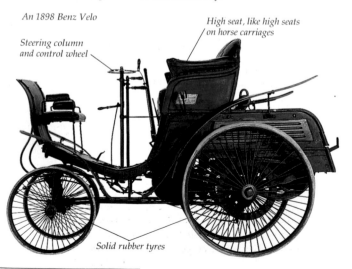

*An 1898 Benz Velo*

*High seat, like high seats on horse carriages*

*Steering column and control wheel*

*Solid rubber tyres*

## Cars Like Cars

By 1900, car makers were turning out cars which looked more like cars and less like a weird type of cart.

## Cars and Carriages

Not everyone could afford a car, and not everyone wanted one. For a number of years, cars and carriages had to share the roads. Horse riders and carriage drivers were not too happy about this as the first cars were very tricky to control.

## Clothes for Driving

Motoring in an early car could be a mucky experience, so a specialist wardrobe (plus extras) was essential. This could cost as much as the car itself. Crazy!

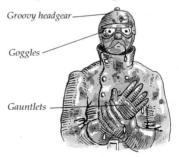

*Groovy headgear*

*Goggles*

*Gauntlets*

## Buses Too

If you can put an engine in a car, then you can put one in a bus too. The result of this was a 46 passenger double-decker bus. Unfortunately, some of these had open top decks, so travellers prayed for dry weather!

# MODERN MOTORING

Motoring took off in a HUGE way when cars became cheap enough for most people to own one. Once the general public had the freedom to travel more or less anywhere, at any time, there was no stopping them. Beep, beep!

## CHEAP CARS

An American, Henry Ford, built cars that everyone could afford, not just the stinking rich. Each person in his huge workforce had a little job to do on each car as it moved along the production line. This made the cars quick and cheap to produce. Brilliant, Henners!

*The **Model T** Ford was the first car to be mass-produced.*

## BELIEVE IT OR NOT...

The Red Flag Act of 1865 was an early law which stopped people from speeding. There had to be two drivers in the car, with a third person walking in front waving a red flag. (Eh?) The act did not survive beyond 1896, (what a surprise!) but new speed limits followed swiftly.

## 'CAR OF THE CENTURY'

The Mini may not have the sporty engine and the good looks of a Ferrari or a Porsche, but it is still known as the 'car of the century'. It is small but it has plenty of space for four people plus luggage. Three cheers for the Mini!

## EARLY TRAFFIC SIGNALS

Before the invention of the handy stop/go devices called *traffic lights*, semaphore-type traffic signals were used. Traffic lights became a permanent feature in Great Britain in 1928, but it was not an offence to disobey traffic signals until 1930. Weird, huh?

## TWO-WHEEL TRAVELLERS

All this stuff about cars..."But what about the bikers?" I hear you cry. When motorbikes came along they were a cheaper alternative to cars, and as far as some people were concerned, they were more fun, too! Vrooooom!

# PEOPLE IN PLANES

You can hop on a plane and travel almost anywhere in the world (pocket money permitting). You have the early pioneers of the skies to thank for this, as they tested the limits of the planes they flew. A BIG "thank you" pioneers!

## WRIGHTS GET IT RIGHT

Who better to make an aeroplane than a couple of bicycle makers. Yes...really! Bicycle-making brothers Orville and Wilbur Wright flew their petrol-engined flying machine 37 m (121 ft) in December 1903. Not a huge distance, but a first flight nevertheless.

*A Biplane*

## TWO SETS OF WINGS

The earliest planes had one, two, three or sometimes more sets of wings. (Sounds a bit over the top, doesn't it?) The best mix of strength, safety and general 'flyability' was in the planes with two sets of wings, called *biplanes*.

## A Channel Crossing

In 1909, Frenchman Louis Blériot became the first person to fly across the English Channel. He performed this fantastic feat in his single-winged plane called a *monoplane*. What a star!

## Atlantic Flier

In 1927, American Charles Lindbergh flew from New York, across the Atlantic and landed in Paris. He was the first person to do this flight solo and nonstop. Top class, Charlie!

## Amazing Amy

In 1930, Englishwoman Amy Johnson flew solo to Australia. It took her 19 days, which was a record at the time. The next year she flew to Japan.

## Get Into Gear

Flying sky-high in a plane with an open cockpit was a freezing cold affair. (Icicles on the end of the nose can be a trifle distracting!) Early *aviators* (aeroplane pilots) wrapped up in lots of specialist gear in an attempt to keep cosy. Brrrr!

Draught-proof leather helmet

Fur-lined leather coat to defy wind

Leather gloves to prevent frostbite

Sheepskin, thick-soled boots

# Jetting Around

The arrival of the modern jetliner meant that ordinary people and not just the wealthy could jet off to foreign parts.

## Old v New

Early jetliners didn't look that different from modern planes, but new technology means that today's jetliners are quieter, more efficient and safer fliers. Phew!

## The Very First

In 1933, a company called Boeing brought out their 247 jetliner, the world's first modern airliner. It could fly at almost 300 kph (180 mph) – faster than most fighter planes around at the time.

*Boeing 247D*

*Engine*

*Propellers help plane go faster and give extra power for takeoff*

## Jumbo Jets

The Boeing 747 can carry over 400 passengers. It is powered by four huge jet engines and cruises along at a height of 10,500 m (34,450 ft). Gulp!

## JET ENGINES

For those of you who are interested, most airliners use *turbofan engines*. The giant fan at the front draws air in where it is mixed with fuel and burned to power the plane.

## FASTER THAN SOUND

Concorde is the only supersonic passenger aircraft. It entered service in 1976.

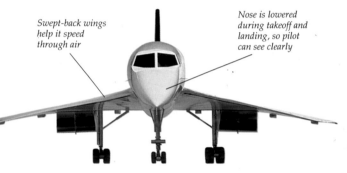

*Swept-back wings help it speed through air*

*Nose is lowered during takeoff and landing, so pilot can see clearly*

Concorde travels at twice the speed of sound and has flown from New York to London in under three hours. Now THAT'S speedy!

*Did you hear something?*

*Nope*

# HOVERERS AND GLIDERS

The aeroplane isn't the only flying vehicle. Hovering helicopters and graceful gliders feature on the flying scene too.

## FANTASY AIRSHIP

In 1863, inventor Gabriel de la Landelle came up with this wacky contraption, inspired by designs such as Leonardo da Vinci's *ornithopter*. Not surprisingly, this fantasy helicopter-style creation was never built, and could NEVER, EVER have flown.

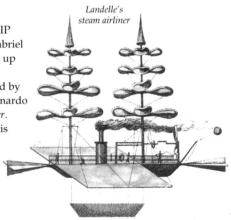

*Landelle's steam airliner*

## EARLY HELICOPTERS

In 1942, Russian-American Igor Sikorsky came up with a pioneering helicopter design. The large rotor on top spun around to move the helicopter, while a mini rotor on the tail stopped the helicopter itself from whirling around.

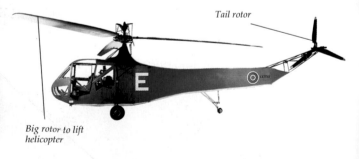

*Tail rotor*

*Big rotor to lift helicopter*

## GLIDER TRIALS

Jean-Marie le Bris made and piloted two full-size gliders.
He based their design on the shape of an albatross
(a big sea bird), but unfortunately they did not fly as
well. CRASH!

## BRAVE ATTEMPTS

In the 1890s, brave German, Otto Lilienthal, built and flew
a series of small, delicate gliders. He controlled them by
changing the position of his body.

Glider popularity decreased after powered
flight came along, but today it is
once again a popular,
elegant pastime.

# TRAVEL ON THE JOB

Travel is a wonderful thing: the thrill of the open road, the speedy ascent of an aeroplane, the gentle (or rough!) swell of the waves on a ferry crossing...and the ploughed field beneath your wheels. Eh? Field? Yes – if you're a tractor driver! Wheeled transport doesn't stop with dull cars.

## BIG BEASTIES

The giant dumper truck is used for building jobs and in quarries and mines, carrying enormous loads of earth and rock. The driver has to clamber up a ladder to the cabin of this 5 m (16.5 ft) high brute.

*This dumper truck can hold 90 tonne loads.*

---
### BELIEVE IT OR NOT...

The largest tyres in the world are made for the giant dumper truck. They measure 3.7 m (12 ft) in diameter, about twice the height of a tall driver! Changing one must be a nightmare!
---

### ON THE FARM

Remember the internal-combustion engine? Well, it transformed farming and made life a lot easier for the animals who had pulled machinery until then.

### ON SAFARI

Next time you go on safari, an *ATV* (All-Terrain Vehicle) is just the thing. It can drive in the most difficult off-road conditions and is fully-equipped with safari gear and survival stuff.
Impressed?

### FIRE! FIRE!

A fire engine with its loud siren and flashing lights is a stunning sight as it dashes to the scene of a fire. Then there is the 41 m (134 ft) telescopic ladder for use on arrival, not to mention the hoses, the water and the foam! So you thought cars were exciting, did you?

# Polar Travellers

The snow and ice of the North and South Poles can be treacherous, but determined polar travellers of the past and present have found ways of getting from A to B in one piece.

## One That Got Away

In 1897, Swedish Salomon Andrée and two other men tried to reach the North Pole in a balloon. Travelling above all that nasty snow probably seemed like a good idea, but the balloon became weighed down by ice and had to land, and the three men died.

## Boats for Hunting

The Inuits (or Eskimos) were the original people to live in Northern Canada, Alaska and Greenland. They had special hunting crafts called *kayaks* for travelling over the icy waters to catch seals and whales.

## Sensible Footwear

Okay – so snowshoes are not exactly a form of transport, but they DO make walking on the white stuff a lot easier. The tennis racket shape helps spread the wearer's weight as evenly as possible, to avoid sinking.

*Snowshoe*

## SKIING

Skis are an ideal way of getting around on snow or ice.
Long-distance travel on these is much easier than on foot.
A must for all polar people.

## SLEDGES

Transport used in the Arctic and Antarctic needs to be
strong for carrying heavy loads but light enough to be
pulled by people or dogs. Sledges with narrow runners
are good for hard ice while sledges with wide runners are
best for soft snow. Got that?

*12 huskies (Arctic dogs) would have pulled this
1930s sledge carrying a half tonne load.*

## SLEDGES ON SKIS

With up-to-date technology, there's nothing to stop you
from whizzing around the icy polar regions. Specially
built sledges on skis, called *skidoos* or *snowmobiles*, are easy
to drive and can pull heavy loads, too. Brilliant!

# BELOW THE WAVES

Not content with sailing OVER the oceans, people also travel around BELOW. The first official expedition to explore the world below the waves took place in 1872. Since then, underwater travel has taken off in a big way. Glug, glug!

## EARLY DIVERS

Before specialist gear was invented, a good pair of lungs was a basic requirement for diving! In the early 1800s, the invention of a copper diving helmet meant that a diver could work 60 m (197 ft) below the surface. The crew up above pumped fresh air down through a pipe.

*This helmet weighs around 9 kg (20 lb)*

## UNDERWATER SUITS

State-of-the-art armoured suits can be worn by modern divers. Just open up, step inside and down you go!

## SUBMARINES

Underwater travel became possible with the invention of the submarine. Some were powered by diesel or petrol while on the surface and by batteries underwater. Modern submarines are nuclear powered and can travel long distances before refuelling.

## SUBMERSIBLES

A *submersible* is a miniature submarine. Some have space inside for pilots and an observer. Extra-thick curved portholes become flat on a dive because of the pressure down below. (Ooh-er!)

*Arm for picking things off sea bed*

*Observation window*

## DEEP SEA SHIP

A special diving ship called a *bathyscaph* can take explorers deep down into the oceans. The one shown here took Jacques Piccard down 11 km (7 miles) in 1960.

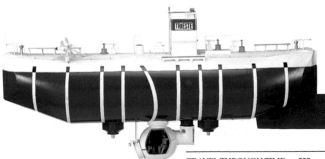

# INTO SPACE

W hen the first aeroplanes were being flown at the beginning of the 20th century, who would have dreamed that people would be travelling into space around 60 years later. Here is a rundown of those first sensational space voyages.

*Saturn V*

## THE FIRST MAN IN SPACE

On 12 April 1961, cosmonaut (a Soviet astronaut) Yuri Gagarin hurtled into space in the *Vostok 1* spaceship. He orbited the Earth at a height of 303 km (188 miles) before returning to Earth. What a hero!

## MOON MISSION

In July 1969, a three-stage *Saturn V* space rocket blasted into space. Each stage burned its fuel and was jettisoned (abandoned). On reaching the Moon, the Command and Service Modules stayed in orbit while two crew members went down to the surface in the *Lunar Excursion Module* (LEM).

## MAN ON THE MOON

On 20 July 1969, the ungainly LEM landed on the Moon and American astronaut Neil Armstrong climbed down the ladder. As he stepped on to the Moon he said, "That's one small step for a man, one giant leap for mankind." Historic words, Neil.

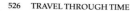

Pressurized helmet with headphones and microphone

Life-support system with oxygen and water

Security line attaches to spacecraft

## SPACE GEAR

Stepping outside a spacecraft is a risky business, so astronauts have to be kitted out in pressurized spacesuits in order to survive.

## MOON BUGGY

On Apollo missions 15, 16 and 17, astronauts used a handy little runabout called the *Lunar Roving Vehicle* (LRV), or *moon buggy*. They travelled around in it on the lunar surface, to collect samples to take back to Earth.

# SHUTTLES AND SPACE STATIONS

Space rockets were a brilliant idea, but they had one tiny little problem – they were not reusable. So scientists came up with the idea of the *space shuttle*, which can fly again and again. Then there's the *space station*, for living and working in outer space...out of this world!

### THE VERY FIRST

In 1981, the space shuttle *Columbia* became the first reusable spacecraft. Its enormous rocket boosters and the fuel tank fell away after takeoff, and its own engines took it into space. When it returned, it landed like a normal plane. Smart invention, eh?

To the nearest space station, please.

### JOBS IN SPACE

A space shuttle is a handy vehicle for doing jobs in space. It can take satellites up or carry a crew to do on-the-spot satellite repairs. If it's transport up to a space station that you need, just catch the next shuttle!

## THE FLYING ARMCHAIR

Early spacewalking astronauts had to be tied to their
vehicle, so they would not float off into space. Now they
can use a flying machine which looks like a hi-tech
armchair. The *Manned Manoeuvring Unit* (MMU) is
powered by jets of gas and the astronaut steers. Nifty!

## MARVELLOUS MIR

In 1986, the Soviet Union launched their space station,
*Mir*. It is now both home and workplace to cosmonauts
who are taken up by shuttle, to stay for months at a time.
Some people have stayed for over a year.

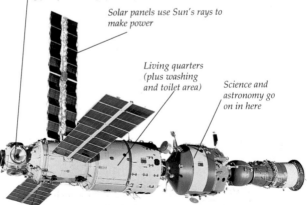

*Decking port for visiting spacecraft*

*Solar panels use Sun's rays to make power*

*Living quarters (plus washing and toilet area)*

*Science and astronomy go on in here*

# Out Of the Ordinary

So...you've got fascinating travel facts coming out of your ears! However, your education would not be complete without taking a peek at a few examples of the more unusual methods of transport that have appeared over the years.

## One-wheeler Record

In 1992, Akira Matsushima from Japan travelled a total of 5,248 km (3,260 miles) on a unicycle. The one-wheel journey took from 10 July to 22 August.

## Believe it Or Not...

Motorized bathtub racing has become a popular sport. Weird, or what? The first of these wacky races took place in Canada, in 1967, and there has been no looking back.

## Solar-powered Cars

Scientists are trying to find a cheap-to-run, pollution-free alternative to the cars you see on the roads today. Solar-powered cars and electric cars are an option, but they don't make it into the speedy supermobile bracket at the moment!

### ELEVATING WHEELCHAIR

Getting around for disabled people could become a lot easier with the invention of the elevating wheelchair. It can travel for 16 km (10 miles) without recharging its batteries and reaches a top speed of 6.5 kph (4 mph). Vroooom!

### PEOPLE-CARRYING KITES

As long ago as 1000 BC, the Chinese began to fly kites. It is rumoured that some of them were so big that they could lift people into the air. Since then, man-lifting kites have been built and used on and off throughout history.

### WATER-WALKING

Rémy Bricka of France, 'walked' across the Atlantic in 1988. Yes...WALKED. He walks on water using special, long ski floats and a double-headed paddle.

### SKATEBOARDING

A personal form of transport in the shape of the skateboard started to take off in the 1960s. Not content with having a fun time zooming around on these things, skateboarders began to do some pretty impressive stunts, too.

**Acknowledgements:** (KEY: b=bottom, c=centre, l =left, t=top)
British Museum; Mark Hall Cycle Museum, Harlow Council; Memorial
Museum of Cosmonautics, Moscow; Museum of Mankind; National
Maritime Museum, Greenwich, London; National Motor Museum, Beaulieu;
National Railway Museum, York; Science Museum, London.

**Picture Credits:** Jean-Loup Charmet: 502; Tim Leighton-Boyce: 531; NASA:
front cover c: 528; Royal Aeronautical Society: 518 t; Science Museum/Science
and Society Picture Library: 486; Seaco Picture Library: 507.

**Additional Photography:** Peter Anderson, Geoff Brightling, Peter Chadwick,
Tina Chambers, Andy Crawford, Peter Downs, Mike Dunning, Lynton
Gardiner, Bob Guthany, Dudley Hubbard, Dave King, Tim Ridley, James
Stevenson, Clive Streeter, Peter Visschev, Jerry Young.

Every effort has been made to trace the copyright holders. Funfax Ltd
apologizes for any unintentional omissions and would be pleased, in such
cases, to add an acknowledgement in further editions.

# WORLD
# FACTS

Written by Fiona Waters

Illustrated by Robin Edmonds

# THE EARTH – OUR HOME

The Earth is one of nine planets circling the Sun. Together they are called the *solar system*. Our nearest neighbour is Venus – which, at times, is a mere 40 million km (25 million miles) away!

We think the Earth is ginormous, but it is actually quite small compared to some of the other planets. It whirls around in space at about 80,000 kph (50,000 mph).

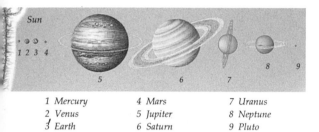

Sun

1 2 3 4

5

6

7

8    9

| 1 Mercury | 4 Mars | 7 Uranus |
| 2 Venus | 5 Jupiter | 8 Neptune |
| 3 Earth | 6 Saturn | 9 Pluto |

## HOLIDAY SNAPS

Pictures of Earth taken from space show a wonderful blue globe in the darkness, with only a red glow from the Sun and the odd pale twinkle of the stars.

*The Earth photographed by Apollo astronauts returning from the Moon*

## Our Big Little Earth

The distance from the North Pole to the South Pole is 12,714 km (7,900 miles) and the diameter of the Earth around the equator is 12,756 km (7,927 miles).

## Flat World?

Many early civilizations believed that the world was flat. The Hindus thought that it was a plate balanced on the backs of four elephants who were standing on a turtle! Eh?

## Big Electricity Bill?

The Sun gives the Earth light and heat, and will continue to do so for another staggering five billion years into the future!

# WHAT THE EARTH'S MADE OF

The Earth has four layers – a crust (nothing to do with a loaf of bread!), a mantle and an outer and inner core.

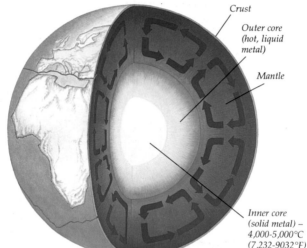

Crust

Outer core (hot, liquid metal)

Mantle

Inner core (solid metal) – 4,000-5,000°C (7,232-9032°F)

## WATER, WATER EVERYWHERE!

Over two-thirds of the Earth's surface is covered by water. The picture shown here is a view of the Pacific Ocean from a satellite. It seems to cover most of the Earth.

BELIEVE IT OR NOT...
All the Earth's land could fit in the Pacific Ocean. Wow!

## ON THE MOVE

Most of the Earth's water is in the ocean. The rest is fresh water in rivers and lakes, ground water (rain which soaks into the soil) and the moisture in the atmosphere (the envelope of air around the Earth).

## THE WATER CYCLE

Not a strange ocean-going bicycle, but the continual, circular journey of water from the sky, to the ground and up to the sky again. Here's how it works:

*3. Water collects as droplets, forming clouds.*

*2. Heated water on land turns into invisible water vapour and rises into sky. (This is evaporation.)*

*4. Big droplets fall as rain.*

*1. Sun heats oceans, lakes and land.*

*5. Rain falls back to land to begin the journey again.*

## GREAT ATMOSPHERE!

The Earth's atmosphere is quite unlike that of the other planets, and is made from the gases originally given out by volcanoes. 78% is nitrogen and the rest is mostly oxygen with tiny amounts of argon and neon.

## DRY AND DARK

The Moon orbits the Earth. (It is a satellite, not a planet.) It has no atmosphere and no weather, and the sky is always black. Maybe not the ideal holiday destination!

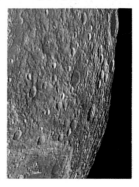

# ROCK ON!

The Earth's surface is made up of three basic types of rock.

*Igneous* – these were the first rocks ever, formed as the Earth began to cool

*Sedimentary* – these rocks are formed out of the bits and pieces of weathered rocks that became squashed in layers at the bottom of rivers and oceans

*Metamorphic* – these are igneous or sedimentary rocks that have been changed either by pressure or heat

## HARD-WEARING
The most common igneous rock is granite. It is often used to build houses as it is very strong and tough, and can withstand bad weather.

*Flint sickle*

## THE FLINTSTONES
Flints are found in a type of sedimentary rock called limestone. Early civilizations used flint to make tools and weapons.

## MARBLE
Marble is a metamorphic rock. Cut and polished, it is very beautiful and used for decorating buildings and sculpture.

*Detail of marble inlay work on the Taj Mahal*

*Taj Mahal*

## Marvellous Minerals

All rocks are made up of elements called minerals. A look at a piece of granite through a strong microscope reveals all the minerals looking quite spectacular!

## Crystal Clear

Many minerals form regular shapes called crystals. For many years, people thought that crystals were ice.

Natural crystals can look very beautiful and are cut to make gemstones such as diamonds, rubies and emeralds.

*These magnificent crystals have formed from hot watery solutions within the Earth.*

*Aquamarine*   *Pink morganite*   *Greenish heliodor*   *Yellow heliodor*   *Cut heliodor*   *Cut aquamarine*

## Fossil Remains

Fossils are the remains of animals or plants that died long ago and have gradually turned into stone.

*This fossil lobster is about 80 million years old!*

# The Continental Drift

The continents are the seven enormous land masses that make up the Earth's land surface. If you were to cut their shapes out of your atlas, you would discover a very curious thing – the continents fit fairly closely together, give or take a few gaps!

## A Closer Fit
Scientists have discovered that between 200-250 million years ago, the continents were probably joined as one huge land mass. They named it *Pangaea*.

## A Vast Continent
The biggest continent is Asia, with an area of 44,485,900 sq km (17,176,090 sq miles). That's REALLY big! In fact, both Europe and Africa would fit into Asia with room to spare.

## INTERNATIONAL CRAWLER

The common garden snail can be found in the British Isles and in the eastern USA. As this would be too far for it to have swum (even if it could!), its early ancestors must have crawled from one place to another when the land was one piece.

*Common garden snails*

## BELIEVE IT OR NOT...

The continents are still on the move – only a few centimetres a year, but the movement can be measured. Yikes!

America and Europe drift away from each other by about 4 cm (1.6 in), and the Rift Valley in Africa gets 1 mm wider every year.

# THE VIOLENT EARTH

Earthquakes are caused by the movement of the giant plates that make up the Earth's crust. In some places, plates slide under each other gradually, but in others they push and push against each other, until one plate suddenly slips over the other. This makes shock waves which we feel as an earthquake.

## THE RICHTER SCALE
The Richter Scale is used to record the amount of energy released by an earthquake. Scientific instruments pick up about 500,000 earthquakes a year. Most are so small they barely measure on the Richter Scale, but about 1,000 each year are newsworthy.

## THE MERCALLI SCALE
The Mercalli Scale is a scale of 1 to 12 which grades earthquakes by observing their effects. For example, 3 = hanging light bulbs swing; 6 = movements felt, pictures fall off walls and windows break; 12 = almost total destruction.

## TOADS AND DRAGONS

The first instrument for measuring earthquakes was invented in China in AD 132. When there was an earthquake, the bronze balls in the dragons' mouths would drop into the mouths of the toads below. Nifty, eh!

*Zhang Heng's seismoscope*

## EARLY WARNINGS

Animals seem to sense when there is going to be an earthquake. Dogs howl, rats leave their holes and horses get restless. Not surprising, really!

## MOONQUAKES

The Moon has quakes, but they are usually caused by meteorites (rock-like objects from space).

# ERUPTION

Volcanoes often lie dormant (quiet and inactive) for hundreds of years, but beware once they become active! They can shoot ash, rocks and gas miles up into the atmosphere, and it becomes as dark as night. People are killed or left homeless and crops are destroyed.

Mount Etna is one of the highest mountains and most active volcanoes in Europe.

## FIRE DOWN BELOW

If you were to journey to the centre of the Earth, you would get pretty hot! 200 km (120 miles) in, the temperature is 1,500°C (2,732°F) but you need to go even deeper before the rocks melt and become (liquid) *molten*. If the molten rock, called *magma*, manages to reach the surface as the Earth's plates shift, it bursts out and is called *lava*.

## PANIC IN THE STREETS

Mount Vesuvius, in Italy, is famous for its eruption in AD 79, which buried the towns of Pompeii and Herculaneum.

Over 2,000 people died in Pompeii as the hot ash poured down on to the town. It all happened so quickly that their remains seem to have been frozen in time, at the moment of death.

The loaf of bread
shown here was
freshly baked –
2,000 years ago!
You can still
see the baker's
stamp.

## REMAINS REVEALED

The ash that fell from Vesuvius set round the bodies of the
unfortunate people and animals who could not get away.
The bodies decayed with time, but their shapes were left
in the hardened ash. The hollows can be filled with
plaster and the tragic victims revealed.

*This mother is trying to protect her child.*

# STORM CLOUDS AHEAD

Storm clouds gathering in the sky can mean that serious weather is on the way.

## THUNDER AND LIGHTNING

Claps of thunder and streaks of lightning can be very frightening – especially if you are outside! Lightning always goes for tall, isolated objects, so never shelter under a tree in a storm.

## NEAR OR FAR?

To work out how far away a storm is, count the number of seconds after seeing the lightning, until you hear the thunder. For every 2 seconds, the storm is a kilometre away.

## BELIEVE IT OR NOT...

US park ranger Roy Sullivan was struck by lightning seven times in thirty five years! How unlucky can you get!

## What's in a Name?

Hurricanes, typhoons and cyclones are all the same thing – they are called hurricanes in the Atlantic, cyclones in the Indian Ocean and typhoons in the Pacific!

At full blow, a hurricane wind will blow at 360 kph (220 mph) and cause absolute devastation.

## Eye Eye!

A great many hurricanes build up over the ocean, which is where the photograph shown here was taken. You can see the 'eye' at the centre of the storm quite clearly.

## I Name This Hurricane...

Names have been given to all hurricanes since 1954. Until the 1970s female names were used, but now male/female names are used alternately!

## Tornadoes, Twisters and Whirlwinds

Tornadoes, twisters and whirlwinds are here one moment and gone the next, leaving a trail of destruction behind.

A tornado can pick things up, send them high into the sky and then put them down quite unharmed hundreds of metres away! Incredible!

# THE WORLD'S OCEANS

Over two-thirds of the Earth's surface is under water. The five oceans make up most of this. They are the Pacific, Atlantic, Indian, Southern and Arctic.

## GRAINS OF SAND

Waves crashing on to the shore can exert a pressure of 25 tonnes per square metre. A human foot landing on the ground exerts a pressure thirty times less! This constant pounding is what reduces huge stones to the finest sand.

## MAKING WAVES

Waves have been recorded travelling at about 900 kph (559 mph). That's much faster than the world water speed record of 556 kph (345 mph), achieved by a hydroplane.

The highest recorded non-seismic sea wave was estimated to be 34 m (112 ft) high from trough to crest.

## SEA MOUNTAINS

Underwater landscapes look remarkably similar to that above! There are mountains, valleys, ridges and plains. The highest underwater mountain is 8,690 m (28,510 ft), compared to Mount Everest, the highest land mountain, which is 8,848 m (29,028 ft).

## OCEAN HARVESTS

70 million tonnes of fish are caught every year, as well as lobsters, shrimps, clams, crabs, squid and mussels.

The sea gives us other useful products such as salt, sponges and beautiful pearls. Deeper down, the ocean floor yields diamonds, coal, oil, gas, sand and gravel.

### BELIEVE IT OR NOT...

• There is more gold dissolved in sea water than there is to be found on land!

• The total amount of salt in the world's oceans and seas would cover the whole of Europe to a depth of 5 km (3 miles)!

# SURROUNDED BY WATER

Some islands are so big they don't feel like islands! Greenland, the world's largest island, is 2,175,219 sq km (839,852 sq miles) across.

Alongside that, Great Britain is quite small at 229,523 sq km (88,619 sq miles).

## I WANT TO BE ALONE

The world's most remote island is Bouvet Island, which is about 1,700 km (1,056 miles) from its nearest neighbour, Queen Maud Land on the coast of eastern Antarctica.

## HIGH TIDE ISLANDS

Each time the tide comes in, some pieces of mainland get cut off by water and become short-term islands, like Mont St Michel in France, for instance.

*Mont St Michel is only an island at high tide.*

# VOLCANIC ISLANDS

Some islands in Hawaii are the tops of volcanoes. When lava poured out of the Kilauea crater of Mauna Loa volcano in the 1980s, it flowed down into the sea and made new land.

Like icebergs, volcanic islands have more hidden below the sea than above. The Hawaiian volcano Mauna Kea is the tallest mountain on earth (from sea floor to summit) at 10,206 m (33,481 ft).

## THOUSANDS OF ISLANDS

Japan is made up of a chain of over 3,000 volcanic islands, but Indonesia has the world's biggest island chain. It has over a staggering 13,000 islands which go through three time zones!

# RIVER DEEP...

Most of the Earth's fresh water is frozen as ice or trapped in rocks. Less than one percent is contained in the world's rivers and lakes. Amazing!

This map shows the largest lakes and rivers in the world, marked in blue. The largest lake, the Caspian Sea, would almost cover Japan, and the longest river, the Nile, could reach from Berlin to New York!

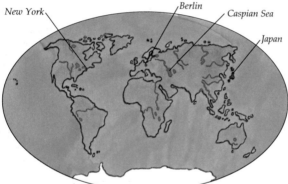

## THE DEEPEST...
The deepest lake is Lake Baikal in Siberia. At 1,637 m (5,371 ft) it would cover five Eiffel Towers standing on top of each other!

## THE LONGEST...
The longest river in the world is the Nile in Africa – 6,695 km (4,160 miles) from start to finish!

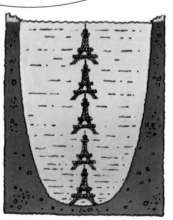

## TRICKLE TO TORRENT
About 180,000 cubic metres (6.4 million cubic feet) of water flows out of the Amazon into the ocean every second. It would take just over a second to fill London's St Paul's Cathedral!

## DRY RIVERS?
Some rivers hardly ever have any water in them!

*The Todd River in central Australia usually looks like this:*

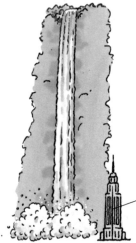

## THE HIGHEST...
The highest waterfall in the world is in Venezuela. The total drop of the Angel Falls, at 979 m (3,212 ft) is almost three times as high as the Empire State Building! The falls take their name from the American pilot Jimmy Angel, who flew over them in 1933.

*Empire State Building*

# ...AND MOUNTAIN HIGH

The biggest mountain ranges in the world are made when the Earth's plates crash together, pushing the crust up into huge folds. Many mountains are still growing, and some of the oldest are slowly wearing away!

## YOUNG AND OLD

The 'young' mountains, like the Himalayas, were formed during the last few million years. 'Middle-aged' mountains, like the Urals, are decreasing in size, because they are gradually *eroded* (worn away). The REALLY old ones are so eroded that only a few low lying hills are left.

### BELIEVE IT OR NOT...

The ten highest mountains in the world are all in the Himalayas.

## ALL CHANGE

The mountains that are volcanoes can change in appearance quite dramatically. Mount St Helens in the USA used to look like this (right).

It erupted in 1980 and now it looks like this (left)!

## MOUNTAINEERS

In 1953, Edmund Hillary and Tenzing Norgay became the first people to climb Mount Everest, the world's highest mountain.

## TOP TO TOE

Mountains are so high that the animal and plant life changes the further up you go! It's so cold at the top that nothing can survive, including human climbers who have to wear special equipment to breathe, see and keep warm.

## AVALANCHE!

When snow and ice accumulate and then crash down the mountainside, it is called an *avalanche*. Avalanches can be very dangerous and can sweep away buildings or anything standing in the way.

Freshly fallen snow is full of air, so people who get buried can sometimes survive. Dogs are used to locate people buried beneath the surface.

*Earthquake shaking may trigger avalanches that were just waiting to happen.*

# WATER FEATURES

$W$ater (frozen and liquid), is responsible
for carving out much of the world's
landscape.

## GLACIERS

A glacier is a thick mass of ice that begins high up in the
mountains and moves downhill at the rate of about 2 m
(6 ft) a day. It can take thousands of years for the ice in a
slow-moving glacier to reach the bottom of a valley.

## THE ICEMAN

In 1991, two climbers found a body frozen
at the top of a glacier in a remote part of
the Alps. Using radiocarbon
dating, scientists
decided that the body,
known as the Iceman,
had died somewhere
between 3,350-
3,300BC, which
made him
the oldest
mummy in
the world!

*The Iceman*

## FJORDS

A fjord is a valley that
has been scoured out by
a glacier and filled with
water when the glacier melted.
The longest one in the world is
Nordvest Fjord in Greenland, which
runs for 313 km (194 miles).